Based on field research in eastern Finland not far from the Russian border, this study examines the connections between farm and family, and their links with wider Finnish society. The author discusses in detail marriage patterns, kinship and succession to farms, and the significance of mechanisation and other modern developments for the persistence of the family as a farming unit. In this and in other contexts, he draws attention to the adaptability of families in a changing world, and to the wide range of collaboration between farming families, whose members nevertheless commonly portray themselves as uncooperative individualists. Another major theme of the book is the relation between law and custom, which is not always what it seems on the surface. In the final chapter, Dr Abrahams explores the ideological significance of family farming within Finnish culture and society, and discusses the problems which arise in the comparative study of family farming systems in different periods and places, both within and outside Europe.

Cambridge Studies in Social and Cultural Anthropology
Editors: Ernest Gellner, Jack Goody, Stephen Gudeman,
Michael Herzfeld, Jonathan Parry

81

A place of their own

A list of books in the series will be found at the end of the volume

A PLACE OF THEIR OWN

Family farming in eastern Finland

RAY ABRAHAMS
Department of Social Anthropology, University of Cambridge

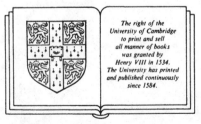

*The right of the
University of Cambridge
to print and sell
all manner of books
was granted by
Henry VIII in 1534.
The University has printed
and published continuously
since 1584.*

CAMBRIDGE UNIVERSITY PRESS

Cambridge

New York   Port Chester

Melbourne   Sydney

CAMBRIDGE UNIVERSITY PRESS
Cambridge, New York, Melbourne, Madrid, Cape Town, Singapore, São Paulo

Cambridge University Press
The Edinburgh Building, Cambridge CB2 2RU, UK

Published in the United States of America by Cambridge University Press, New York

www.cambridge.org
Information on this title: www.cambridge.org/9780521381000

First published 1991
This digitally printed first paperback version 2006

A catalogue record for this publication is available from the British Library

Library of Congress Cataloguing in Publication data
Abrahams, Ray.
    A place of their own: family farming in eastern Finland / Ray
Abrahams.
        p.   cm. – (Cambridge studies in social and cultural
anthropology; 81)
    Includes bibliographical references and index.
    ISBN 0 521 38100 2
    1. Vieki (Finland) – Rural conditions.   2. Villages – Finland – Case
studies.   3. Rural families – Finland – Case studies.   4. Kinship –
Finland – Case studies.   I. Title.   II. Series.
HN534.V54A27   1991
306.85′094897 – dc20   90–24168 CIP

ISBN-13 978-0-521-38100-0 hardback
ISBN-10 0-521-38100-2 hardback

ISBN-13 978-0-521-02645-1 paperback
ISBN-10 0-521-02645-8 paperback

Contents

List of plates	*page* viii
List of figures	ix
List of tables	ix
Acknowledgments	x
1	Introduction	1
2	A strange eventful history	21
3	The origins of modern farming families	47
4	Family and farm	70
5	From generation to generation	112
6	Co-operation between farming families	143
7	Farming families in a changing world	167
	Bibliography	194
	General index	201
	Index of family and farm names	204
	Index of authors cited in main text	205

Plates

1   The fine wooden Lutheran church at Vieki   16
2   A riverside farmstead   17
3   After the storm. Using a chain saw to tidy up a forest   89
    holding
4   Storing timber for the winter   89
5   A recently acquired family combine   91
6   Old methods survive in a tight corner   91
7   Father and son at work   138
8   Holder and heir. House extensions for a transfer between   139
    generations
9   A co-operative task at the planning stage   158
10 Helping out a neighbour   159

Figures

1   Finland and North Karelia   2
2   Vieki and surrounding towns   12
3   Partial genealogy of the Myllynen family   53
4   Partial genealogy of the descendants of Isak Turunen   61
    (b. 1687)
5   Some present and former Turunen holdings in Vieki, 1980   65
6   Partial genealogy of the Kiiskinen family   68
7   Some connections between the Honkanen and other families   96
8   Links between the Savelius and Kainulainen families   97
9   The population of Vieki, 1979   99
10 The descendants of Mikko Saarelainen (d. 1872)   107

Tables

1   Age, sex and marital status of the Vieki population, 1979   40
2   1964 voting patterns in Vieki constituencies and wider   44
    Commune
3   Patterns of succession on Finnish farms   129

Acknowledgments

I have received support from a wide variety of sources in putting together the material for this book. My field research in North Karelia in 1980–1 was funded by a grant from the Economic and Social Research Council, and my summer visit in 1982 was supported by the Crowther-Beynon and Scandinavian Studies Funds of the University of Cambridge. Churchill College has also provided valuable support. The University of Helsinki's Institute of Comparative Sociology provided me with desk space and a friendly institutional base in Helsinki.

As with all such work, my task would have been quite impossible without the generous help of many individuals. Jack Goody has been an important source of intellectual stimulus and advice, and I have enjoyed helpful discussions with Ernest Gellner, Chris Hann, Tim Ingold, Alan Macfarlane, Bill Mead and Frances Pine. Dr P. Wells of Goldsmiths College, London and Professor J. Langbein of the University of Chicago provided useful access to comparative material. Sylvia Hicks, in Churchill College, has given secretarial help and valuable advice on the English terminology of farm machinery. I am also grateful to Heather Murphy in Churchill, and to Anne Farmer, Humphrey Hinton, Mary McGinley and Margaret Storey in the Department of Social Anthropology for secretarial and technical support, and to Barbara Bodenhorn, Mario Guarino and Megan Thorold for help with the figures.

In Helsinki I received extremely helpful advice and support from Professor Erik Allardt, and I am also grateful for the advice which Dr T. Köppä and Dr I. Vainio-Mattila of the Pellervo Institute generously provided. In Joensuu, officials of the Co-operative Dairy, the Co-operative Bank and the National Archives Centre were very helpful, as was Professor H. Kirkinen and other staff of the University of Joensuu. In Lieksa I was much helped by Ms S. Kärkkäinen and other Commune officers. In Juuka, the staff of the Henkikirjoitus offices provided valuable assistance. I am also grateful for assistance from the staff of the Pielisjärvi parish offices, and from the then vicar, Osmo Seppänen, and his wife and staff in Viekijärvi parish.

My debt to the people of Vieki is naturally enormous. Aino and Ilmari Turunen kindly gave me my first home in the village, and Inkeri and Otto Holma generously provided accommodation for me and my family, as did Anni and Teuvo Honkanen. Helka and Veikko Kiiskinen and their family were brave enough to take me in as an unrelated stranger who became a friend. It would be impossible to list all the others who gave me, and my family, help and hospitality, but many will recognise themselves in the text, and I am deeply grateful to them all for their kindness and good company. My wife Eeva was an important source of personal support, in addition to providing invaluable help with the interpretation, and in some cases, the collection, of fieldwork material. I am also indebted to my mother-in-law, Mrs Kristiina Turunen, for her patience as my Finnish teacher during my time in Helsinki, to Pirjo Björkman for her help with transport, and to Reetta and Juha Luukkainen in Kallislahti for their hospitality on several occasions.

I dedicate this book to the memory of Inkeri Holma and Ilmari Turunen.

1

Introduction

This is a book about family farms and farming families. It is focussed upon eastern Finland, where I carried out some fifteen months of fieldwork between 1980 and 1982, but its relevance is not simply restricted to that area. From very early times until quite recently, a large proportion of the world's population has engaged in family farming, and it is probable that a small majority still does so despite the pace and spread of industrialisation. Of course, not all family farming systems are the same. They vary greatly in the details of their property system and inheritance patterns, and in the size and structure of their working units. They also differ in the technology which is available to them and, partly concomitant with this, in the degree and form of their involvement in a wider polity and economy. At the same time there are, not surprisingly, a number of broad similarities between many if not all such farming systems, based as they are upon a combination of land holdings and collaborating groups of kin. Such similarities and differences have been of interest to me in my work in Finland, not least because my previous research was carried out among farming families in the very different setting of East Africa.[1]

As in much of the developed world, the level of mechanisation in Finnish farming is noticeably high, and this has crucial implications for the size of unit that can manage a viable farm under modern economic conditions in that country. To Tanzanian villagers, Finnish farmers would appear quite radically different from themselves in this and many other fundamental ways. They are relatively prosperous, with fairly ready access to substantial credit. They farm comparatively large areas of land, and perhaps more remarkably, they own the land they farm. Yet, while it would be obviously wrong to underplay these features, or ignore the radical climatic differences

[1] See Abrahams (1967 and 1981).

involved, there are two main ways in which the contrast they present needs to be qualified. Firstly, Finnish agriculture has been subjected to immense change and disturbance both in recent and in earlier decades. The high levels of mechanisation are quite new, especially in the more remote parts of the country such as North Karelia, where I worked. Many farmers whom I visited in 1980 had tractors and other machinery on their farms, and telephones, electricity and running water in their homes. Most of them also had a car. Yet the situation was rather different even ten years before, and such things were rarities in many parts of the area not long before that. The second point is that the modern developments in question have themselves been responsible for the preservation and indeed the re-creation of a true family farming system. Husband and wife are a key collaborative unit, full-time hired labour is rare, and there are serious problems in combining the life process of a farm with the developmental cycle of its associated family

Fig. 1 Finland and North Karelia

and the life histories of that family's members. Much of this would be more recognisable to many Tanzanian villagers, as too would the unremitting demands for work and attention which land and herds make upon those who are ensnared in dependence on them for their livelihood.

Fieldwork among one's affines

A variety of reasons lay behind my choice of Finland as a place to study these and other issues. Shortly after my first Tanzanian fieldwork, I received and stored away a friendly warning from a remarkable old anthropologist, Lord Raglan, 'not to be a Nyamwezi all your life'. The idea of complementing work in Africa with work in Europe offered an attractive challenge, and Finland had begun to interest me more generally. Like many other Englishmen with Finnish academic interests, I am married to a Finn, and this has been a major stimulus to extend my research experience in that particular direction.

My fieldwork was in fact conducted in the village where my wife's father was born, and I have been sharply conscious of the fact of doing anthropology among my affines. There is, however, also a more figurative and more interesting sense in which Finland has 'affinal' qualities for an English anthropologist. For Finnish and other European areas of society and culture can be thought of as a sort of half-way house between 'us/self' and 'them/other'. Such intermediate affinal zones, according to some of our own anthropological theories, tend to be apt foci of special behaviour in which taboos, joking and avoidance figure prominently, and it is possible that they may present us in some contexts with the worst of both worlds rather than the best.[2]

Actual affinity in itself created little difficulty for my work, and in many ways it was a help. Finding my first accommodation on a local farm (that of my wife's first cousin) and getting to know local people through informal contacts were much easier than they would have been for a total stranger. Similarly, the fact that my wife and two of our children were eventually able to join me for a substantial period was particularly valuable in these circumstances. Predictably enough, my wife was able to correct or amplify a number of my own impressions in addition to collecting interesting material herself. Her relatives also made a great deal of family 'archival' material available. This mainly took the form of detailed records of

---

[2] On boundaries and taboo see Douglas (1966) and Leach (1976). For other discussions of anthropology in home or near-home areas see Cole (1977) and papers by Hastrup, Hann and others in Jackson (1987). For other studies of rural Finland by British and American authors, in some cases with affinal or descent links to the country, see Gould (1988), Ingold (1984 and 1988), Jarvenpa (1988), Lander (1976) and Roberts (1989). For Finnish village studies by Finns see Ahponen (1979), Sarmela (1984), Suolinna and Sinikara (1986), Tommila and Heervä (1980) and papers by Petrisalo and Siiskonen in Ingold (1988).

inheritance and legal documents concerning the buying and selling of land in the village. Such material was helpful in itself, for the information it contained, and also for the way in which it facilitated access to comparable documents in other families. Not that people were reluctant to provide material of this sort; but my knowledge of its existence and its likely content, and my ability to express a more informed interest in such things, all eased the process of obtaining it. It is of course clear from the experience of others that fieldwork by non-Finns in rural Finland need not turn on such direct connections to a particular community, but it is certainly true that they aided my own penetration into a village whose members are often rather shy of strangers, though by no means hostile to them.

Such help notwithstanding, it is obvious that close connection with, and some dependence on, a particular set of interrelated persons can have limiting effects on the collection and interpretation of fieldwork material. Such people, and others in their personal networks, may hold a particular range of political and religious views, and they may have a particular economic status which could make it difficult to obtain sufficiently broad coverage on various issues. Access to reports on conflicts in which they have been involved could also be unhelpfully restricted.

Dangers of this sort are to some degree a hazard in intensive fieldwork anywhere, and they were certainly present in my Finnish work. However, once I had become more widely known within the village, I was fortunate enough to be able to stay for several months upon a non-related farm, and this provided access to a wider range of information than I might otherwise have gathered. It also gave a welcome opportunity to be a little more myself and a little less my wife's husband, though it would be misleading to lay great stress on the need for this. More generally, the people I got to know reasonably well in the village represented a fair range of experience and viewpoints with regard to many issues in which I was interested. It is true that many, though by no means all, of those I knew were Centre Party (formerly Agrarian League) supporters, but this was true of a majority of farmers in the area in any case.

It has in fact probably been my tendency to concentrate attention upon farming families, rather than involvement with affines and their friends as such, which has led to most biases in my material. I have a broader and more detailed knowledge of the daily lives and problems of such families than about those of some other sections of the community such as timber or electrical workers. It is also fair to say that I have in many contexts learned to see the world of Finnish villages, communes and wider society through the eyes of farmers, and that I have developed a great deal of sympathy towards them in the process. This sort of bias is, of course, a widespread and by no means wholly regrettable part of most fieldwork experience. It will be clear from my discussion in the book that I have been much impressed by the creative spirit of Finnish farming, and by the special combination of economy and family which it presents. I was also impressed by the strong work ethic which is evident in many farming families. At the same time, though, I hope to have seen at least a little beyond such special viewpoints, so as to perceive, for example, that the work ethic may mask the sometimes overwhelming influence of structural forces on the farming sector. I have also been aware that agriculture is a live political issue in Finland, and that farmers' attitudes and self-perceptions may constitute part of their political armoury in the struggle for the allocation of national resources.

Some other problems of 'affinal' fieldwork were less obvious than these, and more difficult to cope with. In 1957, when I first applied to do research in eastern Africa, Audrey Richards asked me if I suffered from shyness, and I replied truthfully, though not especially helpfully, that it depended on the circumstances. Shyness turned out not to be a problem in my African research, but it did affect me during work in Finland, and I am not wholly certain why this was the case. A desire not to worry or annoy people to whom I was connected, and fear of making a fool of myself in front of them were clearly part of the problem. But I suspect too that my special links were partly absorbed into a more general awareness of European commonalities coupled with a self-conscious feeling that I was all the time being judged by canons into which I have myself been deeply socialised. And such feelings were, I think, reinforced by a further consideration. A social anthropologist who wants to work in an African country such as Tanzania needs permission to do so from various governmental and academic institutions. By the time he (or she) reaches a village, he is armed with several high-powered letters authorising the invasion of the villagers' lives. He is also likely to possess considerable curiosity value, and may well serve as a point of access for villagers to scarce goods and useful services, such as letter-writing, medicines and transport. This was epitomised for me in a public debate which took place during my first Tanzanian fieldwork. Some people were complaining about the way in which the local government bus was monopolised by chiefs and other officials, when a man from my own village spoke up. 'I don't understand this fuss', he said embarrassingly. 'Our European's Land Rover seems quite enough for us'. If during my African fieldwork I succeeded eventually in becoming accepted in the community and in making genuine friendships with some villagers, I suspect that this was largely achieved from a position of relative strength deriving from the sorts of factors I have outlined.

Fieldwork in Finland, and in many other European countries, is very different. No official research permission is required, though it is useful in other ways to liaise with a university. If you wish to work in a Finnish village, there is little more to do than simply invite yourself there and hope that people will co-operate. Connections like my own were naturally valuable in this situation. Overall, however, it is easy to feel that you are intruding into the lives of other people to whom you can offer relatively little in return. This feeling of intrusion is intensified by the tendency for so much social life to take place in private space behind closed, solidly built doors. The contrast here with open-style living in Africa is extremely sharp. Far from worrying about gaining access to the life of others, the problem in a Tanzanian village is often one of defining a bounded area of personal space for oneself.

Diffidence and self-consciousness are not wholly bad qualities in an anthropologist, but the inhibitions they create have a deep-seated subjective force which may hinder research to a greater degree than is objectively warranted. During my Finnish fieldwork, I largely kept away from alcohol and heavy drinkers. This stemmed partly from the farming bias in my work, since drinking and successful farming rarely mix well in that area. I also found it hard enough to cope with the complexities and vagaries of sober North Karelian conversation, let alone its drunken counterpart, and it was not clear that the painful expenditure of time in possibly morose drunken company would be very rewarding. It also seemed likely that such behaviour would embarrass people, including affines, with whom I was living and working, and this too was a strong deterrent. Yet it seems in retrospect quite possible that keeping drunken company, as part of research, would have been less embarrassing to my affines and their friends than I assumed. Research is a well-known activity in Finland, and it is probably more respected in the Finnish countryside than in most sections of society in Britain. There are also other contexts where I know more certainly that I was strongly yet mistakenly inhibited from doing things which I felt might give offence or be intrusive. I rarely tape-recorded interviews and conversations, in spite of advice that some people might actually enjoy being recorded – though I suspect that anxieties about tripping up in my wife's language may have played a part here too. I was also hesitant to take funeral photographs, despite the fact that this was to some degree an irrational interpolation of my own cultural experience. For Finnish funerals are probably the most intensively photographed of their rites of passage.

If self-deception was a fieldwork hazard, so too was a more rational awareness that ignorance gave one plenty to be shy about. A European anthropologist going into Tanzania is a peculiar mixture of sophistication and naïvety. Although coming from a quite different cultural background, he is likely to know a substantial amount about such varied institutions as kinship, age-organisation, chiefship, *ujamaa* and ancestor-worship. And if he knows a lot less about some other things, he can at least take comfort from the fact that most other people – apart, of course, from the local population he is studying – are in the same predicament. Moreover, what the local people know is largely unwritten, and the anthropologist becomes a possibly important instrument for the documentation and dissemination of this local knowledge. He is usually working in a relatively unexplored field, and he eventually acquires a wide-ranging if localised and patchy expertise which few others inside or outside the society can match. Theoretical preconceptions may distort his vision – he may discover lineages or dual organisation or class where others might be harder pressed to see them – but he has been taught to beware of this, and the linguistic and cultural otherness of the society is expected to provide a certain amount of shock-therapy for such Procrustean tendencies.

The situation of a visiting English anthropologist in Finland is quite different. Far more is known – though not usually as a matter of course to an Englishman, despite his common European background – and far more has been recorded about Finnish rural society than about Tanzanian villages. There is a large literature in the form of bulky academic monographs by historians and geographers, numerous official and semi-official publications, novels, national and local newspapers, and public records, which amounts to many millions of some of the longest words in Europe. The 'otherness' of the Finnish language may help, as I have hoped it would, to sharpen my perceptions of the culture and society, but notwithstanding my reasonable competence in it, it has often seemed to loom more saliently as a barrier between me and the mass of information available on the past and present of Finland, and its regions and villages. I must confess that I have at times cursed the existence, completeness and accessibility of civil censuses and parish records, and I have listened with some envy to colleagues in Britain who have complained about the hundred-year census rule or the refusal of a vicar to make relatively sparse local records available to them. And, of course, there is not simply one form of 'other' language to be dealt with. The rich inventiveness of rural dialect has somehow to be handled alongside the often turgid academic prose of larger and usually unindexed *magna opera*, which in turn differs from the more archaic language of early records – some of which may be in Swedish – and from the more irritating and opaque forms of journalese.

The welter of available contemporary and historical material on everything from forestry to politics and from household composition to agricultural co-operatives is not the only point of contrast between Tanzania and Finland in this context. Finland's status as a relatively recently independent nation which is anxious to stand up to comparison with Sweden and other northern countries has been an important stimulus to cultural developments there. Finnish villagers are highly literate, and they take a keen and well-informed interest in their own society and culture and in the world at large. They are regular newspaper readers and, increasingly, television viewers, as equally at home with the world news and the Muppet Show as with programmes on the refuse disposal problems of Helsinki suburbs – and, perhaps more surprisingly, they are positively interested in all of them. Rural depopulation is both an important and a relatively recent phenomenon in Finland; and the process of industrialisation, urbanisation and emigration which have accompanied it mean that many villagers have siblings and children living in Finnish and Swedish towns, and further afield than that, as factory workers, office workers, shop assistants, doctors, teachers, engineers and even the odd diplomat. They often keep in quite close contact with these relatives by letter and by telephone, and in many cases they see them at least every summer when they come back to the village for a holiday. So villagers keep well informed about a wide range of issues, events and places, and talk knowledgeably about them as part of their everyday interests; and an anthropologist or other visitor cannot hope to cope simply on the basis of intensive local knowledge, which is itself quite difficult to acquire. At the same time, many urban dwellers, in a wide range of occupations and professions, know a great deal at first hand about rural life, to which they retain ties both through their relationships with villagers and, quite often, through their ownership of forest or other land which was part of the farm on which they grew up. Here, I may add, Tanzania seems more akin to Britain than to Finland despite the rural origins of many urban Tanzanians. For in Britain the longstanding separation of urban and rural society means that many townsfolk are not well informed about the details of rural society, and the anthropologist and sociologist in the countryside is still something of an explorer. In Tanzania, on the other hand, local ethnic diversity, coupled with the alienation from the countryside which many educated urban dwellers have experienced, may well allow a visiting anthropologist to know far more about a particular rural area than most of the urban population he encounters.

In brief, a foreign anthropologist in Finland has to work hard to try to keep up with even a reasonable proportion of the wide range of interests and information which villagers take for granted. He also has to read as widely as he can to try to ensure that he knows as much as possible of what is worth knowing for his work. If he fails to do this, he runs much greater risks than he would in most African contexts of appearing unacceptably ignorant to many people, including villagers and academics, or at best of spending a long time getting to know what they all know already. There is perhaps some consolation to be taken from the fact that many non-Finnish readers will know even less than he does, but this alone scarcely satisfies the wish to make a genuinely valuable contribution to scholarship.

High rates of literacy and the keen interest of Finns in their country and what is said of it have special implications too for confidentiality. Villagers are keen that I should write about them and their community, and many would gladly be named as progressive farmers or committee members. Also, as I earlier implied, official attitudes to confidentiality differ from those which prevail in Britain. Less information is available on some matters, such as suicides, because of the absence of public inquests. On the other hand, civil census material is much more readily available, and I was also granted access to local parish records. This fits both with positive attitudes towards research and with fairly low levels of anxiety about abuse of personal information.

Nevertheless, publication on some topics has its problems. Much more than is the case in many fieldwork areas, I must assume that what I write on Finland may be read by villagers or their relatives, and by others elsewhere in the country. This clearly places a severe constraint on what I write about particular individuals and how I use material which people have passed on to me in confidence. Of course, indiscretions and other issues of research ethics are a problem anywhere, but I have been especially conscious of them in my Finnish work, and by no means only because of my affinal links.[3] Nor is the matter simply a local-level one, though it is true that the importance of local communities is probably enhanced in a country with a relatively small population. Finnish agriculture is a political 'hot potato' at the national level, and there are many who believe that farming families milk the state each time they milk their cows. How such families manage their relations with the state and with the formal economic sector is both theoretically significant for my work and also potentially, at least in some cases, a quite 'sensitive' political question.

There is no ideal solution to these problems, and I have adopted an imperfect compromise which I hope resolves more difficulties than it causes. In keeping with the wish of villagers to see their community 'on the map', I have not felt it right or worth while to try to conceal the identity of the village where I worked, and I have used its real name throughout the book. For similar reasons, I have not always wished to disguise the identity of individual villagers, and I have occasionally named some in the text. At the same time, however, I have been conscious of the need to respect their confidence and protect their privacy from too much outside curiosity on some matters. I have therefore preserved their anonymity in some cases,

---

[3] Barnes (1979) provides a wide-ranging discussion of ethical issues in different kinds of social research.

and I have also referred to some of them simply by their initials in contexts where this seems desirable.

A far country

If Finns know Finland too well for the comfort of a visiting anthropologist, the reverse, as I have hinted, seems more likely to be true of many English readers. There is a substantial range of English writings on the country and its institutions, but most of them are little read, to judge by the variety of garbled images which I have met in conversation.[4] Of course, most people know about the lakes and forests and Sibelius. Sauna too is well known, though it seems to evoke ideas of mild masochism, sexuality and alcohol rather than a highly efficient and pleasantly sociable form of bathing and relaxation. Politically, many seem to assume that the country is part of the Eastern Bloc, while others are hard pressed to distinguish it from Sweden. Its language is commonly known to be 'strange', and as such may be vaguely grouped with Basque or other 'oddities'. In addition to fine athletes and ski jumpers, it is thought of as the home of Lapps and Father Christmas, and their reindeer.

In fact, Finland is an independent multi-party democracy, with an elected Parliament and President. Elections both to Parliament and for seats on local councils are contested by a wide range of parties through a system of proportional representation. The country has a prosperous Western-style economy which nowadays comprises strongly developed industrial and tertiary sectors, with expanding interests in Britain and elsewhere, in addition to agriculture. Finnish belongs to the Finno-Ugric group of languages, of which the best-known other member is Hungarian. Finnish and Hungarian are, however, only distantly related to each other, and the Karelian dialects and Estonian in the Soviet Union are much closer to Finnish. For historical reasons, the country's closest cultural affinities are with Sweden, and a small proportion of Finns (c. 6 per cent) speak Swedish as their mother language. As I discuss in Chapter 2, there has been a long and often conflict-ridden history of links with Russia, which has culminated in the forging of a special relationship of mutual respect and non-aggression. There are reindeer-herding Lapps in the north, but the vast

---

[4] Among the most useful English-language general works on Finland are Hall (1957), Leskinen (1979), Stenius (1963) and Toivola (1960). Allardt (1985) gives an outstanding and succinct account of many of the main features of Finnish society. Mead, who has written authoritatively on a variety of aspects of the country's human geography and culture, has also valuably documented the many images and misrepresentations of the country and its people in English fiction and other literature. See Mead (1958, 1963 and 1982) and also Mead and Smeds (1967). For references to historical works in English, see Chapter 2.

majority of the country's population, and even of Finnish Lapland itself, are Finns.[5]

Finland is a large country (337,000 square km) with a relatively small population (c. 4.7 million), and it is one of the northernmost countries in the world. It stretches over 1,100 kilometres from 59° 48' north to well over the Arctic Circle, but its climate is tempered by the Gulf Stream and Eurasian summer winds, and intensive agriculture is feasible in much of its southern half.[6] The main urban centres and the most fertile land are in the south-west of the country, and the majority of the population (c. 2.85 million) lives there also. Density of settlement decreases noticeably to the north and east, from over 100 per square kilometre in the far south to under 10 in provinces like North Karelia. The village of Vieki where I worked is in the North Karelian Commune (*kunta*) of Lieksa, which borders on the Soviet Union. It lies around 63° 30' north and 29° 40' east. This is one of the poorer and more remote areas of the country in which farming is still possible. As one progresses along the almost 600-kilometre route from Helsinki towards Vieki, one moves out of a zone of relatively mild climate and stone-free fertile soil into a less hospitable, more hilly region. There farmers often tell you that stones are the easiest crop to grow in this *vaara* (hill) country, and the summer – jokingly described to me as shorter than the winter but less snowy – has a short-lived butterfly-like poignancy and beauty.

Seasonal changes are of vital interest to country people everywhere, but this seems to be specially true of rural Finns. When I first discussed my research plans with Finnish academics such as Erik Allardt, I was told that I should try to see a whole year through if I really wished to catch the flavour of the place. This advice did not surprise me after my experience of work in eastern Africa, with its sharp distinction between dry and rainy seasons, but in retrospect it was especially apt for Finland. The stark contrast between summer and winter was particularly notable, with the spring and autumn largely though not wholly seen as constituting border areas between them. Summer is naturally the main growing season, and its short length and the compensating extension of daylight hours which come with it are bound to be of critical significance to farmers, who are predictably keen observers of the passage of the seasons. Weather forecasts are quite the most important radio programmes, and the radio is kept on almost continuously in many households so that none of each day's many forecasts should be missed.

[5] There are about 4,000 Lapps in Finnish Lapland out of a total population of about 200,000 in the region.

[6] See Jäntti (1960) and Mead and Smeds (1967). The country's southernmost point is just below 60 degrees north, and agriculture is mainly practised in the area south of the 65-degree parallel.

Some farmers keep careful diaries of climatic and weather conditions, and the detailed information from these is fed into a 'theoretical' frame of local knowledge and 'country saws' which endows the details with a sort of structural significance. General rules are cited to predict how many days it will be before the river ice starts to break up, or to interpret the likely effects of particular patterns of rainfall or snow cover.

The interest in the seasons is not simply restricted to their many direct implications for farming, since they also very much determine the pace and rhythm of country life more generally. Not surprisingly, summer is particularly looked forward to. The signs of its coming, such as the blossoming of the bird-cherry trees (*tuomi*), are enthusiastically reported, just as the first browning of the alder leaves is noted with regret. Despite its bustle and work pressure, summer is also time for fun, for strolls, midsummer celebrations, and warm days and long northern evenings,

Fig. 2 Vieki and surrounding towns

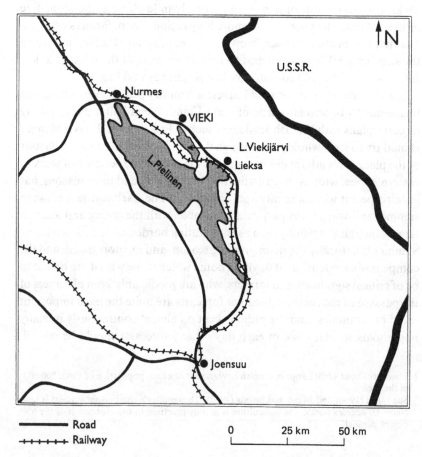

which not even the gnats and mosquitoes can spoil. Least loved is the dull, depressing period of late autumn with its short, grey days before bright snow has settled to relieve the darkness. Little wonder that the Finnish for November, *marraskuu*, means literally 'dead month'. Winter proper can be very long and hard. During my own stay, snow fell in Vieki and nearby villages in October and, untypically, these first falls did not melt away. This had its compensations, since the normal drabness of November was avoided. Discounting drifts, which were much deeper, there was 1.5 metres of snow cover at the height of winter in the area, and skiing was still possible in May, when low fences between fields were just starting to emerge above the surface. Night temperatures went down to minus 39 degrees Centigrade at one point, and minus 20 was quite common during the day. Finnish society is, however, well organised to cope with such conditions. Roads are kept open, rail and air services run regularly, and individuals are used to going about their daily tasks. Cars have special studded winter tyres, and even quite old people get around on foot. Some ski, and many women use a *potkuri* or kick sledge to get to the shops. This clever device is like a chair on runners. The 'driver' stands behind the frame, with one leg on a runner, and propels the sledge with the other leg, rather like a child's scooter. The shopping or an accompanying child can be accommodated on the seat, and the 'driver' rides on the two runners once the sledge has gained momentum.

Most times of the year also have their own outdoor leisure activities. Skiing is very popular, and special scenic tracks are made by villagers for local use. Children are also keen sledgers, and they like to skate if a local rink is prepared. Many people enjoy fishing, in winter through the ice and in summer from the lake shore or from boats, and many are also keen berry and mushroom pickers. Some are enthusiastic hunters of hare or elk, and I have more than once heard it said that there is a hunter-gatherer not far below the surface of most Finns. Even when some of these activities, such as intensive berry picking, can be financially rewarding, it would be misguided to interpret them solely from this point of view, rather than as ways in which villagers take their pleasure in harmony with the changing face of their surroundings.

People generally make the most of what the seasons have to offer, and yet one gets a strong sense that the seasons on their own are not enough. Much more than is the case in Britain, the Finnish year is punctuated by a series of special days. In addition to the main Christmas holidays, New Year, May Day and Midsummer are celebrated; and Mothers' Day, on the second Sunday in May, is particularly important, as is Independence Day on 6 December. There are also many other days, including *Pikkujoulu* (literally 'little Christmas') in mid-December, which are specially recognised. Such days, in addition to their special meanings, serve importantly to punctuate the passage of the year for villagers and other Finns, and their value in this regard seems particularly important when they fall in winter.[7]

Yet there is also a paradox here. Several of the special days in question are relatively modern introductions into rural life. This is naturally the case with Independence Day, but it is interestingly true also of Mothers' Day and *Pikkujoulu*, which are both fairly recent and urban in their origins. This is just one of many areas of life where urban culture has spread into the countryside. Not unreasonably, most people in both town and country would agree that this development has so far been mainly for the good. The benefits of urban life and culture have been gradually made accessible to all, and perspectives are much wider and life more comfortable in rural areas than would otherwise be the case. In addition to more obvious commercial and industrial elements in the situation, schoolteachers and the school system more generally have played a significant part in this process. Many important developments in Vieki, including the foundation of the village's own bank and the building of its church, owe much to the influence of the local schoolteacher, typically in alliance with the pastor, during the first years of this century. I should add that local schools are still important cultural and social centres and, to some extent, provide a source of identity for the communities they serve. They are used for a variety of public meetings and for local gatherings, such as those held on Mothers' Day, and branches of some societies like the women's Martta association are often formed for school areas. Closure of a school and diversion of its buildings to other uses, as village populations fall, can therefore mean much more to villagers than the simple loss of educational facilities for children.

I have already noted that connections between town- and country-dwellers have been intensified through recent patterns of migration. For while many third world village populations are increasing at unprecedented rates, rural depopulation through migration has been a common feature of modern European society, and its recent scale and pace have been particularly notable in eastern Finland. It is arguable that this is of considerable significance politically for Finland, in as much as such connections hinder the development of serious conflicts and communication problems between the urban industrial and the rural world. It is also true, however, that there remains in spite of such connections a longstanding cultural division between town and country which includes an element of self-esteem on the part of urbanites and a genuine tendency to self-deprecation among villagers. Young people going to study in a major town may still feel shy about their country accent and their unfamiliarity with the sophistication of urban life, and this anxiety is by no means simply of their own making.

[7] For a detailed account of the main festival and most other special days in the Finnish calendar see Vilkuna (1981).

The division between town and country is in fact very old in Sweden and Finland, and it was incorporated in the medieval legal system, where a formal distinction between town and country law was recognised in inheritance and other matters.[8] The division and associated attitudes and sentiments have taken different forms at different times, and each period has its own political and economic features which are closely linked to the position of agriculture in the national economy. The fact that large towns are themselves a relatively recent development in North Karelia also probably gives a special flavour to that area as compared to more western regions where the population has had long connections with important urban centres.[9]

There is too another major aspect of the demographic processes which have helped to shape the modern situation. For the population movement, which has helped to cement town and country links, has of course also left many rural communities with at most a small proportion of their former numbers, and with highly distorted age and sex structures. This, with the accompanying loss of local social services, contributes to awareness of the remoteness of such areas from the mainstream of life; and this is not completely compensated for by highly developed postal, telephone, radio and television, and transport connections to the outside world. 'Helsinki would be all right if it wasn't so far out of the way' is a good-humoured quip one sometimes hears in Vieki, and it is interestingly expressive of the ambivalence of belonging to what is, by many Finnish standards, a remote community.

Like deprivation, remoteness is of course a variable and in part subjective quality. From the distant vantage point of the big city, villages like Vieki and even the small towns like Lieksa around which they cluster all easily seem much the same – dull and relatively poor, and moribund if not actually dead. The closer one gets, however, the more complex the situation appears, and there are numerous local centres and peripheries.

The town of Lieksa has a population of around 6,000, and is well provided with shops, garages and public services including schools, a good library and a local-level hospital. There is also a developing industrial area on its outskirts. Until a fire in 1979 the town had an important wooden church which has now been replaced by an attractive modern building. The old church was designed by Engel, an outstanding German architect, who was responsible for major works in Tallinn and St Petersburg as well as for rebuilding Helsinki as the new capital of Finland after a disastrous fire in 1808. People from surrounding villages go into Lieksa for some of their shopping, or to deal with public-service and administrative affairs, though

[8] For the early division between town and country law see Rautiala (1975, pp. 40–1).
[9] Oksa (1985) gives an account of the history of Joensuu and its modern role in North Karelian society.

they may have to go to the provincial capital, Joensuu, for more serious or complex matters.

Villages themselves differ in size and in facilities, and Vieki is in fact quite a substantial centre in its own small world. It lies on the northern border of Lieksa Commune, about 30 kilometres north of Lieksa itself. Although the village has suffered from quite serious depopulation, it has not fared as badly in this as have some smaller 'backwoods' settlements, and it has even absorbed some of the outflow from these. It has its own fine wooden church which constitutes the focus of the parish of Viekijärvi, to which a number of other villages are attached. It still has two primary schools, despite closures, and it has a post office, and there are two bars and several shops. It also still possesses its own bank, which retains a partial independence within the wider framework of the Finnish Co-operative Bank system. There is a small old people's home for villagers, and a day nursery operates in the parish hall. Some veterinary supplies are dispensed locally, though vets themselves have to be summoned from outside and there is no doctor in the village. Petrol and diesel are available at the village centre, and there are good main roads and regular bus services to the towns of Lieksa and Nurmes. There is a nearby main-line railway station which provides links via Joensuu, and also north through Nurmes, to all parts of the country. The nearest airport is also at Joensuu, and there was some discussion at the time of my research about building a new one to serve Lieksa and Nurmes more directly. Vieki itself was suggested as one of a number of possible sites for this, but nothing has as yet come of the project.

Plate 1   The fine wooden Lutheran church at Vieki

A protestant ethic?

A little over 90 per cent of Finns belong to the Evangelical Lutheran Church, and constitute the world's third largest Lutheran community. Slightly more than 1 per cent belong to the Orthodox Church, and almost all of these are from Karelian families which were displaced as a result of enforced territorial concessions to the USSR in the 1940s. The resettlement of substantial numbers of such families in Vieki, as I describe in Chapter 2, has meant that the village has a rather larger Orthodox community than is usual for the Lieksa area and the country as a whole. There is an Orthodox church in the village not far from the Lutheran church. Since 1923, religious freedom has been guaranteed by law in Finland, and individuals can opt to join any religious group they please or none at all. The general trend in the country has been towards greater secularisation of society, though some counter-movement to this may be discernible in the reportedly large numbers of candidates for places on university theology courses.

Most of the farm families which I got to know are Lutheran, and many of their senior members are rather pietist. The extremely pietist Lestadian movement, which is mainly found in northern Finland has very few adherants in the village, and a milder form of pietism than this is the general rule among the 'awakened' (*heränneet*) there. Such pietism, as elsewhere in Finland, is sometimes referred to as *körttiläisyys*, a term referring back to the tailed coats which pietists once wore, but the common expression is *herätys* ('revival' or 'awakening'). There is a long history of pietist

Plate 2 A riverside farmstead

revivalism in the village, dating back to the last century, and many of the present older generation were especially influenced by the establishment of a religious instruction centre in the village in their younger days. This later moved to another village, Kylänlahti, in the area. Such people take a keen interest in the church, and a number of them are in the choir. They hold regular prayer meetings and hymn-singing 'sewing evenings' in each other's homes, and sometimes they listen to tapes of revivalist rallies which one or more of them have attended outside the area. Beyond this they participate, with a broad range of parishioners, in church-sponsored activities, such as fund-raising for mission work, and in gatherings, for example to meet Lutheran visitors from other countries or to celebrate on special days. Not all of them attend church each week, but they listen to church services on the radio if they stay at home. They do not normally drink alcohol.

During my research, I was deeply impressed by the capacity for sustained hard work which such people displayed, and it is tempting to associate this with their Lutheran pietism. I shall discuss the work ethic, and the associated idea of *sisu* (inner strength and guts), in more detail later, but it should be noted here that these are well-known Finnish qualities which the people value very highly. I do not doubt that protestantism has played an important role in fostering these qualities. But it seems mistaken to draw too close an association between them, and Ingold's description of the work ethic as 'bolstered by a strong tradition of evangelical Lutheranism' seems to be an apt characterisation.[10] Certainly, many of the Orthodox Karelian farmers in the area have shown a similar capacity for determined hard work, as have several younger villagers who are nominally Lutheran but in fact have little interest in religion. It is true, of course, that many of these younger people will have learned work habits by example from their more religious parents, and that most of them are sensibly aware that alcohol, whatever else it is, does not mix well with early morning milkings and the successful running of a farm more generally. As such, many of them have a fear of drinking, and only one or two with more cosmopolitan experience feel able to operate comfortably on the principle that excess rather than alcohol itself is the main problem. There has, of course, been a long history of anxiety over drinking in Finland, and this culminated in the introduction of prohibition laws shortly after independence. Even today, there is a state monopoly on most forms of alcoholic beverage, and prices are extremely high compared with those in most other European countries.

Points of focus

A number of the themes which I have touched on in this chapter will be taken up in greater detail later. In Chapter 2, I discuss the historical

[10] Ingold (1984, p. 132).

background to the modern situation in Vieki, including the patterns of population growth and subsequent decline which have helped to shape the village as it is today. Chapter 3 provides more detail to this picture through examining some of the processes of succession, fission, purchase and migration through which contemporary farming families in the village have come to be there.

Chapters 4 and 5 explore the complex nature of connections between farm and family in this area. In Chapter 4, I give an account of the main features of Finnish kinship and marriage as they relate to family farming, and I set out some of the problems which appear to arise from the fact that here and elsewhere the family is a fundamentally dynamic social unit while land itself is static. At the same time, family farming takes place in a wider social and technological framework which can affect the viability of farms and families in important ways, and I describe some of the main features of this framework. Chapter 5 pays close attention to the various succession strategies employed by villagers. These include the use of wills and transfers to children during their parents' lifetimes. Such arrangements provide an important insight into relations between farming families and the state. Some of the documents of transfer, for example, read as if the world of commerce and bureaucracy has penetrated to the very heart of family life, but such documents are not always what they seem.

Chapter 6 analyses the chief patterns of co-operation among villagers both in farming and in other fields of action. There is an element of paradox in such co-operation, since Finnish farmers tend to see themselves as fierce individualists who are poor at collaborating with each other. In fact, they work together a great deal and some even buy machinery together. The chapter explores the important role of trust and choice for their success in this. Less functionally specific patterns of social interaction, such as those involved in visiting and gathering for coffee, are also discussed and are used to highlight the interplay of different and at times conflicting influences and values upon the community and its members.

Chapter 7 examines some of the theoretical and comparative issues raised by the study. The status of family farming as a valid focus of research in different settings is discussed, and it is noted that there are problems of comparison between farmers and their ancestors within a single village, in addition to those which arise from studies carried out in different areas of the world. None the less, it is argued that significant common features do remain despite the undoubted major influence of different temporal and spatial settings. The chapter also examines some of the chief factors which lie behind the persistence of family farming in modern Finnish conditions, which are by no means always favourable to such activity.

It will be apparent that in presenting this account of family farms in Vieki, I have several aims. I hope that it will usefully augment our knowledge of such farming systems generally, while at the same time adding to the awareness of Finland in the English-speaking world. I am also keen to make a contribution to our understanding of the family and other zones of interpersonal relations, and of the nature of their often complex links to the wider world. In this context, I hope that what I have to say about such issues as succession and co-operation will be interesting to social anthropologists and other social scientists who are not necessarily specialists in the study of European or even simply agrarian societies. Beyond this, I hope that the book will be of interest to Finns themselves, and that the naïve eye of the outsider can occasionally see something which those on the inside know, in some sense, and yet miss. Yet what may seem at first sight a more modest aim than to achieve surprise is possibly a more demanding and rewarding one. For it will be a source of special pleasure to me if the many villagers of Vieki who welcomed me to their homes can feel that I have managed to capture and place faithfully on record some of the spirit of their lives.

2

A strange eventful history

From Swedish province to modern independent state

It is a sad truth that few people in the English-speaking world are aware of
even the bare bones of Finnish history. I will not try here in any systematic
way to redress this deficiency, which is in any case substantially self-
imposed. For there are already a number of good accounts in English of the
main outlines of the history of the country.[1] I will, however, try to give
sufficient information, both on Finland's past and on the more particular
history of my research area in North Karelia, to serve as a background
against which contemporary developments can more easily be understood.
At the same time, I am conscious of the problems posed by such a task and
of my limitations for it. The account I present is based mostly on a reading
of the works of others, and it does not claim to constitute a contribution to
historical debate.[2] It is also clear that there is commonly no simple
uncontested history to be summarised, especially in a society which has seen
tumultuous events and sharp and sometimes violent disagreements over
fundamental issues within living memory.

Finland became independent in 1917 after a long period of inclusion
within Sweden and, thereafter, in the Russian empire. Alapuro (1980a) and
Allardt (1985) have both stressed the wide-ranging significance of Finland's
interstitial situation between these two zones of influence. Finland was a
part of Sweden until 1809, when it was formally ceded to Russia, and
Swedish culture, in a broad sense of the term, continued to exert substantial
influence long after that. Swedish remained the only official administrative
language until the 1860s, when Finnish gradually began to be used as well.

---

[1] See Jutikkala (1960a and 1960b), Kirby (1979) and Singleton (1989). There is a useful
further bibliography in Kirby (1979).

[2] My own main sources for this chapter have been Jutikkala (1960a and 1960b), Kirby (1979)
and Saloheimo (1954). Other works are acknowledged in their context.

Russian never occupied this status, though there were fears that it might be imposed on the country towards the close of the Tsarist regime, and some proficiency in the language was required of those wishing to pursue a military or civil service career. Finnish law remained in large part Swedish law, and much though by no means all the post-1809 history of legal developments in Finland, at least in the areas most relevant to this study, has been of the eventual adoption of measures already enacted at an earlier date in Sweden. Examples are the legal establishment of equal rights in land for women (1845 in Sweden and 1878 in Finland), and the abolition of the rights of kinsfolk to prevent the alienation of family land (Sweden 1863 and Finland 1932).[3] A major exception to this general trend was the political enfranchisement of women in 1906. Finland was the first country in Europe, and the second in the world, to introduce this.

Russian influence on Finnish culture has in general been played down by Finns, but it has not been wholly lacking either within or beyond the period of Russian rule. Some customary eastern Finnish patterns of inheritance are said to have had Russian origins, and the Russian Orthodox Church has been important, both in earlier times and more recently with the resettlement of displaced Karelians after the Second World War. In the Russian period, there was also a significant, if limited, awareness in Finland of developments in Russian literature, art and music, and a variety of contacts were established between writers, painters and composers on both sides. In addition, the architectural style of Helsinki, after it became the capital in 1812, had much in common with contemporary developments in St Petersburg. This was, however, mainly due to the neo-classical influence of the German architect Carl Ludvig Engel, who had worked in St Petersburg and other Baltic cities before his appointment by the Tsar as Helsinki's official architect in 1816.[4]

Russian rule appears to have provided both a stimulus to Finnish nationalism and conditions in which it was able to develop a momentum. When the country was officially ceded to Russia, it became a Grand Duchy directly subject to the Tsar himself as Grand Duke. The form of annexation was agreed at a meeting of the Finnish Diet called by Alexander I in March 1809 some months before the war with Sweden was concluded. The Finns swore allegiance to the Tsars, and Alexander announced that he was promoting the Finnish people 'to the status of a nation among nations'. The arrangement seems to have fitted with the views of Alexander's adviser, Speransky, who advocated the creation of an administrative zone where the

---

[3] See Blomstedt (1973, p. 47) and af Hällström (1934).
[4] See Blomstedt (1973, p. 33), Hellman (1989), Talve (1979, pp. 20–1) and Suolahti (1973, pp. 12–15 and passim).

importance of local conditions would be acknowledged and some Enlightenment ideas could be tried before their introduction into Russia itself. Under the agreement, Finns had no part in the government of Russia, and they were not liable to drafting into the Russian army. They had a small Finnish army, a customs frontier with Russia and citizenship rights not automatically available for Russian settlers. Revenue was collected and disbursed internally. A government, composed of Finns and directly subject to the Tsar himself, was established and became known as the Senate, a name which signified its formal comparability with the Russian Senate. On minor matters, the government acted autonomously, but it submitted its views on major issues to the Tsar, through a Finnish minister resident in St Petersburg. The Tsar in turn received advice from the Russian Governor-General in Helsinki. It had been intended that he would serve as Chairman of the Senate, but most holders of the office did not speak Swedish and did not attend meetings. As a result, the Vice-Chairman, a Finn, became in practice a Prime Minister.[5]

With the main exception of Nicholas II, the Tsars largely honoured this special relationship, and they enjoyed substantial loyalty in return. Nicholas II did much to destroy such sentiments, however, through riding roughshod over the established constitutional arrangements as he embarked upon a strenuous programme of russification of all parts of the empire at the turn of the century. The ensuing conflict, coupled with political disruptions in Russia itself, which culminated in the revolution, were a crucial stimulus to Finland's movement towards independence.

The first main developments in this direction had been largely concerned with attempts to establish the respectability of Finnish language and culture in the middle of the nineteenth century. As a Finno-Ugric language, Finnish differs fundamentally from its Indo-European neighbours. It was seen by many as a rough peasant language rather than one suited for administration and the arts in a country with aspirations to participate in the mainstream of European civilisation. The discovery and editing of the Kalevala epic and of other folk poetry played an important part in the counter-movement to such views. Cultural and linguistic nationalism began to be a powerful force, especially in the reign of Alexander II (1855–81). Snellman, the leader of the Finnish language movement, became a Senator. The first Finnish-language secondary school was founded in 1858, and in 1863 the Tsar decreed that Finnish was to join Swedish as an official language. Finnish autonomy was further strengthened at this time in other ways. The Diet met in 1863 for the first time since 1809, and in 1869 the Tsar

[5] Jutikkala (1960a, p. 24).

ratified a new Procedural Law which included rules for holding Diet meetings regularly. By the late 1870s the country had also obtained its own official currency in the form of the gold mark.

Finnish nationalism was not, however, the only force at work in the political arena during this period. Its most powerful early supporters had been Swedish-speaking intellectuals such as Runeberg, but a new 'Swedish' nationalism also began to develop in its wake. A deep rift developed between the two movements, and rival political parties were formed. The main issue was the language one, and the conflict was exacerbated by the relative lack of access of the Finnish-speaking population to the higher strata of society. In addition to these warring language parties, a third force, that of Liberalism, was also of importance in the 1870s and 1880s. For the Liberals, language was a relatively minor issue, and their main concern was to establish greater autonomy for a Finnish government and, in matters such as trade and press activity, greater freedom from government in general. They saw Russia as a backward country from which they wished to be dissociated. Despite the differences between these parties, all three of them appear to have been valuable sources of strength for resistance to the policies of Nicholas II.

In his attack on Finland's developing autonomy, Nicholas II was yielding to Russian nationalist pressures which had already begun to develop under his predecessor, Alexander III. Nicholas's measures aroused strong opposition within Finland, since they threatened to overturn the important constitutional privileges which the earlier Tsars had guaranteed. There were, however, internal arguments about how best to combat them. Direct resistance was proposed by some and shied away from by others, but it did have its fair measure of success. Bobrikov, the Tsar's authoritarian Governor-General, was assassinated by an activist and was replaced by a less dictatorial successor. The general strike of 1905, which had spread from Russia, led to the 1906 replacement of the Diet with a Finnish Parliament in the form of an assembly with political party representatives elected by universal suffrage. By this time, though, the country was itself seriously divided between right and left.

The chief division of importance in the context of this book was that between the 'haves' and 'have nots' of the rural sector, though there were also very serious urban problems as industry and urban settlement developed. Although the details vary from one region to another, the first half of the nineteenth century had witnessed what appeared to be the final stages of the establishment of the Finnish peasantry as a class of relatively free and, for the most part, land-owning farmers. On the other hand, the century was also a period of rapid population growth. This in itself encouraged the development of a substantial landless and tenant contingent, as individuals left family farms which could no longer adequately provide for them. Famine years, especially in the 1860s, also caused havoc to many families. Yet, as in parts of the third world today, more was involved than simply a growing population and the inclemencies of nature. Technological developments in agriculture, which were ultimately of great importance, took place only after immense damage had been done, and the famines reflected not only ecological but also serious political mistakes and problems at both national and international levels.[6] Towards the end of the century, the position of such poorer elements in the rural population began to deteriorate yet further with the development of the timber industry. Land-owners found new uses for their land and became increasingly reluctant to allow tenants to occupy it. In the eastern areas, there was also a related fall in swidden cultivation, which had been an important stand-by for the landless. At the same time, farmers in financial difficulties were often tempted by their richer neighbours and the timber companies to sell up, and although some migrated to the urban areas and beyond, others remained to swell the ranks of the rural poor.

The Tsarist regime's overthrow in 1917 was followed by the restoration of Finland's previous autonomous status by the new Russian provisional government which also, however, claimed for itself the rights previously held by the Tsars. In the aftermath of earlier conflict and resistance, this was not acceptable to the Finns. In July 1917, the Socialist-led Parliament arrogated to itself the Tsar's rights vis-à-vis internal policy, but left rights over foreign policy to the Russian authorities. This measure failed to satisfy the politicians on the right and also many of the people, since it fell short of full independence and it left the country with no clear head of state. The right then gave support to the Russian dissolution of this Parliament, and a new house was elected with a Socialist minority. This increased divisions in the Socialist ranks, and the more radical left began to gather greater strength, fuelled by food shortages and unemployment.

A general strike was organised in November 1917, but it was quickly brought to a close with the help of the more moderate Socialists. Shortly afterwards, Parliament announced its arrogation of all the Tsar's rights, internal and external, while the question of a head of state was left to be dealt with at a later date. A government was formed from the bourgeois parties, and it drafted a declaration of independence. Parliament approved this on 6 December, which became the officially celebrated date of independence, and after some hesitation the new Bolshevik government in Russia was successfully approached for recognition. In the turmoil of the moment there seem to have been many misreadings of the political

---

[6] See Soininen (1974, pp. 402–15).

situation. The Finns apparently assumed that the Bolsheviks would not last for long, and the Bolsheviks thought that a successful Finnish Communist revolution would soon take place. Stalin, who had been in Helsinki the previous month, noted with some discontent that freedom was given 'not to the people, but to the bourgeoisie, of Finland, which by a strange confluence of circumstances has received its independence from the hands of socialist Russia'.[7]

Another task was to remove the last remaining Russian forces from the country. Relations with Germany, as the enemy of Russia in the First World War, were close at this time. The Germans had been giving training to a contingent of young Finnish men, the so-called 'Jaegers', who had originally hoped to organise an insurrection against the Tsar. In addition to promising the return of these men to Finland, Germany also offered to help to expel the Russians with an expeditionary force. Mannerheim, who was leading the government force, at first opposed such help, but it was eventually accepted. His force consisted of the small national army strongly boosted by a largely bourgeois militia, the 'White Guard'. During the campaign against the Russian forces, the revolutionary wing of the Socialists seized power in southern Finland, having formed its own 'Red Guard', and Mannerheim now found himself with two opponents. The war has variously been called a war of independence and a civil war. The fighting lasted from January until May 1918, and atrocities on both sides took their toll in addition to combat casualties. Thousands of executions and deaths through hunger and disease in prison camps meant that Red losses were particularly high in the immediate post-war years. The war was substantially a class war, the Reds receiving their main support from industrial and agricultural workers, while the Whites were mainly drawn from the bourgeoisie and land-owning farmers. Perhaps predictably, tenant farmers were divided, since many had ambitions to become land-owners.

A second major issue after independence was the headship of the state. A monarchy was favoured by most members of the new Parliament, and the first step was to appoint a Regent. Svinhufvud, the leader of the government, and then Mannerheim held this position. There had been hopes that a German prince would take the throne, but the defeat of Germany prevented this. In 1919 a new Parliament was elected. Neither monarchy nor a headless state attracted strong enough support, and a presidency was opted for. At the same time, an attempt to settle the longstanding language issue was made by according official status to both Swedish and Finnish, but arguments about the question persisted into the following decades.[8]

[7] Quoted in Carr (1966, p. 294).
[8] See Jutikkala (1960a, pp. 28–9 and 40) and Kirby (1979, pp. 66–7 and 99–100).

The war left a deep legacy of bitterness of which traces still remain. The fact that there was already a firm base of experience of parliamentary government, though, and the existence of a strong body of political moderates helped to contain most forms of extremism which were later to emerge. The Agrarian Party developed as an important centrist influence at this time. A substantial majority (about 65 per cent) of the working population was still engaged in agriculture, and legislation was quickly drafted to provide at least some ownership of land to crofters and other landless groups in an attempt to weaken class divisions and avert future conflict. It was important also that the less radical section of the Social Democrats regained control of the party. They were the largest single contingent in the Parliament elected in 1919, and in 1926 they formed the government. Compulsory education for all aged 7–13 was introduced in 1921 as a move towards more equal opportunity within society.

Such action in the political centre was none the less accompanied by new polarising trends. The Socialist radicals formed splinter parties of their own, and the right-wing volunteer civic guard (*suojeluskunta*), which had been the mainstay of Mannerheim's force in the civil war, remained active in the maintenance of public order. In 1923 the recently formed Communist Party was suppressed, though it fought subsequent elections through the Workers' and Small Farmers' Party, and all formally Communist political activity was banned in 1930. Political stability was threatened both by the depression and by the example of strong Fascist movements elsewhere in Europe. In Finland the most dangerous development in this last direction was the so-called Lapua Movement, which began to engage in violence towards Communists and other left-wingers in 1929.[9] The movement had a firm grass-roots base, especially among the big and middle-level farmers of Pohjanmaa in western Finland, who believed their independent status and prosperity were threatened both by Communism and by the depression.[10] It also enjoyed substantial government support at first, but it gradually got out of hand and embarked upon an unsuccessful attempt at a coup d'état in 1932. It seems possible that the civil war, the camps and subsequent repressive legislation had paradoxically deprived the movement of the spectre of a truly dangerous radical left wing, through which it might conceivably have won the day even against the staunch constitutionalism of many politicians and lay citizens. However this may be, the movement was itself suppressed under the laws it had supported to deal with the Communists. Some of its followers re-emerged in a new party, the Patriotic People's Movement, which was partly inspired by the German Nazi Party. The

---

[9] See Alapuro (1980b), Alapuro and Allardt (1978), Jutikkala (1960b, p. 45) and Kirby (1979, pp. 83–92).
[10] Alapuro (1980b, pp. 679–81).

Lapua Movement crisis had, however, been enough for the majority of people, and the party failed to make a strong impact on the electorate.

Finland's relations with the Soviet Union after independence were marked by deep suspicions on both sides. These were not wholly allayed by a mutual non-aggression pact in 1932 or by Finnish declarations of intent to join its Scandinavian neighbours in a policy of neutrality should war break out. The country's links with Germany were a major aspect of this situation, since the Russians feared that Finland might allow the Germans to attack them via Finnish territory. The German–Soviet pact of August 1939 assigned Finland to the Soviet zone of influence, and the Russians made demands on Finland for territory and a base which would strengthen their defences. Earlier requests for support had been turned down by Finland, but some concessions were now offered. Even so, they were not sufficient to meet Russian demands, and the country was invaded in November 1939. The strength of Finland's ultimately unsuccessful stand against the Russians is probably the part of Finnish history best known to the outside world. At first, during the Winter War, the Finns fought alone despite offers of help from Britain and France. Later, after a period of crippling Winter War hostilities, the country did in fact turn towards Germany, and Hitler's forces entered via Norway. They were in Finland at the time of the German invasion of Russia, and Finland's efforts to keep out of the Second World War itself were practically at an end, despite its claims to be a 'co-belligerent' of Germany rather than an ally. Its special status was, however, recognised by the United States, which, unlike Britain, did not declare war on the country. It was also recognised to some degree by Russia, which eventually agreed to an armistice with Finland in 1944, rather than the unconditional surrender it had first demanded. Nevertheless, Finland was forced to cede a large part of its eastern territory to Russia, and the resettlement of displaced Karelians from these areas was a major problem of post-war reconstruction. Other territorial concessions in the north were also made. After the armistice, the country had to tackle urgently the problem of removing German troops from Finnish soil. The Germans adopted a scorched earth policy in their withdrawal, and this has left its own quota of bitter memories in the country.

It is all too easy within a brief compass to speak of a whole country or a nation and gloss over vital differences within it. This is particularly pertinent in the present context. For, in spite of the valiancy of the Finnish war effort and the fond memories which many veterans still have for the more spectacularly successful parts of the campaigns, it is clear that broader and probably wiser perceptions of the long-term problems of relations with the Soviet Union were present at an early date. Mannerheim, for example, seems to have held more moderate views than many of his colleagues, whose heightened fears of and hostility to Russia fuelled the government's refusal, without reference to Parliament, to grant early territorial concessions in summer 1939.[11] Even during the war also, the future President Kekkonen was expressing views about the need for readopting the country's earlier neutral stance in due course. Much of Finland's post-war success in creating a stable environment for social and economic development has depended upon the successful pursuit of the foreign policies, towards both East and West, of Kekkonen and his predecessor in the presidency, Paasikivi.[12] A *modus vivendi* with the Soviet Union has been established, and Finland has been able to develop as a fundamentally 'northern' country rather than in any sense a Russian satellite. It has close cultural, political and economic ties with Sweden and the other Scandinavian countries. Like them, it operates a 'free economy' and a parliamentary democracy, and it maintains open, passport-free borders with them. Its border with the Soviet Union is, in contrast, strictly controlled. The Russians have accepted Finland's neutral status, and Finland's special foreign policy responsibilities are spelled out only with regard to any future threats from Germany. Russia and Sweden are the country's main trading partners, and Russian economic connections have been very useful in times of difficulty, for example with regard to oil supplies and the sale of Finnish agricultural products, though there have also been fears of developing too much dependence on such links. The Finnish building industry has also won a number of important Russian contracts. It remains to be seen whether 'glasnost' will adversely affect Finland's favoured trading position as the Soviet Union pursues a wider range of overseas relationships.

The beginnings of modern settlement in the Vieki area[13]
During the fifteenth century the Lake Pielinen area in which Vieki is situated was demarcated as unsettled forest and countryside for the use of Ilomantsi and two other parishes to the south and east. These parishes formed part of the Russian sphere of influence defined in the 1323 Pähkinäsaari treaty with Sweden. By 1500 settlement had started in Lieksa, the centre of the modern commune to which Vieki belongs, and in a few other places. The earliest written records of settlement in Vieki itself date from 1589. By this time fifteen farms had been established in the village. It was already one of the larger settlements in the area, and it has tended to remain so.

The following century was a period of mixed fortunes for this as for many other parts of eastern Finland. Life was frequently disrupted by food shortages and by the long string of wars between the Russian and the

---

[11] See Hall (1957, p. 135).
[12] See Gripenberg (1960, pp. 59–60 and passim) and Kirby (1979, p. 190 and Chapter 8 passim).
[13] My main sources for the early history of the area are Saloheimo's detailed histories of the Lieksa and Nurmes areas (1953 and 1954).

Swedish empires. At the same time, however, the population began to grow as new settlers moved in after the treaty of Stolbova in 1617, which allocated the area to Sweden, and strengthened its westward connections with other Finnish regions. In the course of the century, the population of the area increased almost tenfold, though growth was not an even process. One consequence of expansion from the west was that villages like Vieki became wholly Lutheran during this period, as some Orthodox Christians were converted and others fled. This caused a temporary fall in population in the area, and Vieki's own growth was further hindered for a time by the movement of some residents to new neighbouring settlements.

Towards the end of the century, in addition to their normal fare of troubles, people in the area also began to suffer from the predations of the local tax collector and administrator, Simon Affleck, a man of Scottish descent whose cruelties earned him the nickname Simo Hurtta (literally Simon the Hound). Affleck remained in power for many years in spite of opposition from the people and the clergy, and in 1710 he put down a revolt which was triggered by food shortages the year before. Shortly afterwards, during the Great Northern War, the Lutheran vicar of Pielisjärvi parish, to which Vieki belonged, apparently welcomed the Russians into the area in the hope that they might bring the people some relief from Affleck's tyranny. For his pains, the vicar was driven out by the invaders, and although little detail is available, it appears that the area in general suffered badly at this time from its new masters. Relief came only with the end of the war and the treaty of Nystad (Uusikaupunki) in 1721. By this time Vieki had fourteen farms, of which six were listed as unoccupied or run down, while a further nine had completely disappeared from the record. In the parish as a whole, only 158 farms out of 588 in 1686 were fully functional in 1722, and 226 were in the unoccupied or run down category. Rough estimates of population for the parish at this time suggest that it had fallen to about 1,900 from its 1686 total of just under 3,000, and by extrapolation one might guess that Vieki's 1722 population was about seventy as against more than a hundred in 1686.

The eighteenth century was, however, once again a period of substantial population growth, caused by natural increase and also by new settlement, which was further encouraged during the period. Saloheimo has documented the situation for the Nurmes area in the northern part of Pielisjärvi parish. There, the population was about 550 in 1722 and, despite the transfer of some villages to a neighbouring area, it had risen to a little above 6,000 by 1810. This suggests a population of about 20,000 for the parish as a whole at this time.[14]

[14] Saloheimo (1953, pp. 112–24).

During the seventeenth and eighteenth century the rural population of the area gradually became socially and economically more stratified, though it remained relatively homogeneous compared with regions further south and west. Small groups of labourers and servants are recorded in the seventeenth century, but many of these were sons and daughters of land-holding families (*talolliset*, literally 'house' or 'farm people') and could look forward to a farm of their own in due course. This pattern continued through the eighteenth and even into the nineteenth century, but it was accompanied by the growth of a substantial class of landless villagers. These ranged from stewards (*lampuodit*, sing. *lampuoti*), who ran other people's farms and were in some cases quite prosperous, through tenant crofters (*torpparit*), who occupied either crown land or parts of private farms, in the latter case partly for rent in labour, to small cotters (*mäkitupalaiset*) and a variety of dependent lodgers (*loiset*, literally 'para-sites').[15] The economic security of these groups was to some extent protected in the eighteenth and much of the nineteenth century by the availability of public land for swidden agriculture. Their numbers had increased and their position had deteriorated badly by 1900, when the full effects of mid-century land partition (*isojako*) and the development of field agriculture and commercial forestry were strongly felt.

The nineteenth and early twentieth century in Vieki

The partition and reorganisation of land holdings known as *isojako* (literally the 'big division') was begun in Finland in the eighteenth century, when the country was still part of Sweden, but it was a long process which was not completed in eastern Finland until the middle of the following century. In addition to the rationalisation of farm boundaries, some farms were reallocated to neighbouring villages at that time, and many crown tenants also obtained the freehold of their land.

These developments were already in motion but not yet complete in the Vieki area by 1845. In the *henkikirja*, or civil census, for that year the Swedish-language enumerator lists the village as Yliviegi (Upper Vieki). The name was probably used to mark the difference between Vieki and the older village of Viensuu (literally Viekimouth) which lies to its south at the end of a small lake, Viekijärvi. The lake is fed by the river, Viekijoki, along which some of Vieki's oldest farms were situated.

The village had a population of 654 at that time, and most of these people were living on one or other of thirty-three numbered farm units, which had in many cases been divided into sections. Some 431 men, women and

---

[15] There are detailed discussions of these categories in Saloheimo (1953, pp. 125–63) and Soininen (1974, pp. 29–49). See also Kirby (1979, pp. 9–13). The terms *lampuoti* and *torppari* are derived from Swedish *landbo* and *torpare* (see Harlock and Gabrielson, 1951).

children were resident members of forty-nine land-holding farming families in various stages of development. In addition to their family members, twenty-seven of these farms had a total of thirty-seven resident male labourers between them, and five of these men were married. Seventeen of the farms, including eleven with male labourers, had a total of twenty-five resident female servants, who were all unmarried. Fourteen farms also had resident 'lodgers' who were poor or otherwise unable to look after themselves. They consisted of twelve couples, including seven with children, and three women. One of the women had two children with her.

There was one family which appears to have occupied the whole of another family's farm, probably as *lampuoti* tenants. The owners had another farm elsewhere. There were also seventeen crofting families (*torpparit*). Five of these held crofts (*torpat*) on private farms, and the other twelve were probably on crown land. Only one crofter had a hired labourer, while one other had a female servant. All of the crofts on private land were occupied by couples with young children, though there was also an adult son on one. The other crofting families were more varied in their composition.

In addition to farm families and their servants, labourers and farming tenants, there was a miller in the village living with his wife and children, and an unmarried tailor. Both of these men paid a higher rate of tax than adult farming family members. It is not clear whether they rented or owned property. There was also registered accommodation for travellers in the village, but this was on a family farm and appears to have been an ancillary activity of the farmer.

The village at this time was beginning to show some signs of the future patterns of differentiation. Two-thirds of the population were members of land-holding families, and two-thirds of these kept one or more farm or domestic workers. Although it is impossible to document exactly, some of the labourers and servants were children of local families who could hope to have a farm of their own at some time. On the other hand, it is true also that some labourers were members of former farming families who had fallen on hard times, and the same is true of some of the tenants and most if not all of the lodgers. To the limited extent that I have been able to trace the subsequent lives of such people, it appears that most of them and their children remained relatively poor.

My next data set for the village is the list of 1866–7. By this time the population had grown to 947, and the number of land-holding households had increased to seventy. There were only eight crofting families at this time, and it is possible that some such families had failed to cope with the run of bad years which culminated in the 1867 famine. Resident farm and domestic labour was provided by forty-four men and thirty-seven women, but there was by now also a category of people hired by the day. Sixteen of these were men of whom seven were married, and eleven were women. There was also a poor list for the village which included eleven women, six men and six children, and the number of lodgers had risen to 112 men, women and children. It is clear from later data that many such people were to stay poor or become even poorer, and hard times also lay ahead for many villagers who still had their own farms.

By 1884 the situation had deteriorated further. The village list gives a total of 1,131 people, but there were still only seventy-one land-holding households, and there were now eighteen crofting families. The number of domestic and farm workers was much the same as before, but the number of dependent lodgers (*loiset*) had increased to 142 men, women and children. There was a long list of 196 unattached people (*irtolaiset*) and forty-four poor and incapable of work. A comparable pattern was maintained during the following decades. In 1900–1, there were eighty land-holding and twenty-four crofter households in a total village population of 1,189. This suggests some out-migration in the intervening years, and there was in fact new settlement nearby in Uusikylä. There were 136 dependent lodgers and a list of ninety-four poor and incapable people which included twenty-nine children. The list of unattached people was down to twenty-three, but the previously small category of landless cotters (*mäkitupalaiset*) had risen strongly from eighteen men, women and children in 1884 to 252. By this period, also, the opportunity for such landless and dependent people to fall back on swidden agriculture had been drastically reduced if not completely lost.

It is clear that many individuals and families were impoverished during the nineteenth century, though a few did manage to recover. Famine years, population growth, the development of the money economy and the need for adaptation to new pressures all made it difficult for many families to survive, especially if they were temporarily weakened by the sickness or death of key members. Richer farmers and also timber companies and some shopkeepers were also increasingly keen to acquire land, especially towards the end of the century, and many families were bought out by such people. The possibility of putting land to commercially profitable use also meant that tenancy conditions for crofting families were deteriorating. The situation was not as bad in this last context as in the south and west of Finland, where the numbers of crofters and also of really big land-owners were larger than in North Karelia. But the very factors of relatively poor soil, harsh climate and distance from the metropolitan centres which limited the development of large-scale farming enterprises in the east also meant that it was hard for the small farmers of that area to survive.

It would be wrong, however, simply to see the turn of the last century in

Vieki as a period of increased misery. As in many other areas of rural Finland, it was also a period of important social and cultural developments, including an expansion of the co-operative movement, which have served many of the people in good stead right through to the present. Around this time we find the establishment within the village of such institutions as the Co-operative Bank, a co-operative credit grain-store and a 'Rural Association' (*Maalaisseura*), whose chief stated aim was the development of agriculture.[16] A few years later, the village's own Co-operative Dairy was also opened. These were relatively 'technical' developments, designed to facilitate successful farming in the changing socio-economic circumstances of the period. They were, however, also seen as 'social' developments, through which the village could share in the benefits of modern Finnish and wider European society. As such they have to be considered alongside the formation in the village of a 'Youth Association' (*Nuorisoseura*) and, later, a 'Martta' women's group devoted to the development of the skills and cultural awareness of village wives. The Youth Association was a social club devoted to good works and the provision of suitable entertainments for younger people. Recitals, plays, sports events and dances (in modest numbers) were arranged, and discussion meetings were held on matters such as smoking, drinking and acceptable patterns of relationship between the sexes. Literacy was an important concern, and a library was in due course organised by the society. These local institutions and associations were affiliated in a variety of ways to pre-existing wider regional or national organisations. They were all part of the spirit of the age and of a general movement for the betterment of rural life.[17]

It is interesting in this regard that in Vieki, as no doubt in many other rural areas of the day, there was an intimate connection between such 'progressive' institutions and the development of formal education and the church. A school had been founded in the parish centre, Lieksa, in 1873, and some Vieki children went there. In 1881 a number of influential Vieki villagers, including Johan Turunen, who was active in wider commune affairs, proposed the founding of a local school. There was some local opposition, however, and the commune council would only agree to the proposal if the villagers themselves bore the cost of upkeep. New proposals were made, and rejected, in 1883 and 1884, but the tide turned in 1887. Taavi Kärki, a member of a longstanding Vieki family, had gone bankrupt, and his house and land were bought at auction by a Lieksa merchant, Fredrik Hämäläinen. He, perhaps partly in an effort to establish good

[16] See Saloheimo (1953, pp. 395–400 and 517–22) for similar developments in the Nurmes area. For Finland generally see Soininen (1974, pp. 337–42 and 347–9.)
[17] Fox (1926, pp. 45–50 and 124) discusses some of these institutions for Finland generally. See also Saloheimo (1953), pp. 429–30).

relations in the village, generously offered the buildings and also some land to the commune for use as a school over a period of fifteen years rent free. The land included an area of forest to provide firewood and building timber, and also some arable and meadow land. In return the commune was to cover the costs of running the school. This was agreed, and the first pupils entered in September 1888. The first teacher, Antti Kinnunen, stayed till 1891 and is credited among other things with starting a school choir, out of which the village church choir later developed. He was, it seems, a devout Christian and a stern disciplinarian. Kinnunen was followed by a number of short-term appointments and secondments, until 1894, when Oskari Alen was appointed. Alen, who later adopted the Finnish name Ahola, remained in office for twenty years, and he appears to have had an immense influence within the village. He worked closely with a number of 'enlightened' villagers, and played a particularly strong role in the founding and development of the village bank and credit grain-store. He was later joined in many such activities by the local pastor, Emanuel Kolkki.[18]

Vieki was part of the Pielisjärvi parish until 1948, when it became the centre of a new separate Viekijärvi parish. The fine wooden village church was built in 1908–11, and the building was the culmination of a process which began in the 1890s. Already at that time many villagers, including those who had supported the new school, were keen to have their own church and independent parish. A meeting to propose this was held in the school in December 1892, and by 1897 it was formally agreed by the parish authorities that Vieki might have its own resident curate (*kappalainen*). Kolkki was appointed in 1901, and he actively supported the request for parish status and, more successfully, the planning and building of the present church. This last task was itself a major co-operative venture in the village. Land was given by Petter Turunen, and the timber, which was provided by the state, was shipped down the river by local villagers. Many villagers are also said to have lent a hand with the building work.

The role of school and church as focal points of village identity, and that of Alen and Kolkki as pivotal figures in new developments, are very clear. The enthusiasm of the two men, and their education and trustworthiness were vital at a time when relatively few villagers were literate or had much experience of the wider world. Alen was on the committee which founded the co-operative credit grain-store in 1897, and he was the first keeper of the storehouse. The meeting at which it was agreed to found the Co-operative Bank was held at the school in 1905. Alen was once again one of the founders, and was elected chairman and secretary of the first management

---

[18] I am grateful to Ilmari Havia, who was headmaster at the time of my research, for a copy of his manuscript on the history of Savolanvaara school, For schooling in the nearby Nurmes area see Saloheimo (1953, pp. 599–641).

committee, the first meeting of which was also at the school. A first meeting of the members of the new bank was held at the vicarage in 1906, and Kolkki was elected treasurer and keeper of accounts. It was decided also to keep the bank's funds at the vicarage. Kolkki later became an inspector of accounts for the credit grain-store, and the two men were also involved in the youth association. Both men were initially outsiders to the village, but they made it their own and they are still spoken of with warmth and affection by many older villagers. Of course, they could not have achieved anything without local support, and it is important to recall that active villagers had made their presence possible in the first place and collaborated with them in planning and realising the developments I have discussed. A variety of names recur in these different contexts, and several of those involved were members of the Kiiskinen, Kärki, Kärkkäinen, Saarelainen and Turunen families, whose background is described in Chapter 3.[19]

Most of these families were at that time relatively well-off land-owners, though some, like the Siltavaara Kärkis, were former land-owners who had become crofters after falling on hard times. As I have noted, this was a period when the gap between 'haves' and 'have nots' was at its most apparent in the village, and it is not clear to what extent the developments concerned were mainly relevant to the more prosperous elements in the community. Certainly, here as elsewhere, it was easier for such people than for the poor to exhibit the creditworthiness and respectability which were a precondition of full participation in the network of cultural and economic institutions centred around school and church. Some evidence for this on the economic side appears in the records of the credit grain-store. In 1922, these listed 46 outstanding debts in Vieki and the outlying settlement of Uusikylä, which the institution also served, and 43 of these were in Vieki itself. The household status of two Vieki debtors is unknown. Seventeen were land-owners, and twenty-two were crofters and cotters. There were also a tailor and a tanner. Eleven of the land-owners, as against only three of the twenty-four crofters and others, were given extensions or additions to existing loans. Again, on the social side, the Youth Association had forty-six members in 1917. Thirty of these were from land-owning families, and one was a shopkeeper's son. Four are described as workmen (*työmies*), and three as female servants (*palvelijatar*). Five others were crofters' children, another a shop assistant, and the status of two others is unclear. It is, of course, of interest in itself that the list actually recorded the 'status or profession' (*arvo tai ammatti*) of the members. All this was not surprisingly

---

[19] I am grateful to E. Mikkonen, a former manager, for a copy of his manuscript (Mikkonen, 1975) on the history of the Vieki bank. I discuss the more recent history of the bank in Chapter 6.

accompanied by a leaning towards political conservatism amongst those concerned. The records of the credit grain-store are also revealing in this context. In 1917 the committee donated 2,000 marks to the White Guards, and in 1924 it gave 4,000 marks for the erection of a (White) heroes' statue in the village.

At the same time, it is important to note that the gap between the landed and the landless was less stark in this area than in the *kartano* zones of the west, and there is for the most part relatively little evidence of sharply drawn class conflict there. The ambition of many tenants to become their own masters once again, and join the landed classes, was both seductive and realisable. In addition, as some of the latter group rose in the world, there were plenty of examples in the 1920s and 1930s, as there had been earlier, of families failing to survive successfully in farming despite the advantage of a landed birthright.

Even at the time of the civil war, violence was relatively limited as compared with many other parts of Finland, though it is clear that the crisis was a source of great anxiety and considerable bitterness for many people. As in Finland generally, an attempt to gain a clear picture of the civil war in Vieki and nearby areas is complicated by the partisan nature of existing reports and the reticence of many people, who are anxious to let old wounds heal. It is for the most part only after the war with Russia that a predominately right-wing picture of events has been tempered by accounts more sympathetic to the left. Coupled with this, memorials to those who died on the Red side were only then erected within Lieksa town and at some other sites. A number of local men on both sides lost their lives in battle elsewhere in the country. Locally, the White force and its supporters were dominant, and a number of known Socialists in Lieksa town and in some villages were subjected to considerable harassment and even, in some cases, executed by the White authorities. In one well-known incident, four brothers were hunted down and murdered by a self-appointed right-wing posse which reputedly included one or two Vieki farmers. A number of captured Reds also died in camps after the war.[20]

Independent farmers in an independent state

As elsewhere in Finland, land reform was a main feature of the early years of the post-independence period in Vieki. By the late 1930s, crofters and cotters had been allocated smallholdings of their own, though there was one exception to this in the village. Oskari Pyykkö, who had been a crofter on the large Mustola farm, refused steadfastly to give up this status, and he

---

[20] There are interesting accounts of Red sufferings in the war in the Lieksa area in Nykänen (1977).

developed a local reputation for being Finland's *viimeinen torppari* ('last crofter'). His stand on this was clearly quite eccentric, but it is also perhaps interesting in other ways. It suggests that there was not always much for an individual to choose between the crofter's lot and that of the small independent farmer. Structurally, too, it is consonant with the fact that the land reforms of this period appear in retrospect as short-term palliative measures which replaced one set of problems with another. The former inequalities between the landed and the landless were now superseded by a sharp growth in the number of small, independent farms whose viability in the changing modern world was put to an increasingly stern test. Also, rural population growth continued to exert pressure on existing land resources, though admittedly the pace was slowing down. The village population had increased by over 40 per cent between 1901 and 1921 (from 1,189 to 1,681), and the increase between 1921 and 1938 (1,681 to 1,812) was only slightly above 7.5 per cent as people moved away, especially during the depression years.

The population of the village began to grow rapidly again after the war with Russia. Many older present-day farmers fought in the war, and it is clear from conversation that it was a vitally important personal experience, of great hardship and excitement, for many of them. As in other areas, several families suffered losses, but a majority of men returned to their families and the harsh uncertainties of farming. In addition to returning sons and husbands, the war also brought newcomers to the village. Following the 1945 Land Act, several war veterans (*rintamamiehet*) from other North Karelian villages were allocated farms in Vieki, and a substantial group of Karelians, mainly from the Suojärvi area, were also resettled there after the boundary revisions following the peace arrangements. Several Karelian families were allocated land in central Vieki, but many were settled in the northern area of the village. This area is usually called Loukku these days, after the name of one of the original Vieki farms there, but it was commonly called Egyptinkorpi ('the Egyptian wilderness') at the time of resettlement, and the name continues in use to the present time. As the name suggests, resettlement involved a massive clearing operation of so-called 'cold farms'. The total area of the new settlement zone was 2,730 hectares, and a little under 500 hectares of this was suitable for cultivation. Only a small proportion of this land was already in use, though, and the rest had to be cleared. The clearing was done by the state, and also through the medium of a voluntary international work camp. The state also saw to roads and drainage works, and to the provision of saunas which the settlers used, in traditional fashion, as base camps from which to build their farmsteads. Building materials were also given by the state. Most of the land had belonged to the Enso Gutzeit company, but other land came from the state, the Commune, the Kaukas timber company and individual land-owners.[21]

The process of resettlement was extremely difficult both physically and psychologically for the newcomers, and their arrival was tolerated rather than wholeheartedly welcomed by some local residents. There is still occasional slight evidence of resentment among some of the latter, and as far as I can tell this stems originally from the large quantities of aid, with an ultimate cancellation of debts, which the displaced families received from the state at a time when many local farmers were struggling to make a go of things. One occasionally hears statements that many of the Karelian newcomers (*siirtolaiset*, literally 'migrants') were technically poor farmers, and that some of them had never even farmed before. It is also sometimes said that they were keen to sell up their newly acquired farms as soon as they could. There is in fact little ground for most such claims, and much the same proportion of Karelians as of previously settled villagers (*paikalliset*, literally 'locals', or *kanta-asukkaat*, literally 'original settlers') have remained in Vieki as farmers. Moreover, such occasional grumbles have not inhibited a considerable amount of intermarriage or the development of valuable technical co-operation with Karelian neighbours. It is, of course, significant that the latter still tend to retain an 'ethnic' identity of their own, so that they have not simply merged into the local cultural landscape. Almost all of them are members of the Orthodox Church, as opposed to the Lutheranism of the *kanta-asukkaat* and, linguistically, there is some tendency to maintain their own dialect forms or to move from them to standard Finnish rather than to North Karelian speech patterns.

There has also been a more general interest within North Karelia, and to some extent beyond, in the maintenance of Karelian culture and traditions. This has received substantial academic support from Karelian experts in the University of Joensuu, and some people have also been quick to realise the commercial tourist potential of fine national costumes, special cooking and weaving traditions, folk dances, orthodox ceremonial and large log buildings based on old extended family houses. The Bomba House hotel complex just outside Nurmes successfully embodies a number of these attractions, though an attempt at the development of one or more commercial 'tourist villages', as elsewhere in the region, has not so far been made in the Lake Pielinen area of North Karelia.[22] The various emphases on Karelian culture and its maintenance have also occasionally been a source of irritation to some local people, and one man recently wrote to the

---

[21] For accounts of the creation of the Egyptinkorpi settlement see Salpakari (1963) and Lieksan Pääkirjasto (1985).

[22] See Petrisalo (1988) for a critical discussion of attempts to develop a Karelian village and its culture as a commercial tourist attraction in Tuupovaara Commune.

Table 1 *Age, sex and marital status of the Vieki population, 1979*

Born	MALE Married	Unmarried			FEMALE Married	Unmarried		
		Divorced	Widower	Never		Divorced	Widow	Never
Pre 1910	32	0	6	6	12	0	36	2
1910–19	62	2	3	11	45	0	31	7
1920–9	65	4	3	20	75	1	21	10
1930–9	37	2	0	18	49	0	4	6
1940–9	31	0	0	32	28	2	0	8
1950–9	20	1	0	110	29	0	0	33
1960–9	0	0	0	101	0	0	0	88
1970–9	0	0	0	44	0	0	0	42
Total	247	9	12	342	238	3	92	196
Total males			610		Total females	529		

Lieksa newspaper to ask, somewhat petulantly, what 'culture' is and why it is something which only Karelians in the area seem to have.

The coming of the Karelians brought the last main increase to Vieki's population before the period of large-scale emigration out of Finland's rural areas in the 1960s and 1970s. The village was strongly affected by this widespread exodus, but it did not suffer as drastically as some of the surrounding small communities, and its facilities have even attracted a few settlers from these in recent years. In the nearby but more 'backwoods' area of Uusikylä, for example, the population dropped from 230 in 1960 to 37 in 1979, and some of those who left went to live in Vieki. There the population dropped from its highest point of 2,477 in 1960 to 1,827 in 1970, and from there to 1,139 in 1979. This drop was accompanied by severe distortions in the age and sex structure of the village, as Table 1 reveals.

As the table shows, there were 609 villagers between twenty and sixty years of age in 1979, and 266 of these were women. Twenty-five of the women were widows, three were divorced, and fifty-seven had never been married. Three men were widowers, seven had been divorced, and 180 had never married. According to official figures, there were still 116 working farms in Vieki in 1980, with an average field area of 10.45 hectares and an average forest holding of thirty-nine hectares.[23] The farm workforce was listed as 264, or a little over two persons per farm. A combination of these figures provides a rough estimate of the proportion of the population of working age engaged in farming in the village at that time, i.e. about 43 per cent. The same source notes the existence of a further 110 people (c. 18 per

[23] These figures were kindly provided for me by the Agricultural Adviser's office in Lieksa.

cent) working in other occupations, including thirty-one forestry workers, fifteen shop workers, ten church employees, five bar staff, four taxi drivers, four bank workers and four postal workers. In addition, 107 of the people listed as engaged in farming were also engaged in some ancillary activities for longer or shorter periods of the year. These included thirty-nine engaged in timber work, and fourteen doing agricultural or dairy work for others. These figures probably also include a small number of men working for a new sauna and shed construction company which had recently been started in the village, and there were also a few mechanics, carpenters, builders and other technically skilled individuals who provided services within the village and sometimes beyond. It is not clear what proportion of the remaining number were also employed part or full time in or outside the village, but there is evidence to suggest that perhaps a further fifty were living on pensions tied to farm closure schemes, and there were several former farmers and workmen on sickness pensions.

As in other rural areas, the decline in the Vieki population up to 1980 was partly due to falling birth rates, but it mainly stemmed from movement into urban areas of Finland and abroad. Emigration from the villages was fuelled by difficulties at home which were coupled with new levels of expectations based on educational expansion and a more general broadening of villagers' horizons. The pattern has differed for males and females. Women have tended to move to the service sector, while man have gone more often into factories in Finland and also in Sweden, whose developing motor industry has attracted many immigrants, Many younger women were anxious to escape from the reality or looming threat of unrewarding farmhouse drudgery on a small farm and perhaps under the eye of an unfriendly mother-in-law; and men were finding it increasingly hard to make a living. Many village men, and especially those with smaller holdings, were used to supplementing income in the winter months through work for timber companies. The post-war development of the Finnish timber industry, however, included its rapid mechanisation, with the introduction of petrol-driven saws and increasingly large and complex vehicles and machines for loading and transporting timber. Less manpower was needed, and a vital source of income was lost to many village men.

Many of the main effects of industrialisation and mechanisation on rural society were well understood in political circles, and there was substantial support from Social Democrats and others for the new developments. Agriculture itself was thought likely to benefit from them in the longer term through increased efficiency, and the effects on the economy as a whole were also seen as mainly beneficial.

There was clearly some truth in such arguments, though the situation has been less straightforward than some seem to have expected. The agricultural sector now accounts for about 10 per cent of the country's working population after slimming down from a figure of about 50 per cent in the 1950s, and it has become much more efficient. The increased productivity involved has been necessary for maintaining farmers' incomes at a reasonable level relative to others, and this indicates that some cutback in numbers, especially of smaller and less viable farms, was essential.[24] Total production figures have indeed increased in some sectors, such as meat, and they have kept up with their early post-war levels in the crucial dairy sector which has, as elsewhere in Europe, an awkward tendency to over-production. This has been a recurrent source of political debate and conflict which has been exacerbated by the subsidies and other forms of support for farmers won by their parliamentary and professional lobbies.

It might be argued from this that the process of retraction simply has not gone far enough, but there are also reasons to fear that it has already gone too far. Although emigration in itself is much less of an immediate problem these days, the damage it has done to village population structures still remains. The figures which I have presented for Vieki are reasonably typical of many villages in this and other parts of Finland, and they do not seem likely to be much offset by the return of former migrants or the arrival of new settlers, though there are a few of these. Such a population is doomed to decline further through mortality, and its ability to reproduce itself and to achieve an equilibrium is seriously impaired. During early 1981 my wife and I lived quite close to the church in Vieki, and the regular ringing of the bells was a sombre reminder of the death rate in a population of this sort. Already these developments have had quite serious effects on the quality of rural life. Although some mobile services such as a library bus and mobile shops have been provided, villagers are keen whenever possible to keep their locally based services. Many village schools, shops and other public- and private-sector facilities have been declared uneconomic and have been closed down. In these circumstances, earlier complacency about the running down of agriculture seems much less appropriate. Present levels of subsidy are quite high, and the potential welfare burden and the real distress behind it which the uncontrolled collapse of rural society could involve are

---

[24] See Toivonen and Widerszpil (1978, pp. 109, 112). The calculation of farmers' incomes and their relative evaluation against other incomes at home and abroad is very difficult. Available figures suggest that average farmers' earnings were close to average manual workers' earnings in the 1970s, but this conceals considerable variation between large and small farms and between regions. In 1976, earnings per household on medium-sized farms were reportedly higher than the national average for all households, but farm households were relatively large and earnings per household member were lower than the average. A higher percentage of farmers on middle- to large-sized farms owned cars, telephones and fridges than people in most other occupations, but this seems likely in part to reflect their relative isolation. Most farmers in Vieki had relatively modest cars. See Valkonen et al. (1980, pp. 128, 129–34, 141–2). In general, Finnish living standards are among the highest in Europe.

frightening. Nor has it helped the situation that industrial development has recently been in the doldrums, though it is true that it has picked up once again, at least in certain sectors. It has no doubt been easier with hindsight than it was originally to realise that there was no guarantee that industrial expansion and prosperity were a long-term or a stable prospect. Nor was there sufficient control available to ensure that the effects of economic change on the decisions of farmers and their children to give up or continue farming could themselves create a balance between the conflicting tendencies of sectionally and nationally perceived economic needs.

Some aspects of the double nature of the problem are neatly illustrated by the variety of modern official agricultural pension schemes which have become increasingly important as the average age of Finnish farmers has gradually reached its present figure of almost fifty-five. Apart from simple old-age pensions, there is an arrangement whereby farmers are tempted to retire early and close down their farms. At the same time, a further programme attempts to bring 'new blood' into the farming scene by facilitating the inter-generational transmission of farms from ageing owners to more youthful successors. This includes credit facilities for renovations and for buying out co-heirs, and pensions for the retiring farmer and his wife. Not surprisingly, interested potential successors are more common on more profitable middle- to large-sized farms. It seems clear that the number of farms will drop substantially further before a plateau is reached, and it is probable that the fall will be steepest in poorer and already hard-hit areas like North Karelia.

The influence of some of the demographic and structural changes which I have discussed is also visible in the local government election voting patterns of Vieki villagers.[25] In 1930, the Agrarian League (*Maalaisliitto*), which later became the Centre Party (*Keskustapuolue*), polled just under a third of votes in the village. As its name implies, the party was particularly concerned with the interests of farmers. It played an important role in the post-independence land reforms, and at the time of this particular election it was campaigning hard for debt-relief for farmers who were badly hurt by the depression. The Conservatives (*Kansallinen Kokoomus*, literally 'National Coalition') polled about one-fifth, and the Social Democrats and other Socialists just over half. This reflects both the mixed nature of the village population and the large number of small farmers who still relied at that time on timber work and labouring for others for much of their income. In fact, the Social Democrats were heavily reliant upon rural workers for support in Finland generally during the 1930s.

By 1953 the Social Democrats were still well supported, but the Agrarian

[25] I am especially grateful to Viljo Turunen in Vieki and to Ms S. Kärkkäinen in Lieksa for providing me with information about early local elections.

Table 2 *1964 voting patterns in Vieki constituencies and wider Commune*

Area	Vieki (centre)	Siltavaara	Savolanvaara	Commune[a]
Party				
Conservatives and People's Party	30 (10%)	—	6 (2%)	863 (10%)
Small Farmers' League (later SMP)	53 (18%)	14 (19%)	42 (17%)	476 (6%)
Agrarian League	111 (38%)	29 (40%)	118 (49%)	2040 (24%)
Communists etc.	20 (7%)	2 (3%)	7 (3%)	1955 (24%)
Social Democrats	78 (27%)	27 (38%)	70 (29%)	2995 (36%)
Total	292 (100%)	72 (100%)	243 (100%)	8329 (100%)

Note:
[a] Rural Commune and Township constituencies combined

Party had also developed strongly, and this appears to reflect the tendency for a larger proportion of villagers to perceive themselves as land-owning, independent farmers. Figures for the Savolanvaara area of the village, which was largely agricultural, showed the Agrarians with 119 votes (44 per cent), the Social Democrats with 129 (48 per cent), the Communists and other left-wing groups with 19 (7 per cent) and the Conservatives with 4 (1 per cent). In the Vieki centre (*kirkonkylä*) area for that year, the Conservatives polled 35 (13 per cent), the Agrarian League 109 (41 per cent), the Social Democrats 120 (45 per cent) and the Communists and similar groups 3 (1 per cent).

Figures for 1964 are set out in Table 2 for the three voting areas of Vieki centre, Siltavaara in the north of the village, and Savolanvaara, and they are compared with voting in the Commune as a whole, including Lieksa town and its neighbouring areas of industrial development.

The table shows a substantial fall in the Socialist and Communist vote in the rural areas, and this relates to the onset of substantial out-migration of some of the smaller farmers in these areas. There is a contrast between Vieki centre and the outlying constituencies of Siltavaara and Savolanvaara, for example in the size of the Conservative vote, which reflects the more mixed nature of the *kirkonkylä* population, with its shopkeepers and officials in addition to farmers. The size of the Social Democrat vote in Siltavaara is partly a reflection of there having been a well-established popular candidate in that part of the village, but it is noticeable that the two 'farming' parties none the less polled 59 per cent of the vote there, and 66 per cent in Savolanvaara. The contrast between the figures for these rural areas and for the Commune as a whole stems from the much larger number of votes cast for both right- and left-wing candidates in the densely settled urban and industrial area in and around Lieksa.

Figures for the 1980 elections show a continuation of these general trends. Thus in the Vieki voting area the right-wing parties polled 8 votes (3 per cent), the Centre Party (formerly the Agrarian Party) 126 (53 per cent), the Finnish Countryside Party (SMP – a small farmers' party) 42 (19 per cent), the Social Democrats 48 (20 per cent) and the Communists 13 (5 per cent) out of a total vote of 237. In Savolanvaara the figures were: right-wing parties 8 (4 per cent), the Centre Party 104 (54 per cent), the Countryside Party (SMP) 31 (16 per cent), the Social Democrats 48 (25 per cent) and the Communists 2 (1 per cent): total 193. The Finnish Countryside Party (SMP) has been a maverick party which has attracted varying degrees of support from farmers who have felt dissatisfied with the larger and more powerful parties such as the Centre Party, which easily appear distant and too much involved in opportunistic bargaining in Finland's complex multi-party governmental system. The figures for SMP and Centre Party combined votes (72 per cent in Vieki and 70 per cent in Savolanvaara) reflect the extent to which migration has left active and retired independent farming families as a main element in the community.

I shall discuss a variety of aspects of the histories of some such families and their farms in the next chapter, and I shall take up some questions of the comparability of modern family farming and its antecedents in the area in Chapter 7. It is already clear from my discussion that many changes have occurred in North Karelian farming over the last hundred years or so, and it may be worth while here to highlight some of these to close this chapter. Firstly, there has been a process in which the number of farm-owning families has increased and then diminished in the village, and this has been accompanied by an associated rise and fall in the number of small farms. At the same time there has been a tendency for farm families to work their own farms with very little if any outside labour, and this has been facilitated by increased availability and use of farm machinery. A further and in part connected change has taken place in the significance of forests in the lives of farmers. While opportunities for paid timber work have steeply declined, the viability of modern farms has turned increasingly upon a farmer's private forest holdings. In some cases these have been inherited, but many farmers have also been able to acquire a substantial holding by purchase from the state on what have proved to be extremely favourable terms. Timber grows relatively slowly in this area of Finland, and the more successful farms in the village tend to have considerably more forest than the reported average of 39 hectares, which I quoted earlier. The judicious development and harvesting of forest holdings has been important for the financing of new capital developments on farms, such as drainage, soil improvement and the purchase of new buildings and machinery, though here again the availability of favourable credit has also been of considerable help. Lastly, I should make explicit here the fact that modern Finnish farming has changed significantly from its origins as a source of self-provisioning for rural families. Modern farms tend to specialise in milk or livestock production, and much of their arable land is given over to the production of fodder. One farmer in Vieki even successfully concentrates on the production of flowers and houseplants. Moreover, many farming families supplement their income with work off the farm. Predictably, this is particularly true of those whose farms are relatively small, but a number of farmers with larger holdings also acquire extra income through outside work for neighbours, and especially hiring out some of their more powerful machinery, with themselves as drivers. One farmer whom I know is a skilled builder of log houses, and he and one of his sons have developed a considerable reputation in different parts of Finland for their hand-crafted buildings, from which they earn a substantial income in addition to that gained from farming. Despite such cases and developments, however, there has been no simple shift from 'farm' to 'firm', and Finnish family farming still retains a fundamentally domestic quality which differentiates it sharply from most other modern forms of livelihood.

3

The origins of modern farming families

Introduction: roots and shoots

As in other parts of Finland, many North Karelian farmers are descendants of earlier farming families in the same or nearby villages. A few contemporary Vieki families, such as the Savolainens, go back in the village to at least the seventeenth century, and there are many others whose roots there can be traced to the eighteenth and early nineteenth centuries. Matti Kärkkäinen represents the eighth successive generation of his branch of the Kärkkäinens to hold his lake-shore farm since 1722, but most cases of connection between family and locality are less clear-cut than this. Farms have passed through daughters into other surname groups, and they have often simply been sold to other families. Even Matti's case is not as simple as it sounds. He owns only part of the large original ancestral farm, which has gradually been carved up into sections with a wide variety of owners, and he has himself acquired land from others. At the same time many members of the family have moved to other farms or out of Vieki altogether. Overall, approximately half of the farming and land-holding families of the village in the early nineteenth century still have direct descendants of the same surname who own, and have at least till recently, farmed land there. Moreover, the degree of continuity between earlier and modern populations traced through males and females equally is much higher than appears simply from such figures based on surnames, and a high rate of intra-village marriage through the generations contributes to this.

From time to time, of course, there have been newcomers. In 1980, for example, although the large majority of adult villagers were born in Vieki, just over 20 per cent of them were born outside the Pielisjärvi Commune within which the village lies.[1] Some of these were born in Nurmes villages

---

[1] Since 1973 Vieki has been part of Lieksa Commune, which was formed through joining Pielisjärvi rural Commune and Lieksa Township. Despite its large rural area, the new Commune technically has the status of a Town (*Kaupunki*).

directly bordering on Vieki, but the main contingent of them are members of the resettled Karelian and war veteran (*rintamamiehet*) families which I discussed in the last chapter. This concentrated influx of newcomers was unprecedented in the modern history of the village, though we have seen that its population also fluctuated noticeably during more unsettled periods of the seventeenth and early eighteenth centuries. Usually, however, immigrants have come in at a fairly gentle rate, either as individuals or as family units.

Such arrivals, coupled with departures from the village to elsewhere, provide some qualification to the simple picture of longstanding continuity which at first sight seems to mark the village population. A significant factor is the tendency for families to maintain their links to local farms at the cost of sloughing off those members who, for one reason or another, cannot be fitted into the chain of connections between the family and its land. The need to do this has varied from time to time and farm to farm, depending on such variables as the number and sex of a farmer's children, the size of holding, and wider economic and other influences on the viability of local agriculture. Of course, not everyone who leaves a village farm has had to seek his fortune outside the community. A son unable to remain at home may sometimes buy a holding elsewhere in the village if its owners no longer require it or cannot cope with its upkeep. Or he may find a wife within the village, and if she lacks brothers to inherit the parental holding, he may be welcome to reside uxorilocally and take over the farm after her parents' retirement or death. Failing this he might in the past have remained in the village as a crofter or a labourer on someone else's land.

It would also be mistaken to assume that a strong tendency to equilibrium exists between departures and arrivals in a village. Decisions concerning such movement are not made by the village as a unit or community, but are taken typically by individuals and their families, often under the external influence of political and economic developments in the wider society. Village populations have grown and declined here as elsewhere as a result of population movement and of shifts in birth and death rates. As we have seen, the overall pattern in North Karelia has been one of early fluctuations followed by substantial population growth from at least the late eighteenth century until the early 1960s, when a serious decline took place. Such growth was interrupted and impeded from time to time by adverse conditions, like those of the 1860s famine years, but the overall upward trend was very clear. Nor have all settlements grown or declined at the same rate. The modern development of Lieksa as the administrative and commercial centre of the area, for example, has largely taken place at the expense of its surrounding villages. Again, in recent years, Vieki's population has dropped more slowly than that of more remote rural communities, and the village has taken in new settlers from these as its own population has declined.

Sources and problems

In my discussions of the history of some Vieki farming families in this chapter, I mainly use the Christian names which figure in the documents of the period in question. It should be noted that in earlier documents these names usually have Swedish forms, although in everyday life the people themselves will have used Finnish versions of them. Towards the end of the last century, there was an increasing tendency to shift to the use of Finnish name forms in official documents, along with the more general use of Finnish in administrative matters at that time. This creates a problem of choice for the modern analyst, as the names used for particular individuals change from one set of documents to another, and the problem is also slightly complicated by the fact that late nineteenth-century documents are not always consistent in their choice between Swedish and Finnish forms. Again, many of the Finnish name forms in question are themselves only likely to have been used in formal church and governmental contexts, while within village society more familiar forms will almost certainly have been current. Thus a man listed as Johan in early documents may appear as Juho in a later text, and he may well have been known locally as Jussi. In these circumstances, I have found it difficult to maintain a wholly consistent pattern of usage, and I have sometimes felt constrained simply to choose one form or another as clarity of expression and the context of discussion have appeared to demand.

This question of names, though small in itself, relates quite closely to a number of other substantive and methodological issues. It is clearly connected with the wider history of relations between officialdom and village life as these have developed under Swedish, Russian and independent governments, and some features of this history are discussed in other chapters. It also raises questions about the general nature of the source materials from which Finnish village family histories can be reconstructed, and it will be useful to say something in more detail here about these.

In Finland, there are various sets of public records which are relevant for such enquiries. These include the civil authority registers of village populations, the so-called *henkikirjat* (literally 'spirit-books'), which give a year-by-year account of village residents and their dependants. Then there are the parish registers, which provide a detailed list over the years of all members of the Lutheran Church. There are also court records of litigation, and there are the records of the Land Registry Office. In the course of my own research, I have made substantial use of the first two sets of documents, and I have only consulted court and land registration papers which are in private ownership or which, occasionally, are cited by writers on the North Karelian area such as Saloheimo. More generally, in this as in other contexts, Saloheimo's work has been an important source of historical information and insight for me, as too have the works of Jutikkala and Voionmaa and some legal studies.

I have found the *henkikirjat* and parish registers extremely useful for exploring several aspects of the history of individuals and families, but the information they provide has often needed further elucidation from other documents such as contracts of sale, court records of inheritance matters, and some wills. As I discuss in Chapter 5, such other documents themselves have also to be interpreted whenever possible in the light of interviews and informal discussions with villagers themselves.

Although I have consulted a few Vieki *henkikirjat* from earlier in the nineteenth century, I have found those from around mid-century onwards to be more informative. The lists vary somewhat both in the quantity and in the nature of the detail they provide. Thus the list for 1845 gives the official number of the farm, the Christian name and surname of the household head, the Christian name of his wife and children and other close kin and a definition of his relation to them, and also the Christian name and surname of any other residents and their relation if close, for example son-in-law, to the head. Labourers, maids and lodgers are identified as such, and some professions and statuses such as 'miller' and 'crofter' are specified. Neither this list, nor the 1867 one, give dates of birth. The 1867 list also includes the maiden names of married women, whereas this is omitted from most subsequent lists until relatively recently. Many later lists provide the dates of birth of adults, but unfortunately omit both the Christian names and dates of birth of minors. Modern lists, such as those from the 1960s and 1970s, are much fuller. They include the birth dates and full names of all residents, the maiden names of married women and some information on the relation of household members to the household head. The lists for the 1960s also provide information about where people have come from or moved to since the previous list. Most lists over the last hundred years have also given brief details about land transactions.

Some of the gaps of detail in these civil lists can be filled in by reference to parish registers and other documents. The parish registers for Vieki go back to the eighteenth century. Some of the early records were destroyed by fire, and in any case they only begin to provide systematically detailed information about farm residents from the late 1700s. From then on, valuable information is available on the names and ages of all villagers, and also on their movements. The privately held documents which I have mentioned often provide further helpful genealogical information in addition to data on a variety of transactions of family members both among themselves and with other villagers.

Many of the problems which arise in the study of such sources, and also their potential value for elucidating different aspects of family life and kinship, are broadly similar to those which have been well discussed by Plakans in his studies of late eighteenth-century rural society on the southern Baltic littoral.[2] He is worried about two main issues. One is the problem of detecting and interpreting from certain types of documentary data the presence, form and extent of people's involvement in extra-familial kinship linkages including membership of lasting and bounded descent groups. The second is a more general problem which in part encapsulates the first. How can one safely make the leap between knowledge of genealogical relationship and a confident assertion of its salience and customary content within a kinship system?[3]

Part of Plakans's anxiety on the first point arises from the synchronic nature of much of the available material, and from the focus on dyadic ties rather than wider group structures and boundaries which has characterised many censuses. He is also concerned about the significance of a possibly immense cultural and linguistic gap between the enumerators and those enumerated in the Baltic 'soul revision' data he examines. Although there is occasional evidence of such a gap in some of the early Vieki *henkikirjat*, it does not seem to have been as wide as that obtaining in the very different circumstances of southern Baltic society, where peasants lived on feudal estates under often oppressive foreign ownership and control. In Finland, the issue was more likely to be one of urban versus rural culture, and it does not seem to have caused widespread serious problems of misunderstanding in the records I have studied. With regard to wider kinship groupings and relations, a considerable amount of information about connections between families emerges from the Vieki material, and the continuity and time depth of the data are predictably extremely valuable in this regard. Detailed connections are, however, more readily traceable within and between the subdivisions of a common surname group than between such groups themselves, though more information than I have so far obtained on such links could be gleaned from a more thorough perusal of the parish records. I should, however, add here that my own research experience in Africa has led me to be more wary of the dangers of seeing descent-group systems where they do not exist, than of missing them where they do.[4] It is possible that in Finland also the existence of 'patrilineal' surnames, and the tendency to pass land downwards between males, demand similar interpretative caution. I shall discuss some further aspects of this question towards the end of this chapter, and more generally in Chapter 4.

Plakans's second and more general question is a vexing one. In this context, he draws a sharp contrast between a documentary data base and

---

[2] See especially Plakans (1984).   [3] See especially Plakans (1984, p. 249).
[4] See Abrahams (1978b) and also Chapter 4 below.

one obtained through intensive anthropological field research. I myself have similarly been conscious of the qualitative differences between material on kinship which I have collected through participant observation and discussion with villagers, and the data to be got from 'cold' census collections, whether they be old or new. In terms of a familiar metaphor, the latter have a skeletal quality and lack the flesh and blood of real life. One knows all too little about the customary rights and obligations, and about the positive and negative emotions which inform relations between 'census kin', and with historical material there may be little or no way of adding these important features to the dry bones of one's lists of names and numbers. Much, of course, depends on what one wants to do with the material. The reconstruction of the form and content of an historical kinship system is an ambitious project which entails the kinds of difficulties spelled out by Plakans. My own aim, at least in this chapter, is less ambitious and more easily achieved with skeletal material. I mainly wish to look at what has happened to some of the farming families in the village with the passage of the generations, and to look at the related question of what has become of some of the early family farms in the course of the last century or two. There are naturally gaps in my knowledge of these processes, but some broad outlines are clear, and hints of answers are also available to some more difficult questions.

Chains of connection and points of departure
A few examples from longstanding families in the village will illustrate some of the commonly recurring routes to farm ownership by contemporary farming families. I do not have detailed information on the sizes of all the early farms in question, or of all their later subdivisions. Nor am I certain of the exact relationship between the size and location of very early holdings in the village and those set up under *isojako* rationalisation and reparcelling. It is at least clear that the land areas of the *isojako* farms were generally quite large. Figures available to me range from just over 200 to 800 hectares, but only a small part of such farms was kept under cultivation in the late 1830s, while the rest was variously divided between fallow, forest and often quite substantial areas of land unsuitable for agriculture.

The Myllynens are a relatively simple case of a long established village family (see Figure 3). There are records of Myllynens in Vieki dating back at least to 1679, but it is not clear from the data at my disposal how, if at all, these earliest bearers of the name relate to each other or to present residents. We know, however, that by 1794 Isak Myllynen (1757–c.1820) was in charge of half of what became Vieki farm No. 43, which was formally attached at that time to the neighbouring village of Kuohatti. He later (1815) seems to have taken over farm No. 16. This was previously held by

Paavo Toivanen, and it is possible that the transfer stemmed from Isak's marriage to Helena Toivanen, who may have been a relative of Paavo. All modern Myllynens in Vieki appear to descend from Isak, and most of them occupy sections of farms No. 16 and 43. Isak himself seems to have had four sons and at least three daughters, but little is known about these with the exception of the eldest son, also Isak (b. 1786), who stayed on the farms. The census of 1845 lists him and his wife and children as living on farm No. 43 and owning farm No. 16.

Isak (1786) died some time prior to 1850 and left a widow and several children. There were three sons, Isak, Petter and Påhl, in addition to three daughters, who all married out. Between 1856 and 1862 a number of deals were concluded between these siblings. The sisters and their husbands were bought out, and the holdings were divided between the brothers. Isak (b. 1826) was left in charge of farm No. 16, and Petter and Påhl each had half of the family's holdings in farm No. 43. Påhl later sold his part of No. 43 to outsiders (the Turunens, who owned the other half of No. 43) and moved to

Fig. 3 Partial genealogy of the Myllynen family

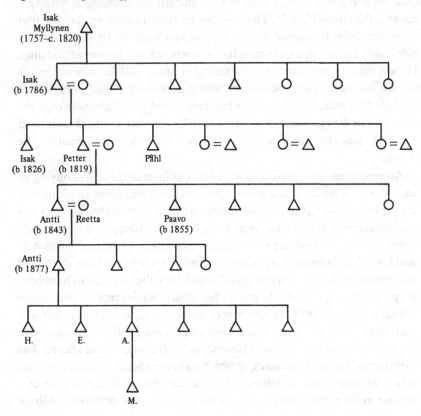

farm No. 27, which he bought. By 1900, the Myllynens had lost this last farm, though some of them were still living there as *loiset* (landless lodgers). Some of the descendants of Isak (1826) are still on parts of farm No. 16 today, and Myllynens descended from Petter (b. 1819) still live and farm on parts of No. 43.

Petter (1819) had four sons and a daughter, but towards the end of the century his farm had been divided equally between two of the sons, Paavo (b. 1855) and Antti (b. 1843). By 1921, Antti (1843) had died, and a small portion of the farm (about 15 per cent) was in the hands of his widow, Reetta, who lived there with an unmarried daughter, Anna. The remainder was now owned by two of his three sons, but by 1938 it had passed, along with the mother's portion, into the ownership of one of these, Antti (b. 1877). The farm was a substantial one of about 65 hectares, including about 12 hectares of arable land. Antti was extremely long-lived (1877–1970), and he had six sons and no daughters. In 1959 the farm was divided between three of Antti's sons, H., E. and A. The other three were bought out and went to farm elsewhere. E. and H. were still alive in 1981, the former married and with children, and the latter a bachelor who had two of A.'s children living with him. A. died in 1969 and left eleven children, with ages ranging then from 12 to 31. Their mother had died in 1961. His farm at first remained under H.'s guardianship. Its present owner, M. (b. 1940), was the eldest son, and he appears to have had no ambition to take over at that time. He was married and working in the timber industry while his wife worked as a shop assistant in another village where they lived. It had always been thought that one of M.'s younger brothers would eventually take over the farm, but he died in a timber accident in 1975. Another brother briefly tried to run the place but gave it up, and M. somewhat reluctantly agreed to take it over.

An agreement was reached by M. and his siblings on the cost of buying up their shares of the farm, and he paid them all the agreed price. In addition to the expense of doing this, he also needed to extend the cowshed and increase his hectarage of arable land by clearing forest. He obtained a loan to help cover the cost of these improvements and he also sold the house which he and his wife had been living in before moving back to the farm. Although his siblings agreed the price of transfer with him, they are said to have been surprised at the good price he got for his house, and this created some strain between them. In 1981, he had two tractors, one of which was rather old, and other machinery, including a baler and a trailer; and he participated in the usual patterns of reciprocal lending and borrowing between farms. The farm covered some 72 hectares, of which eight were fields. Most of the forest which he owned was obtained from the state by his father as part of a scheme in the early 1960s to allow farmers to increase their forest holdings.

With the additional help of some rented land, he was able to support a herd of eight milk cows and several calves and some beef cattle. His main on-farm income came almost wholly from meat and milk, and he strongly felt the need for more land on which to grow the necessary fodder. He would have been glad to buy more if he could, for instance from his uncle E., who no longer farmed himself but simply rented out some of his land to neighbours and was unwilling to sell. M. found this frustrating, since there seemed to be no other land that he could buy nearby. In addition to farming, M. sometimes did winter timber work, and he also earned a little from snow-clearing for some of his neighbours. He and his wife have three children, the oldest of whom is a son born in 1965, followed by sisters born in 1967 and 1977. It was unclear whether the boy or his younger sister would wish to stay on the farm, but M. and his wife were of course still relatively young themselves. Meanwhile they were potentially a little vulnerable in their labour supply, especially if one of them became ill for any length of time.

There are several examples in the village of families like the Myllynens with a long history of uninterrupted ownership of an area of land, though this typically depends on the division of holdings and the sloughing off of many family members over time. There are also less straightforward cases where families themselves survive in the village, but the nature of their holdings changes. The Kärkkäinens on farm No. 35 provide a relatively simple example. There are many families with this surname in Vieki, which is in fact one of the two main areas of its concentration in eastern Finland, the other being Iisalmi in northern Savo. No links are traceable between many of these Vieki Kärkkäinens – though there are more connections than most villagers appear to realise – and the parish records for the 1760s already list a number of different residents of that name in the village. The present family on farm No. 35 are direct descendants of earlier owners of the land, but the family lost their freehold ownership of the farm at the end of the nineteenth century, and lived there as tenants. They then regained the place after the land reforms which followed independence. The present owner no longer relies on farming for a living, but runs a successful plant and flower nursery.

A second and more complex case concerns one of the Vieki Kärki families. There are at least two longstanding families with this surname in the village, and they appear to be distinct, though it is possible that they had a common origin prior to arriving there at different times in the early nineteenth century. The group in question are descendants of a Joran Kärki who became the owner of farm No. 2. The family became bankrupt in the 1880s and lost their land, but a number of them stayed on in the village in various capacities as crofters, day labourers and dependants. Joran's youngest son, David, had left the family farm to live as an in-marrying son-in-law on farm No. 22, and he eventually went to settle in another, nearby village from which his descendants later returned to buy part of Vieki farm No. 12 in the 1930s. Some of them still farm this holding.

Other descendants of Joran are also farming in the village these days. Thus, Matti Kärki farms what was originally a croft (*torppa*) on the Turunen part of farm No. 43. When the family became bankrupt, Matti's grandfather Sakari remained in the village and lived as a tenant on different Turunen holdings, ending with the present farm, Huuro, in the early part of the century. In 1927 the family took advantage of post-independence legislation and acquired ownership of the farm, which was passed down to Sakari's son, Yrjö, and from him during his lifetime to his only son, Matti. Hard work and a modest life style have helped the family to develop and increase their original holdings to their present substantial proportions. In 1981, they had just over 20 hectares of arable land and 78 hectares of forest. An important development for them was their purchase of about 10 hectares of arable land from a Karelian neighbour who simply kept a house site and his forest holdings for himself, and they also rent some land. They had eleven milk cows and some calves and chickens. Matti's father was no longer able to do much work on the farm, but his mother still helped out, especially with housework and with the cows. Matti and his wife are both exceptionally hard workers. They have five children. The oldest lives away – he is a mathematics teacher and married – and their youngest was at university in Joensuu at the time of my research. The other three, two daughters and a son, were in their twenties and lived on the farm. None of them was yet married. The son at home, Martti, was scheduled to inherit the farm in due course, and at least one of the daughters was also very keen on farming. All, like their parents, are extremely hard workers. The farm was well supplied with machinery, and it was awarded a prize for the regular high standard of its milk production by Nurmes Co-operative Dairy, which serves the farms in this part of the village.

When the Kärki family lost farm No. 2, it passed after several deals into the hands of other villagers. One of these was Matti Kainulainen, who bought one-third of the farm from the family and moved there in the mid 1880s. He then appears to have given half his holding to his brother Pekka. Like their father before them, both men were tailors, and they travelled around from one village and one farm to another making clothes for local families, who would accommodate them during the work. Such men were always popular visitors, bringing news and gossip from other places, and providing some variety to the dull round of a sometimes isolated family. Before buying the Kärki place, Matti had a small cottage (*mökki*) near the modern centre of the village on No. 9 farm land belonging to the Mustonen, and subsequently, Ryynänen families, to which the Kainulainens were connected through marriage.

The later history of this No. 2 Kainula farm is quite complicated, and I give only a brief outline of it here. By 1981 part of Matti's holding, along with other land, was owned and farmed by his grandson Leo. Leo's father, also called Matti, was born on the farm in 1891, but moved away in 1914 shortly before his father died. He moved to Ilvesvaara, a remote settlement a few miles east of Vieki, and married Anna Savelius, a widow who had been left a large farm by her husband, Erkki Meriläinen (see Figure 8).[5] In 1915, however, all the buildings at the farm were burned down accidently after a fire in the cowshed, and the family then returned to Vieki to Jokela, part of farm No. 10, which they bought. Leo was born on this farm. In 1926–7 the family then moved out of the main village once again, this time to Issaanvaara, through an exchange of farms. Leo, however, came back to Kainula from Issaanvaara in 1951. He left because the land was difficult to farm. The soil was stony, and there was little clay soil and no meadow land. Access to the farm was very steep, and it was a backwoods settlement.

The Kainula farm itself had remained undivided until shortly before Leo's return. On division, some forest and some meadow went to his father's sister, who was married and lived with her husband, Juho Turunen, on the nearby Männikkölä farm (see below), and Leo obtained a little over 20 hectares, including about 9.5 hectares of fields, partly by inheritance and partly in return for a pension agreement for his father's bachelor brother, who had stayed on the farm. Leo's own brothers forewent their share of inheritance of this farm, though like him they also had rights to inherit other land their parents had acquired. Leo has also added to the farm by purchase. At the time of my visit he had an impressive holding of over twenty-three hectares of fields and about 177 hectares of forest, and a herd of fifteen milk cows. He owned two tractors and a combine harvester. Much of the forest holding came into the family through his mother, Anna Savelius, and it has been crucial to Leo's success. He has had to borrow relatively little, taking state loans for fertilising forest land and for drainage. Everything else, including the cost of machinery and of renewing buildings, has come through the sale of trees.

A further case is that of the Kiiskinen family, who farm part of farm No. 32. Hannu Kiiskinen and his father Veikko are descendants of a Johan Kiiskinen who came to Vieki in 1814 from the village of Viensuu at the southern end of Viekijärvi lake. Johan came to the Wallius family farm,

---

[5] The story of Anna Savelius's inheritance is well known among the families concerned, and has all the makings of a classic rural drama. She is said to have been a domestic servant (*piika*) on the large Meriläinen farm, where she was courted and married by the young master. When he died, his kin are said to have wished to keep the property within the family, but she was given good advice and made her claim successfully at the right time.

which was also on the lake shore, as an in-marrying son-in-law (*kotivävy*). He went on to inherit the farm, which became No. 12 on the *isojako* lists. A number of his descendants still live on No. 12 holdings, after a series of divisions and departures which are comparable to those outlined for the Myllynens.

Veikko Kiiskinen, whose farm concerns me here, was born in 1927 on a small No. 12 holding. His father, Iivari, did some farming, but he was also one of a small group of Vieki men who were actively involved as villagers in new developments. He worked for some time as a carrier for the nearby molybdenum mine at Mätäsvaara, and he was also actively involved in the running of the Vieki Co-operative Bank. One of Iivari's colleagues on the bank committee was Arvid Saarelainen, and Veikko in fact married Arvid's daughter Helka.

Iivari had several children, and it was clear that there was insufficient land available for the young couple from his holdings. Veikko therefore took a modest sum of money as a pre-inheritance, and with this he bought a small neighbouring farm. He thought at one point that he might not farm at all if other opportunities presented themselves, and he even tried factory work for a time, but he found he did not like it. The farm itself proved too small and unproductive for the family's growing needs, even when their income was supplemented by winter timber work. Fortunately they were able to sell it to the state and move to Helka's parents' farm, Saarela, elsewhere in the village. This was part of a larger No. 32 farm which had been bought in the 1880s by Helka's great-great grandfather, who came to Vieki from the village of Höljäkkä, just over the border in Nurmes Commune. The previous owners of the farm had apparently been unable to keep it up successfully.

Veikko and Helka bought the farm from her parents, with the agreement of her siblings in a typical pre-mortem transfer involving arrangements for the continued residence of the retiring couple and their support in old age. Veikko and Helka have themselves now formally transferred the farm to one of their sons, Hannu, and his wife, though they continue to live there and help with its running. The other sons are working away in the urban industrial sector, and their two daughters are married, one to a local farmer and one to a soldier. Veikko was keen to expand the farm over the years, and he was eventually able to obtain some extra local land from the Commune authorities. The fact that he had a young and energetic successor ready to take over was an important factor in the success of his application for this land. The farm is still not large, but it is viable. There is a reasonably good range of machinery, and plans for modernisation for which subsidised funding is available.

This case involves considerable movement from one village and one farm to another, but my collection of material on the Kiiskinens was also interesting for some continuities of settlement which it revealed. The parish archives for early nineteenth-century Vieki noted the arrival there of Johan Kiiskinen, but uncharacteristically failed to indicate where he had come from. The 1980 telephone directory revealed the answer. It showed that, in addition to Vieki, the village of Viensuu is a modern local centre of the Kiiskinens in the Lieksa area, and sure enough the Viensuu records for the earlier period report Johan's residence there and his departure.

Lastly, I turn to some of the Vieki Turunens. As with the Kärkkäinens, there are many different local families with this name, which is in fact quite widespread over North Karelia and Savo and beyond. When I first moved to the village for research, I stayed on the farm of Ilmari and Aino Turunen. Ilmari was my wife's first cousin, and I was naturally interested that there were so many other Turunens around. Some of these were clearly relatives, but I was told that most, including some close friends, were not.

The history of the friends' family, which I refer to as the Lehtola Turunens from the name of their home farm, was quite well known since a local vicar had been kind enough to trace their roots back for them in the parish records. They came to Vieki from the village of Vuonislahti on Lake Pielinen. This village also has a large number of Turunen families, including that of the well-known Finnish writer Heikki Turunen.

Antti, the father of the present senior generation of the Lehtola group, was born in 1886 and died in 1964. He came to Vieki at the beginning of the century after he and his brothers had lost their land, apparently to relatives, when their father died in 1894 shortly after his own father's death. Antti's brother Mikko also moved around this time to the Nurmes area.

At first Antti had no land of his own in Vieki. He married into a family of smallholders there, and he became a tenant steward (*lampuoti*) on land which the Cederberg timber company had acquired. He became an independent owner of the small Lehtola farm in the land redistributions of the early 1930s, and he and his wife lived there with their four sons and two daughters. Two other children had died very young in 1911 and 1913. The family was poor but religious, hardworking and respectable. In 1935 the eldest son, Veikko, married and left to run and later purchase a small farm nearby. The Lehtola farm was encumbered with debts at this time, and Veikko was simply given a cow and released from responsibility for the farm's debts as a form of pre-inheritance when he left. Since then he has managed to prosper. He and his wife gradually improved and expanded their holding, and they have now retired, though they still live there. The ownership of the farm has been transferred to one of their nine children. He has bought it from them and provides them with a pension, and he has also bought out his siblings with the help of a state loan. The farm now covers over 80 hectares of arable and forest land.

Viljo, the second son of the family, married in 1940. When the father, Antti, died in 1964, Viljo moved away and bought another nearby farm from a war veteran. This man was apparently without a potential successor. He did not advertise the place, and I was told that he was not keen to squeeze the highest possible price from Viljo, whom he knew quite well. The farm, Harjula, is now quite prosperous. In 1980, there were fifteen milk cows and substantial areas of field and forest. Viljo and his wife, Helmi, had handed the farm over to their son, Unto, and his wife, Kaarina, though they still helped to run it. The other children were bought out, and they all live outside Vieki. There were five altogether, and some of them have had successful urban careers. The family have worked hard to develop and expand the farm. In 1980, the two couples were living in and sharing the same house, though Viljo and his wife had their own bed-sitting room and kitchen upstairs. Since then they have built an apartment attached to the old house but with its own separate entrance, and Viljo and Helmi now live there. Unto and Kaarina have two children, a son, Timo, and a daughter, Susanna. At the time of my research, Timo was in his early teens. Susanna is a few years younger. It was not clear that either of them would wish to continue the farm, but Unto and Kaarina were themselves still relatively young and active. Kaarina was a keen participant in village affairs in addition to her farm and household work. She sat on various committees, and she was awarded the title of Farmwife of the Year in a Commune-wide competition.

Of Antti's other children, one daughter also married and left home to live with her husband elsewhere in Vieki. The other three siblings have remained at Lehtola. Only one of them, Pentti, is married. In 1980 Pentti and his wife owned half shares in the farm, and his brother Martti owned the other half. Their sister Aili had no formal share but was entitled by mutual agreement to bed and board during her lifetime. Martti received a war pension. He helped out with the farm and occasionally bought equipment for it. Aili also helped out, though she did not normally do dairy work. She earned additional income from catering for private and public functions such as birthday parties and parish gatherings, and she was also a dressmaker. Pentti married in 1949, and he and his wife Eevi have three sons and a daughter. One son, Pertti, is a research geologist and lives away at Rovaniemi. A second, Markku, works as a postman and also runs a small farm elsewhere in the village. He has obtained this through his mother and her siblings – she is Veikko Kiiskinen's sister – to whom it had belonged by inheritance. The third son, Juha, is a young unmarried man, and he may find it hard to marry when village girls are scarce and often do not wish to become farmers' wives. He has recently taken over formal ownership of the farm, though the members of the senior generation continue to work on it and help out. The farm, which has been extended through the purchase from the state of extra forest land, consists of about 15 hectares of fields and 60 hectares of timber, and it had a herd of 16 milk cows in 1980.

It is interesting that despite statements to the contrary, several of the other sets of Turunens in Vieki are actually related to each other. Such denials of relationship appear mainly to reflect a genuine ignorance of linkage and a form of structural amnesia. With the passage of the generations, the identities of the different groups have become separated. As I discuss in Chapter 4, it is arguable that the tendency to deny relationship rather than assume its presence provides testimony to the importance of land holdings as a boundary marker between families.

Isak Turunen, who was born in 1687, came to Vieki from Juuka on the other side of Lake Pielinen in 1728. He appears to have had at least three sons, Anders (b. 1728), Olof (b. 1733) and Thomas (b. 1739) (see Figure 4). There are also records of three other men who may have been his sons. These were Christer (b. 1749), Johan (b. 1753) and Nils (year of birth

Fig. 4 Partial genealogy of the descendants of Isak Turunen (b. 1687)

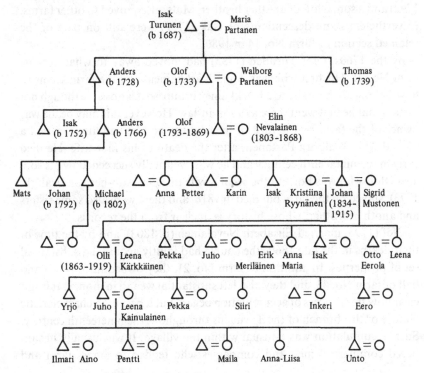

unknown), and they were recorded in the parish records as living with Anders during the years 1781–90. Christer and Thomas both had sons, but I have not been able to trace them beyond the early nineteenth century. They mainly appear in the records of the holdings of their close relatives and, unlike Anders and Olof, they did not establish long-lasting farms of their own in the village.

Isak (1687) came to a large Viekijärvi lakeshore farm which was then No. 8, and the divisions of which became farms No. 13 and 14 after *isojako*. Anders (1728) stayed on this farm, and it was eventually divided between the descendants of his two sons, Isak (b. 1752) and Anders (b. 1766). As I discuss below, farm No. 13 was bought by descendants of Olof (1733) in the latter half of the nineteenth century. The holders had got into difficulties and had to sell in order to survive. Later, part of farm No. 14 was also sold to the same group. Some members of these sections of the family (the descendants of Isak and Anders) moved to other farms as tenants or labourers. Some others had already gone as owners to new farms elsewhere. Thus a later Anders (b. 1826), who was a great-grandson of Isak (1752), moved to farm No. 38, which his descendants occupied for many generations. Michael (b. 1802), who was a son of Anders (1766), moved to farm No. 28, which was then inherited by his daughter and her husband, whose descendants stayed there till the early 1900s. Michael's brother Johan (b. 1792) and a son, Olof, of another brother, Mats, also moved to other farms. Nevertheless some descendants of Isak (1752) were still on part of the retained section of farm No. 14 in 1980.

By the 1760s, Olof Turunen (1733) had moved away to what became farm No. 21. His first wife was Anna Kärkkäinen, and the farm seems to have belonged originally to a Kärkkäinen group, so it is possible though not certain that he first went there as a son-in-law. However this may be, he was owner of the farm by the turn of the century, and he had also married a second wife, Walborg Partanen, after the death of his first wife. He died early in the nineteenth century and he was eventually succeeded by his son, also Olof, who was born to the second wife in 1793. Another son, Isak (b. 1773), stayed on the farm but died in 1816, and there were also some sisters and another brother, whose history is unclear from the records.

Olof (1793) married Elisabeth Nevalainen (b. 1803), and by the time of their deaths in the late 1860s the couple had jointly acquired a substantial set of properties. In addition to farm No. 21, they owned farm No. 4 and half of farm No. 43, and they also left substantial wealth in money. It is not clear how this process of accumulation began, but it became a characteristic feature of this branch of the Turunens throughout the nineteenth century. Such accumulation was unusual within the village. It was usually urban-based commercial men and companies who tended to amass farm and forest holdings in this period, and this was mainly confined to the end of the century. One possibly significant element in the situation was the structure of the family at this time. Olof and Elisabeth somewhat unusually left a will, and this allocated money to their daughters and land to their sons. There were three sons, Petter (1828–1907), Isak (1833–1906) and Johan (1836–1915), and of these only Johan married. Although some property was acquired by them individually, most of it was held jointly, and it was in fact all treated as joint property when Isak and Petter died. The property which they amassed was thus not subject to the usual divisions between siblings and their wives and children until the next generation, when Johan's children and grand-children received individual shares.

In 1869, the year of their father Olof's death, the three brothers bought farm No. 11 from its owners, Lauri Räisänen and his wife Anna. Possibly as a result of the preceding famine years, Räisänen seems to have become insolvent. He died in 1878, and his widow was on the village poor list in the 1880s. Several members of his family, however, stayed as tenants, labourers and dependent lodgers on the farm, and some of his descendants were crofters and eventually smallholders there until the 1960s. In 1933, one great-grandson, Eino, moved as son-in-law to his wife's farm in a nearby village, and his daughter Lilja now lives in Vieki, where she farms with her husband on the latter's family land.

In 1872 and 1876 the three brothers also bought three quarters of farm No. 13, known as Turula, which belonged to their distant Turunen cousins descended from Isak (1752). They later bought the remaining quarter from Paavo Heikura and his wife, who had acquired it not long before. In addition, Petter (1828) bought just under half of farm No. 14 from the descendants of Anders (1766) in 1891 and 1900, and he also acquired a watermill in the village. Lastly, as noted earlier, the brothers also bought a further quarter of farm No. 43 from the Myllynens in 1877.

The turn of the century saw these Turunen holdings at their peak of size and concentration as a jointly held estate. The family was undoubtedly by far the richest in the village at this time. Isak's death in 1906 and Petter's in 1907, however, led to a substantial subdivision of the property among the members of the two succeeding generations.

Johan had married Kristiina Ryynänen in 1862, and they had a son, Olli (the Finnish form of the name Olof), in 1863. Kristiina died in 1867, and in 1870 Johan married Sigrid Mustonen. They had three sons, Pekka (b. 1871), Juho (b. 1873) and Isak (b. 1879) and two daughters, Anna Maria and Leena, who survived to adulthood. The two girls were married, Anna Maria to Erik Meriläinen, a local man, and Leena to Otto Eerola, who worked for the family as a book-keeper. Olli and Juho were married and had children by the beginning of the nineteenth century, and Isak married shortly after and had several children. Pekka married relatively late (1917) and remained childless.

Isak (1833) and Petter (1828) both left wills, and I shall discuss these in some detail in Chapter 5. The two men died within a short time of each other and the distribution of their property took place in 1909, by which time Juho's wife Sigrid was also dead. The main beneficiaries of the distribution were Juho's children, to whom Juho sold his own share of land at the same time. The total estate was valued for this process at over 370,000 marks, of which a little under 150,000 was in land, and about 220,000 in money and movables. The divisions were made carefully, with lots drawn to avoid difficulties of choice. The estate was divided into multiples of one-hundred-and-eightieth shares, and the final result based jointly on the sale and on the wills was as follows:

1. Olli received 22 shares and his sons were allocated 15 shares.
2. Pekka received 37 shares.
3. Juho received 22 shares and his sons were allocated 15 shares.
4. Isak received 37 shares.
5. Anna Maria received 16 shares.
6. Leena received 16 shares.

Not surprisingly, the fortunes of the family began to diversify during the following decades. Apart from differences of luck and character, the growth of the public education system and new developments in the political and economic life of the nation provided a new range of opportunities for both success and disaster within the different branches of the family. Olli Turunen, for example, went bankrupt in 1916, and he died of influenza in 1919. His eldest son, who was expected to become a doctor, had by then fallen in the civil war, but his other children mainly prospered. One daughter became a village schoolmistress in Vieki and other villages, and another worked for a time in commerce before becoming incapacitated through illness. One son became a civil engineer and a director of the Finnish Railways, and another became one of Finland's leading mining engineers and geologists. The oldest brother, Juho, who had relatively little formal education, stayed behind and farmed, but he also ran the Vieki Co-operative Bank for a period and turned down an opportunity to move full time into bank management.

Ilmari Turunen, with whom I stayed, was this man's eldest son. He first bought part of old farm No. 21 (plot 21.47 in Figure 5) with his father's help just after the war. The land belonged to his paternal grandmother and a brother and two sisters of his father, and it had been part of the earlier allocation to his grandfather Olli. There had apparently been a risk that the

Fig. 5 Some present and former Turunen holdings in Vieki, 1980

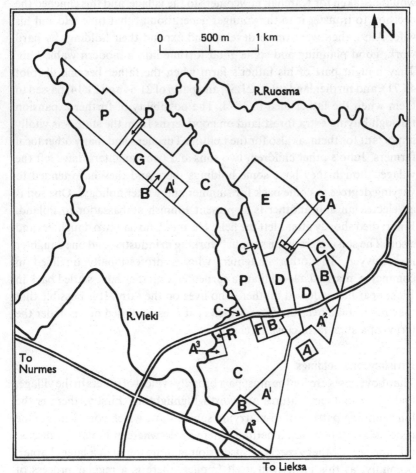

Key

A Owned by Ilmari Turunen
  (A1 = 21.47, A2 = 43.71, A3 = 21.14, 21.51, 21.54)
B Owned by Ilmari Turunen's siblings
C Formerly owned by Juho Turunen (half-brother of Olli, 1863) and now in
  other hands
D Formerly owned by Isak Turunen (half-brother of Olli, 1863) and now in
  other hands
E Owned by a son of Isak (D)
F Owned by descendants of Juho (C)
G Owned by Ilmari Turunen's father's brother's family
P Donated to parish by Pekka Turunen (half-brother of Olli, 1863)
R Rented from relatives by Ilmari Turunen

land, which was used as a meadow for a few cows kept by his grandmother, would be taken for Karelian newcomers to the village, and this clinched the decision to transfer it to the younger generation at that time. He and his wife, Aino, then went on to develop and expand their holdings by hard work, good planning and some good fortune into a modern viable unit. They bought part of his father's farm when the father became ill (plot 43.71), and further land (plots 21.51, and parts of 21.54 and 21.14) passed to them when the father died in 1974. The possibility of further expansion through buying extra forest land on good terms from the state was vitally important for them, as also for the Lehtola Turunens and many other local farmers. Juho's other children, two sons and two daughters, have left the village, though they have some holdings there and they have tended to varying degrees to come back for summer and winter holidays. One son is an electrician and another is at present Finnish ambassador to Poland. Ilmari died shortly after I left the field. He and Aino had two daughters and a son. The son is a graduate scientist working in industry, and one daughter is a lawyer. The other daughter, who is professionally qualified in commerce, married a local man, a carpenter, and they have settled back in Vieki near her widowed mother, who lives on the farm. It is possible that they might take over the farm, which is at present closed down under the terms of a state farm-closure scheme.

Divisions and holdings

The above cases are for the most part broadly typical of others in the village, and some of their features are worth highlighting. Firstly, there is the longstanding pattern of in-marrying sons-in-law, which complements the processes of father–son inheritance here as elsewhere in Finland. I discuss this and some other aspects of succession in more detail in a later chapter. Secondly, as this pattern in itself implies, there is a regular process of 'shedding' of family members which accompanies the transmission, and often the division, of farm holdings from one generation to another. Such shedding is partly a function of the relationship between farm size and the number of potential heirs, but it has also been very much affected by economic and political factors external to an individual farm and often, indeed, external to rural society itself. The legislative enfranchisement with rights to land of previously landless villagers in the 1920s is one of a large number of such factors which have influenced the patterns of family continuity and rural settlement in villages like Vieki.

Another point of some significance is that while there are substantial numbers of people farming land which once belonged to their ancestors, the process of transmission has involved considerable division of the earlier large farms into much smaller holdings, not all of which are held by relatives. This has been a complex process in which very diverse factors such as improved agriculture, farm failure and bankruptcy, excessive fragmentation, the creation of subsequently redeemed tenancies, land transfers for convenience, and urban migration have all played a part. In looking at such shifting patterns of connection between farm and family, I am reminded here of the possesive-pronoun forms in some African languages. The words in question consist of two syllables, and each of these is variable. The first represents the noun class of the possessed object, and the second that of the possessor. The system thus provides a series of binary forms flexibly geared for highlighting the variability of each of the two main elements in possession – the holder and the held. In broad contrast, the idea of a family farm, persisting in the 'same hands' over many generations, tends to mask the extent to which such variation actually occurs.

The most active period of such farm division and diversification has been the present century from about 1910 to 1960. This appears to have followed legislation which removed some of legal trammels upon subdivision.[6] Since then, though, new attempts at the consolidation and rationalisation of holdings have done something to reverse this trend. These processes, and the accompanying factors I have mentioned, mean that one obtains a rather different picture of developments over time if, instead of concentrating on the link between a family and an area of land, one takes either of these elements as one's focal point. As I have said, an examination of the history of a family in itself typically reveals that the connection with a farm is only maintained at the cost of sloughing off many of its members elsewhere. Similarly the history of a piece of land itself often reveals a picture of fragmentation coupled with an increasingly complex pattern of diverse ownership. A further corollary of all this is that a modern farm holding is only rarely made up purely of inherited land or land acquired from close kin who had been actual or potential co-inheritors. None of these perspectives needs to be considered more significant than the others, and all of them have to be taken into account in an attempt to gain a rounded understanding of the situation.

To close this section, I will illustrate some of these points by reference to the history of ownership of a particular land area in the village. In some other cases, the degree of change involved has been much greater, but the present example will suffice to bring out the basic patterns of continuity and discontinuity in farm–family relationships. The area in question is farm No. 12, to which Johan Kiiskinen had come as an in-marrying son-in-law in the early nineteenth century. In 1866, after the land consolidation realignments of the *isojako*, the farm covered an area of around 340 hectares. It was by

---

[6] For details of the removal of constraints on farm division in the late nineteenth and early twentieth centuries see Jutikkala (1958, pp. 303–5).

then divided into three equal sections. On the first section was Johan's son
Antti and his wife Agneta, and their three sons, Johan, Isak and Antti (see
Figure 6). The first two of these were married and Isak and his wife had a
daughter, also called Agneta. Also on the farm was Isak Wallius, the
mother's brother of the owner, Antti. Wallius was unmarried and too old to
pay taxes. In addition there was a poor lodger, Petter Toivanen, with his
wife and a young step-daughter.

On the second farm was Johan's son Johan with his wife and three young
children. There was one male labourer and two maids. In addition there
were two poor lodgers and their wives, and a young child of one of the
couples. On the third farm was the widow of Johan's son Erik, and their
three sons, who were of age but not yet married. A daughter of Johan had
left home by this time.

By 1884, Antti's sons Johan and Isak had already left the first farm for
other land in the village. Their youngest brother Antti with his wife and five
young children had remained, and their old parents were also still living on
the farm. There was a labourer and a maid, and also a crofter with his wife
and child. By that year also, the original Johan's third son, Johan, had also
left and the remaining two thirds of the old farm were reamalgated in the
hands of two of Erik's sons, Antti and David. Their brother, also called
Erik, had left by this time. Also living on this farm was the widow of a
formerly unrelated holder of a plot there, a male labourer, two maids, a
dependent lodger and his wife, and a tanner and his wife and two young
children. The situation had not greatly changed by the turn of the century,
but there were considerable diversification and division after that. By 1921,
there were six main subdivisions of the original holding ranging from about
15 hectares to about 85 hectares in area. Four of them were held by
members of the Kiiskinen family, one by an in-marrying son-in-law, and
one by a member of another family in the village who appears to have

Fig. 6 Partial genealogy of the Kiiskinen family on Farm No. 12 in the
nineteenth century

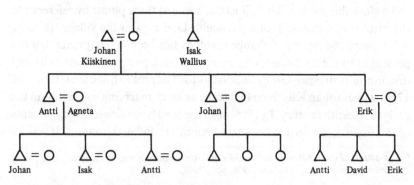

bought the property. One holder was a schoolteacher who lived away from the village. In addition to the main holders and their families, there were a number of cotters and dependents living on the farms. Altogether, there were 50 people living there, of whom 17 were adults of tax-paying age, and 10 of these were cotters or dependent *loiset*. Three of the remaining 33 were over-age and the rest were children.

By 1962, before large-scale migration from the village, there were 26 registered divisions of the old farm and there were 64 people (26 adults, and 38 children under eighteen years of age) living there. The largest unit was about 55 hectares, but some were now less than one hectare in size. Only six holdings, including the largest one, were in hands of Kiiskinens, but four further holdings were owned by descendants of a man who had married a daughter of the family. Sixteen holdings were not lived on. They were mostly rather small, and some of them belonged to people living on other sections of No. 12 land. Some, however, belonged to people living on neighbouring units (farm Nos. 13 and 20), and now constituted parts of their own working farms. Similarly, at least one of the Kiiskinens still farming parts of No. 12 land had acquired some additional land in the neighbouring village of Varpanen. By this stage, large parts of this and the other original numbered farms in Vieki had become fragmented, and individuals who wished to continue farming, like the one just mentioned, had to buy, rent or borrow land from kin or neighbours in order to obtain a viable holding. This need for more land did not arise for everyone, however, since some of those who owned and lived on these and other village plots were mainly reliant on forestry and other work rather than on farming for a living.

4

Family and farm

Structures and functions

Kinship, marriage and the family have long been the special stock-in-trade of social anthropology. As linked domains of more or less unchallenged expertise, they have served both to mark off the discipline from others and to provide an arena in which the experts themselves can engage in exclusive academic debate on a wide range of theoretical and comparative questions. Their discussions have occasionally led to bitter conflict, as widely different viewpoints are espoused and forcefully expressed about such matters as the universality of kinship, or the unilinearity of descent and the applicability of models of alliance. Yet much of the argument has taken place against a background of common understanding and assumptions which are only rarely voiced these days.

In his Radcliffe-Brown Memorial Lecture (1985), however, Jack Goody interestingly lays bare and criticises some of these assumptions. He complains that, in the field of kinship, social anthropologists have excessively, if more or less unwittingly, dichotomised both their theoretical interests and the social world itself. He points to a heavy emphasis on synchrony and system, and a related tendency to play down the activities of real live people striving to cope with their mortal lot. This has been accompanied, he argues, by the creation and maintenance of an exaggeratedly sharp boundary between a 'primitive' and a 'modern' world. Systems, whether of lineage or alliance, loom large in the first, while individuals and families seem to form the basic analytic units in the second. He notes regretfully that many students of European kinship have found it hard to draw successfully upon the theoretical armoury of mainstream social anthropology, and he comments that this is scarcely surprising when a concept like that of the 'household' has received relatively scant attention in the major literature.

There are, of course, notable exceptions, such as the work of Arensberg and Kimball on Ireland, and Gulliver's study of the pastoral Jie and Turkana of East Africa, in addition to Goody's own comparative work. Chayanov's ideas on the logic of peasant family work patterns and their relation to developmental cycles have also made a strong impression on a range of sociologists and social anthropologists, including Sahlins, whose model of a 'domestic mode of production' extends these theories from the peasant sector to traditional African and Pacific agricultural systems.[1] Yet Goody's point is still likely to ring uncomfortably true to many social anthropologists who have tried to take seriously the fact that they are working among farming families. Goody himself plausibly suggests that the gap in question can be bridged by an approach which looks at familial institutions and behavioural strategies as problem-solving 'potentialities' for societies and as 'possibilities' for their members. Such an approach, which reminds us of the simple fact that structures usually have functional implications, certainly makes sense to me for both my Tanzanian and my Finnish research areas. In both cases, families are important work groups, and their creation, maintenance and dispersal are intimately connected with patterns of land holding and land use. In both cases also, customs change and individuals have choices. Neither side of the connection between form and action can be said straightforwardly to be determinant of the other, yet neither can be properly understood alone.

It may be useful at this point to say a little about the idea of a family farm in general. When the two English words 'family' and 'farm' are thrown together in this way as a catchy and convenient shorthand label, it is easy to gloss over ambiguities and shifts of meaning. It is easy too to forget how complicated the family farm's intrinsic combination of social, technical and material elements can be. In addition, the concept naturally tends to draw attention to the farming unit itself and away from the quite crucial fact, which I will return to on a number of occasions, that farm families and family farms never exist for long if at all in a political and economic vacuum.

Even ignoring the broad spectrum of cross-cultural comparison and variation, it may be noted that the term 'family' has a number of interestingly different referents simply within the confines of ordinary English usage. In the opening sentence of her introduction to *Some Elmdon Families* (Richards and Robin, 1975), Audrey Richards writes of 'six well known families which have been represented in the village for a very long time, in fact as long ago as the seventeenth century in two instances'. The sense of the term 'family' here is clearly very different from that of the family

[1] Arensberg and Kimball (1961), Gulliver (1955), J. Goody (1976a, 1976b, 1983, 1984), Chayanov (1986, pp. 53ff.) and Sahlins (1974, Chs. 2 and 3).

as a marriage-centred reproductive and domestic group. Significantly in the present context, the distinctive connotations involved here are partly tied to types of property in England. The expression 'family car' seems most likely to evoke the idea of the relatively short-term elementary family. The term 'family farm', on the other hand, is a more ambiguous concept, since it suggests both the connection of the farm to a living family, and its inter-generational transmission within the longer-term framework of Richards's quoted usage.

This, of course, relates to some of the special qualities which land at least potentially possesses as a form of lasting property, and which have long been of interest to economists, lawyers and social scientists. The crucial point in the present context is the ability of land to outlast human beings, and thus its immediate implications for transmission from one generation to another. At the same time, we know that the heritability of rights in land (and by implication farms) varies greatly both within and between societies, and that differences in this regard can be closely related to other aspects of the connection between farm and family. It seems clear, for example, as I discuss in Chapter 7, that the high mobility of Nyamwezi villagers is linked to the lack of well-developed hereditary rights to land among them, and it has been interestingly suggested by Voionmaa that there were historically important differences in inheritance practice between eastern Finnish swidden cultivators and their western compatriots who engaged in fixed-field agriculture.[2]

Families are dynamic groups, however else we might define them, and they always have their own developmental processes and inner conflicts. These are naturally centred on the human life-cycle and the complex pattern of relations between different life-cycles, and they by no means automatically fit well with the demands of farming. The issues involved can be seen extremely clearly with regard to land, and some of them also emerge interestingly from a comparison between land and livestock as familial resources. Livestock, as their name implies, are an intrinsically dynamic form of property. Thus, many of the basic questions of the relation between livestock and family in pastoral societies turn on the extent to which the dynamics of herd growth can be adapted to the comparable processes which the family itself undergoes. The fact that livestock holdings can be used both as a capital resource and as a consumer good, and the ability of herds to reproduce themselves, make for considerable adaptive flexibility in this regard. In addition, livestock are both mobile and relatively easily divisible, and this matches fairly well with the mobility of human beings and the fissive tendencies of families at different junctures in their developmental cycles.

[2] Voionmaa (1915, pp. 379–80, 429–34, 449–51).

Land is not completely lacking in dynamic potential, since it can sometimes be rendered more productive through new crops or new agricultural techniques. None the less, it has intrinsically strong tendencies to stasis. A piece of land will not move, grow or reproduce itself, and this does not bode well for its relations with a living human group. If more land is wanted, it has to be sought elsewhere, and this can adversely affect the efficiency of a family farm if extra land is not available close by. The availability of land is also clearly an important factor for the family in other ways. If it is freely accessible, problems and conflicts over inheritance are likely to be less common and less bitter than if it is scarce. And even if land shortage does not lead to actual conflict between heir and holder, or between heirs themselves, one none the less finds recurring conflicts of principles, and an ultimately irresolvable question constantly arises for the parental generation. How can one maintain the unity of a viable farm without depriving some of one's children of a birthright in the land?[3]

Farming in situations of restricted land availability seems bound to militate against the unity and equality of siblings. It also tends to mean that the idea of a family farm, persisting as a unit over several generations, depends heavily upon the shedding of at least some family members as the generations pass. This is usually partly catered for by the out-marriage of some children, commonly daughters, but there may also be more drastic action through patterns of primogeniture or ultimogeniture, or more flexible forms of choice and heir restriction. We have already seen some examples of such processes at work in Vieki in the material discussed in the last chapter. Non-inheriting sons in such a system may be forced to move away altogether, sometimes to towns or even to another country, though not always to their disadvantage. Or, they may begin to form the basis of a rural tenant-farming group or labouring proletariate. Sometimes, as historically in parts of Finland and elsewhere in Europe, a form of compromise is reached where some sons who remain on a farm do not marry, and their adult status vis-à-vis the younger generation is defined by 'unclehood' rather than parenthood.[4] The main alternative to such strategies is of course to divide the farm between several or all heirs, with a subsequent risk that the viability of holdings will be seriously impaired.

In addition to such effects upon intra-generational fission and differentiation, relative land scarcity may also seriously affect the extent to which parents can exert authority over their children, whose dependence on them is likely to be closely linked to land. In practice this is often a quite complicated issue. It partly turns on how much choice parents can legally or customarily exercise about which of their children will inherit, and it also

---

[3] J. Goody (1976b), p. 5); Barnes (1957, p. 54).
[4] J. Goody (1976c, p. 25). For an example of a comparable uncle/bachelor connection in the Góral dialect of Polish see Pine (1987, p. 154).

ties in closely with the needs which parents have for support in old age. None the less, one can easily see a potential link between land scarcity and parental power.[5]

Relatively fixed land holdings will also adversely affect a family's ability to compensate for changes in its composition. Apart from simple changes in group size, there is also the question of changes in the ratio of hands to mouths. The birth of children is naturally a key element here, but so too is the ageing process of the senior generation. Changes may also occur through the permanent or temporary departure of an able-bodied adult member.

The problematic nature of the farm–family connection is, however, importantly mitigated by more positive features of the family as a farming group. Families are by nature highly flexible work units, and they can often respond successfully to difficulties and pressures by working harder and tightening their belts.[6] Even dispersed members may return home to help in a crisis, and a more regular combination of farm work with a paid job or other extra-farming activities is quite common. Such flexibility is impressive, though recent Sahel famines painfully remind us that it is by no means unlimited. In an extreme case where mouths are many, hands are few, land is scarce and poor, and climate is unfavourable, the results may, of course, be disastrous for farming families. Groups may become involved in a spiral of misfortune leading to extinction through hunger and disease, or they may dissolve as members try to find relief elsewhere.

Even in circumstances of this latter sort, however, kinship's common axioms of permanent ascriptive bonding and marriage's tendency to be a relatively lasting tie may help families to survive quite damaging disruptive interludes. Families may reunite after long periods of dispersion during which their members have sought refuge in neighbouring areas as labourers or domestic servants or in more general client roles. In the late 1950s, I was surprised to discover a couple of young women canvassing around the Nyamwezi village I was working in, and offering themselves as 'wives'. They were from a neighbouring drought-stricken area and they had been left at home while their husbands went to look for food elsewhere. They had eventually given up waiting for the men's return and had set off on the mission in question. This was quite common practice in such circumstances, and I was told that the women would almost certainly leave any new 'husband' and return home once things got better there.

Beyond its use in crises, family flexibility also fits very well with some of the demands which farming can make even at the best of times. For farming is not typically amenable to neat and simple organisation on a regular and

---

[5] See Gulliver (1964, pp. 212–13) for an African example of this.
[6] See Chayanov (1986, p. 87 and passim) and Sahlins (1974, p. 89).

unchanging basis through the year. Unless it is highly specialised and mechanised, and often enough even when it is, farming needs a flexible workforce to cope even with regular seasonal change and the resulting pattern of quiet periods and hectic labour bottlenecks. And to this must be added all the vagaries of climate and other unexpected pressures which seem to be intrinsic to a farmer's lot. Short of coercion, or the lack of alternative forms of income, it is often hard for an observer to see how people can be willing to put up with the uncertainties and stresses of a farming life, even when, as in modern Finland, they are working for themselves rather than as others' labourers and tenants. There are, of course, a variety of arguments about the persistence, and indeed the regeneration, of family farming in the modern world. Are farming families, and their rural communities, simply left by 'capital' to carry the unwanted burdens and to take the risks of farming, or do they have a special capacity to adapt to the demands of agriculture and even perhaps outperform a large concern, as Warriner has suggested, for example, with regard to livestock keeping?[7] However one resolves such issues, the arguments on both sides point towards positive features of the fit between farming and a family workforce, and these help importantly to compensate for the more problematic aspects of compatability between the two which I have also outlined.

Distinctions and ambiguities

Many of the general points raised in the previous section are of critical importance in the Finnish case, and a number of them will be taken up in detail in this and succeeding chapters. First, however, it is useful to explore in outline some of the terms, concepts and values which are central to the family farming pattern there.

The ambiguities of the English term 'family' are largely avoided in Finnish through the use of separate terms, though the language also contains its own interesting zones of multiple and diffuse meanings in its kinship and domestic-group vocabulary. The distinction between family as a marriage-centred unit and as a multi-generation surname grouping is relatively clearly marked in Finnish by the terms *perhe* and *suku*, though there is slight overlap between them. *Perhe* is essentially a short-term concept, mainly denoting family and household as narrowly prescribed groups of living people. There is an air of domesticity about it. The family car is *perheauto*, a family doctor is *perhelääkäri*, and family life is *perheelämä*. A 'family man' is *perheellinen* (adjectival form) *mies*, and an 'extended family' is *suurperhe*. The term *perheviljelmä* is sometimes used to refer to a family farm, but the main emphasis in such a case is on the more synchronic aspects of family residence and labour, and perhaps ownership.

[7] Warriner (1964, p. 148).

Suku is different in its emphasis, though it also seems to have a wider range of meanings than *perhe*. One set of these is 'strain, stock and descent line', and it is often used in this context to refer especially to a surname (*sukunimi*) group. Here one finds a certain agnatic bias in the term since surnames are transmitted, as in Britain, via the father, and one also sometimes encounters a slight tendency, which is also found in Britain, to talk as if character and other personal features are mainly transmitted along surname lines.[8] This is not altogether surprising since it is much harder to express generalisations about other sets of kin for whom no unifying term, such as a surname, exists. Surnames have been used in Finland for some centuries, and their origins are by no means wholly clear. Some of those found in the Vieki area, such as Meriläinen or Nevalainen, appear to be fairly evenly and widely distributed over many parts of eastern Finland and beyond. Others are more localised, as for instance Kärkkäinen, which I discussed briefly in the previous chapter. As elsewhere, when people have become dispersed from their original communities, some surname groups in Finland nowadays hold gatherings from time to time. Such a gathering is known as a *sukukokous* (literally '*suku*-meeting'). Large numbers of bearers of the name Eskelinen, for instance, gather occasionally from far and wide in the Nurmes Commune village of Höljäkkä, from where they claim originally to have sprung. In contrast, the term *perhekokous* would most likely refer at most to a small meeting of the dispersed members of a formerly unified nuclear family with their own spouses and children. In the same vein, a term like *sukuhistoria* refers to family history over the generations, and *sukututkimus* is the word for 'genealogical research'. The term *sukutila* is sometimes used for 'family farm', but here the emphasis is clearly on the fact that such a farm has been passed down through the generations from one family member to another.

The contrast I have so far stressed between *perhe* and *suku* is comparable to that often drawn by anthropologists between 'family' (in a narrow sense) and various ideas of 'descent'. I should note here also that a unilineal emphasis is arguably present in some other features of the Finnish kinship system in addition to the handing on of surnames. At the level of more detailed kinship terminology, for instance, modern Finnish still retains an idea of 'avunculate' in the distinction between *eno* (mother's brother) and *setä* (father's brother and other 'English' uncles), even though it has shed several other traditional terms. Again, as I discuss below and in the following chapter, customary practice has in general tended to support the land entitlement of males more sharply than the law insists, even in cases

---

[8] Strathern (1981, pp. 148–9 and 161–9) has an interesting discussion of the relation between surnames and bilateral kinship in an English village. She notes the tendency there to ascribe special identity and character to surname groups.

where the law already discriminated in their favour by allocating larger portions of inheritance to them than to females.

At this juncture it is perhaps worth asking whether *suku* in some contexts represents a form of patrilineal descent group. There is some evidence to support such a view, though the question is a complicated one which has to be examined over time, and any answer has to be hedged round with limitations. As I noted in the previous chapter, some writers on the family in historic Europe, such as Plakans, have worried that persistent features of a wider kinship structure, including descent groups, might be hidden by the types of data which the scholar has available for use. At the same time, one must bear in mind the lengthy and at times quite bitter arguments about the presence or not of descent groups in societies where a whole generation of anthropologists had been accustomed to seeing them. Barnes and Leach made it quite clear that the concept of a unilineal descent group could not simply be transferred from Africa to New Guinea and Sri Lanka, and their work also sowed major doubts about the validity of this framework of analysis for much of Africa itself.[9] One of the points they stressed, which appears relevant in the present context, is the difference between true 'descent', as a right-generating link to an ancestor, and 'cumulative filiation', which involves a replicated series of right-generating parent–child connections back through time. Another, to which I return below, is the distinction, especially strongly marked by Leach, between 'statistical' and 'normative' patterns of relationship. Goody, on a different tack, has argued that the apparent similarity between the 'lineage' of social anthropological descent-group theory and European forms and concepts such as the French *lignage* can be seriously misleading.[10] He also stresses, very aptly for the Finnish case, that agnation in the context of inheritance of land may form part of a wider pattern of bilateral inheritance. This implies some system, customary or legal, of 'diverging devolution' which may include the use of dowry as a form of female pre-inheritance of other forms of wealth such as livestock or money. Certainly, there is nothing like a 'segmentary lineage system' in Finnish rural society either today or in recent centuries, and it is not clear that there ever has been, although some writers assert that strongly corporate kinship groups were a major feature of early northern European social systems. There is uncertainty and argument, however, about the structure of such groups, and in any case any substantial power they had seems to have been weakened in the Swedish region by the time of the early medieval legal codes.

[9] See Barnes (1962), Leach (1960, pp. 116–17, 120 and 123) and Abrahams (1978b, p. 67–8).
[10] See Leach (1960, p. 124) for a discussion of the distinction between statistical and normative approaches to kinship systems. His ideas on this are dealt with at length in Leach (1961). See J. Goody (1983, pp. 222–39) for the distinction between 'lineages' and *lignage*.

Paradoxically, although it may have its archaic counterparts, the recognition of a large surname group as a sort of clan, as in the case of the Eskelinens which I have mentioned, appears to be a modern development. It is probably best understood as part of a contemporary search for roots among urban dwellers and other dispersed members of rural communities and their descendants. Many such people nowadays like to peruse the various village records preserved in the National Archives in Helsinki and elsewhere, and there are published guides to such material and its investigation which are designed expressly for the amateur genealogist.[11] Such behaviour seems to be an interesting if minor counter-reaction to the narrowing of the range of active kinship links and the accompanying tendency, at least in many areas of social life during the last century or more, to place greater emphasis upon the rights, obligations and potential of the individual. A full discussion of this complex and uneven process of increasing individuation is beyond the scope of this study, and indeed beyond my academic competence, but I will return to certain aspects of it and complications within it both here and in my subsequent discussions of inheritance and of co-operation between farmers.

As I have implied, villagers themselves, with their feet firmly planted in a real rural community, are generally less interested in finding and getting together with large groups of kin. Admittedly, some individuals are more interested in tracing genealogies than others, but I have been struck by the tendency of rural dwellers, like the Vieki Turunens described in the last chapter, to deny their kinship links to others with the same surname even in cases where archival searches can fairly easily reveal direct connection. It is true that Turunen is an extremely common name in this area, and it is quite widespread elsewhere in Finland. It is also true that the name Kärkkäinen is even more common in the area, and that the statements I encountered that most of the families of that name within the village were of diverse origins are true as far back as parish and other records permit one to trace. These factors may go some way to explain assertions of unrelatedness as simply overgeneralisations of a statement that is often though not always true, and I must confess that the denials of linkage which I encountered were by no means passionate. None the less, they go beyond the agnosticism which ignorance of connection might more rationally dictate, and even if they are seen simply as evidence of 'structural amnesia', this in itself is noteworthy. Certainly, they mark a contrast with the common tendency I have encountered in East Africa for people to be keen to search out kinship links between themselves and others. I should add that I have occasionally been told by Vieki people in the course of my enquiries that they have heard they

---

[11] See Mäkelä (1988) for an example of a popular text of this sort published in a widely read Finnish yearbook.

may be related to some other families of the same name, but that they are not especially interested in the matter. This fits well with my understanding of the role of wider kinship links more generally within the village, where they seem to constitute a possible basis rather than a structurally defined imperative for help and collaboration.

Coupled with this is an apparent tendency for *suku* (as surname-group) linkage to be most salient when it is combined with a connection through land holding. Once the land rights of one section of such a group have ceased to be meaningfully connected with those of another, there is relatively little else to link the two together more strongly than any other set of kin. Significant relationship through land takes various forms. Most directly there are shared rights to an area of land between siblings, or between a person and a sibling's child, or occasionally between siblings' children. We are thus dealing here typically with people who at most share common grandparents. Beyond this it is possible to detect a sense of linkage to those kin who own, or have owned, land which is known to be part of a formerly undivided holding. Nowadays, of course, this also commonly involves relationships with siblings and with cousins in the towns, and there are some advantages for both sides in the maintenance of such links. Town-dwellers may welcome the opportunity to take cheap rural breaks, and villagers may find it advantageous to have one or more urban points of contact, in addition to more generally enjoying the sense of connection to the wider world through such ties. Urban kin are especially welcome visitors on a farm during labour bottlenecks such as haymaking, and one farm-wife told me that there is a fairly sharp distinction between kin who come at such times and those who do not. As far as I am aware, such feelings of connection rarely extend beyond the level of living second cousins and their children, and a tendency for such relationship to fall within a *suku* as a common surname group arises from the customary patterns of inheritance. Legally, rural land in Finland has been inheritable by women for many centuries, but there was an agnatic bias in the law until the late nineteenth century, and women were entitled until then to only half as much as men. Often, moreover, they received their share of an inheritance in other forms such as livestock and money, and the eventual legal equivalence of male and female shares was in any case not always recognised in practice. It is true that custom also recognises the possibility that daughters and their husbands may usefully inherit land in certain circumstances, as I discuss in the next chapter, but the common and preferred pattern of transmission is to sons.

Custom, then, has tended to generate fairly small-scale 'agnatic' groups focussed on existing or earlier joint interests in land. It is possible, moreover, that a further feature of the legal system has also varyingly influenced the range of kin sharing such interests at different times. Some aspects of this point have been highlighted by the Finnish jurist af Hällstrom in his discussion of the historical inalienability of inherited land (*perimysmaa*).[12] This is a very complex issue, about which Finnish lawyers themselves have not always been in agreement, and I treat it only in broad outline here. It involves a form of rights in family land which have commonly been referred to, even in English writings upon kinship and inheritance, by the French term *retrait lignager*. The use of this French term in English probably derives from the fact that the customary and legal forms in question have been long suppressed in England, with the exception of special entailments, but it may be noted that even in France the system was abolished with the revolution. The equivalent term in Finnish is *sukulunastusoikeus* (literally 'kin redemption right'), and the rights in question persisted in a limited form in Finnish law until the present century. Since early times, Swedish law had recognised the right of individuals to own land, but it had also empowered certain kin to prevent the transfer of an inherited holding outside their own ranks. In the early law, including the revised legislation of 1734, the relatives who were so empowered were the owner's children or other direct descendants, parents and grandparents, siblings and first cousins. If the owner tried to pass such land outside this range, one or more of the kin concerned could protest within a year and a day and obtain the land by offering a sum equal to that involved in the transaction. The law of 1734 was repealed in Sweden in decrees of 1857 and 1863, but it remained in force in Finland until 1878, when it was replaced by a restricted form until its final abolition in 1930. In the 1878 regulations the rights of collateral kin to prevent a transfer were abolished, and the range of those empowered to do so was narrowly restricted to the owner's children and parents. It is not clear to what extent this shift reflected the views of the lawmakers more than those of villagers, but it was in keeping with the liberal individualism of the times, and in any case it seems unlikely that it would have exercised no influence at all upon the sense of mutual involvement of the kin concerned. As with inheritance, the laws of land redemption recognised the rights of women as potential holders and transmitters of land but, as my earlier discussion implies, relations between agnates are most likely to have been involved.

Such a likelihood in this and other contexts is none the less significantly different from the consequences of a simple jural rule of agnation. Agnatic grouping in rural Finland thus represents a mixture of the 'normative' and the 'statistical', qualities which Leach and others, including myself (1978b), have found it useful to keep analytically distinct. The legal rules, with their

12 af Hällström (1934).

former recognition of male rights to a larger share of the inheritance, have historically had a distinct agnatic bias, and custom has often gone beyond this to the point of excluding women from inheritance of land when male heirs were available. At the same time a substantial degree of flexibility has been and still is maintained by farmers in the handling of the devolution of their farms, so that choice within a framework of cultural preferences has played an important part in actual practice. This will emerge more clearly in the following chapter, both in my discussion of inheritance by daughters, and more generally in my account of the transmission of farms *inter vivos*.

It is important to note that, in addition to the problems of delineating *suku* as a type of unilineally skewed group, there are some further areas of ambiguity in the concept. For *suku* also seems to carry certain implications of kinship more generally as a bilateral and often ego-focussed system of relationship. This emerges most clearly in the everyday noun *sukulainen*, which is originally an adjectival form directly derived from *suku*, in much the same way as *suomalainen* ('Finn') or *karjalainen* ('Karelian') are derived from Suomi ('Finland') and Karjala ('Karelia'). *Sukulainen* simply means 'relative' or 'kinsman', and the person referred to can be linked through intermediaries of either sex, in any combination, and as such is not expected to share the same surname with the speaker. Such kinsfolk, as in English, may be near or distant, and they may be of the same or a different generation (*sukupolvi*, literally '*suku*-knee'). They may also be of the same or the other sex, for which the standard term is interestingly *sukupuoli* (literally '*suku*-half') although, at least in modern usage, it covers much the same range of referents as the word 'sex' in English. Most adult villagers are aware of a substantial number of such cognates, typically up to the range of second cousins and some of their children but occasionally beyond, and especially those who live or have till recently lived in or near the village. Such awareness of one's more distant cousins does not in itself mean a great deal if it lacks the stimulus of interaction which is itself largely the result of chance and choice. Intermarriage. which I discuss below, and also friendship and collaboration in work or leisure activities may create significant additional connections between more distant kin, though it should be added that they also commonly occur between unrelated villagers.[13]

Turning now from kinship and the family to the farm itself, some other features of linguistic usage are worth noting. I mentioned earlier the use of two terms *viljelmä* and *tila* for a farm. The first derives from the verb *viljellä*, which means to 'cultivate' or 'till the soil', and is the more direct and literal of the two terms. However, *tila*, which literally means 'room' in the sense of space, and the slightly more explicit form *maatila* (literally 'land space') are

---

[13] See the entries under *suku* in Hurme et al. (1984) for the range of meanings of this term and its derivatives.

more often used. The word *talo* (literally 'house') also had this connotation in the past, no doubt through the intermediary idea of a farmhouse and its occupants, and it can still be used in this sense in a rural context. Similarly, although *maanviljelijä*, literally 'land cultivator', is a quite specific and quite common term for farmer, other words which refer more to social role and status have been very widely used. In the old days, distinctions of status within the rural community were understandably more important than the designation of a farmer's occupation, and it is interesting that many of the terms used to denote these did so primarily by reference to culturally graded types of social space. The word *talonpoika*, literally 'house son', was the standard word for 'peasant farmer', and as we have already seen, terms like *talollinen* (house- or farm-owner and literally 'house-person'), *torppari* (crofter) and *mäkitupalainen* (literally 'hill-cotter') were among the main words used. Even the word *loinen*, which was used for the lowest-ranking villagers, is ultimately of this sort. The term literally means 'parasite', and it appears to be connected in its etymology with the word *luona*, which means 'at the home of'.[14] In addition, both today and in past usage, common words for a farmer and his wife are *isäntä* and *emäntä*. These relate respectively to words for 'father' and 'mother', and they can reasonably well be translated as 'master' and 'mistress'.

There are probably many reasons for such slightly vague and diffuse usage. It is plausible, for instance, as I have implied, that exact reference to farming is less necessary in a rural community. It is also perhaps possible that the spatial component of older status terms discussed might have served to soften the differences involved, though I would not wish to push such a suggestion very far. In the case of words for 'farm' and 'farmer', it seems likely that the diffuse usage partly relates to the fact that farmers and their families tend to engage in a range of economic activities to supplement their farming income. It is also arguable that this is simply one aspect of a more embracing fact that farming in Finland, as in many other countries, is not simply an occupation or profession like that of a welder or a lawyer. In addition to the question of other income sources, which is also relevant for other sections of the population, there is the point that even on their farms, farmers tend to be a bit of everything – mechanic, woodworker, plumber and so on.[15] More important than this 'do-it-yourself' tendency, though, which others in any case increasingly share with farmers, is the fact that a farm is not only a place of work and source of income but much more besides. It is also the place, focussed on the farmstead, where the full variety of family life is lived. In short it is 'home', and farming itself is part of home

[14] See Hakulinen (1961, p. 114). Newby (1980, pp. 34–5) has some interesting general comments on the social organisation of space as a key element in rural society.
[15] See Galeski (1971) and Mendras (1970, Chapters 3 and 6).

life. It is perhaps also worth noting in this context that a farm family is often referred to simply as *väki* (people), so that, for example, *Lehtolan väki* will be used to refer to the family on the Lehtola farm. This word *väki* is itself of quite considerable interest, since it also has connotations of 'force' and 'power' as well as being a standard word for 'people'. The intimate connection between work, strength and social group which characterises family farming is thus neatly encapsulated in this little word.

While it is true that education and movement to towns may affect the degree of overlap between the set of family members who have rights in a farm and those who live on it and work it, the general connection between farm and family is still strong. The ownership and internal organisation of a farm, and relations between it and other farms, are still essentially intra- and inter-family matters, and to some extent the farm and farming also give a family its identity. Thus, although it is partly a matter of convenience, given the frequent incidence of many local Christian names and surnames, the tendency to identify people by the name of their farmstead – which is often loosely used as the farm name – cannot be explained purely in these terms. People from other farms speak readily of Turulan Teppo or Lehtolan Aili (Teppo of Turula and Aili of Lehtola), and this kind of usage is also sometimes extended to refer to, and no doubt retain a sense of contact with, members of farm families who have long since left the area to embark on urban careers. As I discuss in Chapter 7, it has even been the custom in some parts of Finland for new owners of a farm to change their surname to that of the farm, though this has not been so in North Karelia.

The vocabulary and usage which I have discussed mark a close and pervasive link between farm and family in this area. I have outlined some of its main features here, and I hope that I have said enough to suggest convincingly its fundamental place in Finnish rural society. The connection is in fact more complex than I have so far described, and I will deal with further aspects of it in the course of my account.

Households and workers

As in other contexts of activity, marriage is conventionally the pivotal relationship in the Finnish family (*perhe*) as a farming unit. The traditional division of labour between the sexes is the simplest expression of this fact, with the man's work focussed upon field and forest and the woman's upon livestock. These days, especially with the coming of complex machinery, and with changes of ideas also brought in from outside through magazines, books, television and through personal contacts, old attitudes are gradually changing. Such change ultimately goes well beyond the narrow field of agricultural labour, and a few village women are interested to question the traditional definition of their place within society more generally, and even the assumed 'masculinity' of God. Change can and often does take place, however, in particular areas of practice without needing the acceptance of a wholesale ideological revolution by those involved. For the most part this is what is happening in Vieki. It is no longer very surprising there to find an *isäntä* helping to look after livestock on a modern farm, or even doing most such work, and women may occasionally drive tractors and do other jobs traditionally thought of as men's tasks. It is well known that the 'mucking out' of cowsheds is one of the most physically taxing jobs, and husbands who do not help with this – especially if it has to be done manually – are nowadays the subject of much critical comment, particularly from more fortunate wives on other farms. Some women also say a little ruefully that it was only the advent of milking machines that made men willing to help them with the cows. Yet the idea that the standard work team on a farm is a married couple still survives, and not without good cause. A husband and wife team which is hard-working, and in which the spouses provide both physical and emotional support to each other in an atmosphere of mutual respect, is in fact a formidable workforce, as I saw on many occasions in the course of my research.

In Vieki, as anywhere, however, there are considerable risks in such arrangements, and evidence suggests that these are often borne by women. Of course both husband and wife can become temporarily or permanently incapacitated by illness. Back troubles among men seem to be extremely common, and women seem often to suffer from hand and wrist problems among other occupational ailments. There has also been a long history of heart trouble in the area, though the incidence of this is now diminishing as people have become more diet-conscious and work patterns have changed. But problems arising through defects of character – and especially those associated with alcohol – seem often to be male ones. There are a number of cases I have come across, both past and present, where such problems have put farm and family at considerable risk, and even wrecked them, and the efforts of wives to salvage themselves and their husbands from such situations are a well-known theme of local gossip. Such efforts commonly involve a wife's conscientious struggles to economise, and perhaps to find a part-time job to bring in extra money. Sometimes women have been known to set up their own small enterprises, such as a coffee stall in Lieksa in one case, in order to try to make ends meet.

Although a married couple is the ideal core of a farm workforce, the ideal is not always realised. A widow may try to keep up a farm after her husband's death, though this is especially hard if there are young children to look after and no resident adult help. Survival may be possible, however, in such circumstances, if help with heavy work can be provided by relatives and neighbours, and I have come across the odd case where this has happened. On one farm the widow has managed to keep things ticking over in this way, at least to a limited extent, while waiting for her teenage son to become old enough to get things moving properly. In another case a widowed mother helps her unmarried adult daughter to run a farm with several cows, about seven hectares of arable land and a substantial forest holding. They had no tractor of their own at the time of my research, and had to rely on help from nearby kin and neighbours. On another farm, there was a widowed mother and her two unmarried adult sons, and they were making a satisfactory go of things for the time being. Their position was, however, precarious since the mother was quite old, and the two men had health problems. Indeed the younger brother died of a heart attack not long after I left the field, and the older one also had a history of heart trouble. In some cases, a sort of halfway house arrangement is achieved. A husband may work regularly off the farm, perhaps as a forestry worker, and his wife will run the place with part-time help from him. This is an extension of the earlier extremely common seasonal pattern of winter timber work for men, and it depends very much on the availability of machinery and possibly of help from children and other kin in order to succeed. In yet another case, an old widow remained on a small farm which her son looked after at weekends and during his holidays from work as a schoolteacher.[16]

In such cases, we are, of course, dealing with examples of two crucial general features of the family which I have already stressed – its mutability and flexibility. I will deal in Chapter 5 with questions of succession and the co-residence of two adult generations, as a major juncture in the developmental cycle of farm families. It will be clear more generally, however, that children who stay on a farm are likely, as in the past, to become an increasingly important element in the labour force as their parents age and they themselves mature. As I have mentioned, however, there has been an increasing tendency for the movement of younger people away from the rural areas, and this has been associated with such developments as higher levels of general education, increased industrialisation and growing pressures on the viability of small, old-fashioned farms. In recent years, villagers have also begun to be more aware of allergies to cattle and to grain dust, and these have become acceptable excuses for children to avoid involvement in the running of a farm, and to move off into other sectors of the economy.

The fact that children are in other jobs does not, however, automatically prevent their regular participation in the running of a farm, as the above

---

[16] For discussion of the combination of farming and other economic activities in Finland see Nygård (1983) and Uusitalo (1979). Such combinations have been common both historically and in modern times and they have taken many forms. Cf. Mendras (1970, pp. 236–7), Newby (1980, p. 100) and Löfgren (1974, p. 28, and 1980, p. 191).

example of a schoolteacher shows. More often, though, help will be available less regularly, but none the less extremely valuably, in times of crisis. Thus a well-educated son, with a good urban job, may well travel long distances every weekend to help out if his father is ill at a busy period of the farm calendar, and children may in any case return for major labour bottlenecks such as haymaking.

The composition of farm households and workforces has changed radically over the last century or so, as my earlier discussions have made clear. Nowadays such households are much smaller units than they were during the nineteenth century, and their structure is also much simpler. The fundamental change has been the narrowing of the range of household composition almost wholly to the members of a single family, and the disappearance of the categories of *renki* (labourer), *piika* (maid) and various forms of lodger from the lists. Again the absence of crofters and cotters from modern farms, even though they used to have their own accommodation and smallholdings, has removed a once significant source of labour for farm-owners. According to a survey conducted in the mid 1970s in the Lieksa area, there were only eighteen farms (under 2 per cent of those surveyed) on which there was permanently employed labour, and in almost all cases only a single employee was involved.[17] I myself only came across a couple of such cases in the Vieki area. In one, the worker was a young man who was fostered by the family concerned, and in the second, the worker was an old man who had died shortly before my research began. He had originally been taken in as a young man in distressed circumstances, and he stayed on for the rest of his life. Temporary employment of outside labour was more common and occurred according to the survey on a little over one-third of farms. In the very large majority of cases such employment was for one to twenty-five days only. My own information suggests that many such cases involve the short-term hiring of a fellow farmer for some special task, perhaps as the driver of his own machine such as a combine harvester, or simply for help with heavy work. As I describe in Chapter 6, farmers are usually extremely careful to respect each other's dignity and independence in such cases and to avoid any hint of meanness on their part. Those who fail to do so will usually find it hard to recruit help when they need it, and this can make life very difficult for them. I have encountered a case where a prosperous farmer hires a retired villager to do odd jobs for him from time to time, but even here, where it is clear 'who is boss', the farmer in question is careful to behave generously and appears to treat the man more like an old acquaintance than an employee.

[17] Lieksan Kaupunki (n.d., pp. 32–3).

A man and his wife and two tractors

The development of ownership of farm machinery, and especially tractors and their large variety of attachments, has been vitally important in this context, and a modern Finnish farm cannot in fact survive without machines. A wide choice of machinery is readily available, and access to spares and servicing is good even in a relatively remote area such as Vieki. It is a paradox of modern agricultural development in Finland, as in many other countries, that mechanisation has been crucial to the maintenance and, indeed, the resurgence of the family as the main farm workforce. As we have seen, the modern farmer, at least in this part of Finland, hires very little outside labour. He also often lacks the help of a group of resident children, though such help is still of great benefit when it is available. It is the farmer's stock of machinery which fills such gaps, and which makes it possible for him and his wife to manage a farm more or less alone for a considerable number of years.

The introduction of machinery has been an important part of a more general process of technological development in Finnish farming since the latter part of the last century. Other elements in this development include ditching and drainage, the use of improved crop varieties, and the spread of more effective forms of ploughs, rakes and other tillage implements. The diffusion of this new technology was greatly aided by the Pellervo society and by associated Farmers' Societies at village level.[18] As with other new developments, some pastors seem to have played a role in their introduction, as too did some of the more 'enlightened' local farmers. Mowers were among the first machines to come into this part of North Karelia, and they were quickly followed in the early 1900s by threshing machines and the occasional potato-lifter, commonly owned by small groups of farmers, and also some mechanical winnowers. Steam power was at first used for larger machines, and this was gradually replaced by internal combustion engines and even electrical power in some parts of the area. The horse was the main source of mobile power, both in agriculture and in forestry, and it remained so well into the middle of the present century.[19] Figures for Finland as a whole show a gradual decline in the number of horses from 399,000 in 1921–5 to 346,000 in 1951–5. Ten years later the figure had dropped to 215,000, and by 1979–80 it was down tenfold to only 22,000. This most recent decline is clearly connected to the overall decline in farming as well as to increased mechanisation. The horse has, of course, given way to the tractor, and the increase in tractor use has been one of the most noticeable

---

[18] For the local history of early agricultural improvements see Saloheimo (1953, pp. 382ff.). Fox (1926, pp. 45ff.) has a discussion of the history of the Pellervo Society.

[19] See Saloheimo (1953, pp. 391ff.) for early mechanisation in the neighbouring Nurmes area.

features of recent decades. Nationally, the number of tractors rose from 75,000 in 1959, when rural populations were at their height, to 155,000 in 1970 and 204,000 in 1979, when they were at their lowest.[20] North Karelia was one of the slower areas to take up the use of tractors initially, and the rate of increase there in relatively recent years has almost certainly been steeper than the national average.

Some notion of the range of machinery on modern Vieki farms can be gained from the following two examples. The first is a medium- to large-sized farm, and the second is closer to average size. Neither farm had a dairy herd at the time of my fieldwork. On the first, there was a herd of pigs which had been brought in instead of cattle a few years before, because of the ill health of the farm wife. Keeping pigs is a less strenuous task than looking after cows, though the strong smell of the piggery makes it unpleasant work. The farmer mainly looked after the herd himself. On the second farm there was a small beef herd and one milk cow. In this case, husband and wife both participated in looking after the livestock.

Männikkölä

The Männikkölä farm contained about 20 hectares of fields and a little over 70 hectares of forest at the time of my research. Most of the arable land was planted to barley, but there was also some hay. In addition to his own fields, the farmer, Ilmari Turunen, also rented some land from an urban relative. The core of the farm was longstanding family land (see Chapter 3), but a large part of the forest (some 33 hectares) was bought from the state in 1966. At the time of my research Ilmari was aged fifty-five and ran the farm with limited help from his wife, Aino. Despite some previous heart trouble, Ilmari was unusually strong. He had always been keen on machinery, however, and was one of the earlier tractor owners in the village. He was also very positive about machine sharing.

In 1980 Ilmari had the following equipment of his own on the farm:

> 2 tractors
> 1 plough and 2 harrows
> 1 mowing attachment
> 1 raking machine
> 1 drainage plough
> 1 snow-plough and rotary snow blower
> 1 chainsaw
> 1 manure buck-rake
> 1 wood-splitting machine
> 1 stump hook

[20] Agricultural Information Centre (1981, p. 9), Pellervo Seura (1981, p. 269).

Plate 3 After the storm. Using a chain saw to tidy up a forest holding

Plate 4 Storing timber for the winter

1 cultivator
2 trailers
1 tractor sled
1 cold-air dryer
2 grain augers
1 hygrometer
1 tractor-drawn road leveller

In addition, he had part shares with other farmers in a fertiliser drill, a set of field rolls, a crop sprayer, a potato harvester, a slurry tank, a winch, a ditching disc and a combine harvester.

Kiiskilä

This farm was owned by Veikko and Helka Kiiskinen at the time of my research, and has since then been transferred to one of their sons. The farm was originally in the hands of Helka's parents, as I have described in Chapter 3. The farm had about 9.5 hectares of arable land and a little over 30 hectares of forest, but the forest holdings were increased by the purchase of a further 10 hectares from the state in 1982. In 1981 Veikko had the following equipment:

1 tractor
1 plough and 1 harrow
1 spreader
1 mowing attachment
1 raking attachment
1 wooden field roller (home-made)
1 chain saw
1 trailer
1 manure buck-rake
1 warm-air dryer
1 snow plate
1 tractor sled

Veikko was not involved in any joint-ownership groups with other farmers, but he occasionally borrowed a winch, a ditching disc, a sled and a stump hook from other individuals to whom he in turn lent things which they did not possess. He has hired a combine harvester from other farmers in recent years. I will discuss joint ownership and borrowing arrangements in more detail in Chapter 6. Here it may be noted that Veikko has a basic set of equipment of his own which is less comprehensive than Ilmari's, and he has none of the equipment in which Ilmari has joint-ownership shares. It is hard to place a value on such equipment, since it has been acquired at

Plate 5 A recently acquired family combine

Plate 6 Old methods survive in a tight corner

various times and not all of it was bought new. At a rough estimate, and at 1979 new prices and exchange rates, the equipment listed as fully or part owned by Ilmari would have cost about £50,000 and Veikko's something over £20,000.

As these two examples suggest, there is considerable variation in the range of equipment on farms in the area, and this largely turns on hectarage and on the capital available to a farmer. At one extreme only the largest enterprises are likely to have combine harvesters in single ownership, and there are one or two such in Vieki. On the other hand even a fairly small working farm is likely to have a tractor, though there were still some without in 1980. The following additional figures are taken from a 1978 survey of farms in Lieksa and several other North Karelian Communes which supply milk to the Joensuu Co-operative Dairy.[21] Seventy-six per cent of the farms had their own tractor, and about seventy per cent had their own milking machines. Lieksa farmers were a little below the average, with figures of 68 per cent and around 60 per cent respectively. Figures for the total area show that over 90 per cent of medium- to large-sized farms (with ten or more hectares of arable land and/or seven or more head of dairy cattle) had their own tractor, and almost all such farms had one or other form of milking machine, though only the larger ones tended to have systems which piped milk into a storage tank. On over ninety per cent of farms with nine or fewer milk cows, manure was still shifted daily by hand, and it was only on farms with fifteen or more cows that a majority of those surveyed had mechanised systems for dealing with this task. The survey noted the increased use of machines in recent years, and it seems safe to assume that this tendency has been continuing since then.

Marriage patterns and connections

I have no doubt that many marriages have been made in the village with at least *some* thought for their economic implications. Marrying into a family with good resources in farm land and especially timber, and the possibility of combining these with one's own holdings at some stage, are ideas which can scarcely fail to enter people's heads when marriage plays so prominent a role in a domestic economy of this sort. Moreover, there have been one or two more obviously one-sided cases in the past, in which villagers clearly countenance the possibility that one of the spouses had a sharp eye for the main chance. I am thinking here especially of the odd occasion when a hired labourer has married the daughter of a family with a valuable farm when there were no sons to inherit it, but there have also been cases here, as elsewhere, in which a poor woman has managed to get herself a wealthy

[21] Honkaniemi (1979).

husband. More generally, I have been told that in the past, and as far as I can tell especially in the period from the latter end of the last century to the late 1930s when social and economic stratification had become a salient feature of village society, members of better-off families were extremely keen that their children should marry well. This does not seem to mean, however, that marriage in the village has typically formed part of a clear strategy of land accumulation and consolidation, as appears to be the case in many societies, even though opportunities for this have increased as daughters' rights in property including land were legally enhanced and gradually received more local recognition. Rather, it has meant that sons and daughters have been encouraged to marry people of the same social and economic standing as themselves, and especially that the child of a landed and respectable family should if possible marry someone from a similar group. I have also heard it said that in the past marriage was preferred 'off the farm'. This amounts to much the same rule, since it was quoted to me in relation to one of a number of early cases where the son of a land-owner married a young woman who was working as a maid on the farm. In the early nineteenth century, such domestic help was more or less exchanged between families, but by the turn of the century it was often provided for richer households by the daughters of poorer families. I was also told of one young woman who ran off to town with a labourer on her family farm because her family would not give permission for their marriage, and I have heard that some women in such circumstances have been forced by family pressure *not* to marry a particular man, and have ended up unhappily married to someone more 'suitable'.

During the same period, there is also said to have been a particularly harsh attitude to women who had illegitimate children, and it seems likely that social considerations of respectability in such cases were reinforced by the development of religious pietism around this time. It appears to have been mainly poorer women who have had children out of wedlock in the earlier history of the village, but one case is known to me in which this happened to a daughter of a landed family. She was born in 1890, and she had an illegitimate son in 1914. It is not clear who the father of the child was, but the woman is said to have been ostracised by her parents and especially by her mother, even when she was eventually married by another man with whom she then had several children. This man was a landless labourer, and he is said to have been a difficult husband. The couple found it very hard to manage economically, and the woman's mother is said to have turned her away when she tried to get help from her parental home. At the same time, there appears to have been a rather softer attitude towards some illegitimate children themselves, especially if they were of good character. In the present case, the girl's father provided a sixth share of the farm for his illegitimate grandson in his will, and the will was countersigned by his wife, the girl's mother. In another case, the illegitimate son (b. 1883) of a poor woman eventually became a crofter, and his descendants now own their own farm. He himself became a respected villager with a wife and several children, and as a widower he later married the widow of an established local landowner. His descendants volunteered the information to me about the circumstances of his birth, though it is not apparently something which is very widely known in the village. The volunteering of such information partly reflects the lapse of time and the successful rise to respectability of the man in question and of his descendants. At the same time, it probably also reflects some important changes of attitude which have been taking place in recent years. These have followed in the train of the many new connections which have been established with the modern world outside the village through migration and the penetration of mass media.

A small number of village couples these days live together without being formally married, and such unions are not uncommon in the towns. These arrangements are rather conveniently described in Finnish by the term *avoliitto* (literally 'open union'), which is but a single vowel away from *avioliitto*, the standard word for marriage. In the past such unions were looked upon with deep disapproval if they occurred at all, and strong social pressure was brought to bear on individuals by kin and neighbours to try to get them to abandon them. I am told that an important special factor in the modern situation in such cases is that *avoliitto* unions are economically advantageous for retired people who are in receipt of pensions, and this has led to greater tolerance when older couples live together in this way. There are also, however, a few cases where younger couples live together without marriage. These are still frowned upon by older villagers, and especially the more pious churchgoers, but their attitudes are mitigated, as in other contexts, by a sometimes grudging recognition that the world is changing.

Similar views are also taken of divorce, which was extremely rare in the experience of villagers in the past, but is these days recognised as a regrettable but inescapable fact of life – a 'new fashion' (*uusi muoti*), as one old man called it. Although divorce is still uncommon in the village, especially in families which are actively engaged in farming, everyone these days knows of a few cases either locally or among relatives and acquaintances in town. In Finland as a whole divorce rates have risen strongly since the 1930s, and especially during the post-war years, though not as steeply as in England and Wales. At the same time, rural Finnish rates have been consistently much lower than those for the towns. Rural conservatism, a concern for reputation and the ties created by joint involvement in farming are all likely to be influential factors in this context, and rural rates are also likely to be lower when a relatively large proportion of the married population of a village is over fifty years of age. In 1930 there were 1,106 divorces in the country as a whole, and 514 (46 per cent) of these were in rural communes in which 82 per cent of the country's 3.67 million population was living. This gave a national rate of about thirty divorces per 100,000 people, and just under two per 1,000 extant marriages, but the rural rate was only about seventeen per 100,000 people and just over one per 1,000 marriages. By 1974 this rural figures had risen to around five per 1,000 marriages, which was less than half the urban rate, and it had risen to about eleven per 1,000 marriages by 1985. These figures exclude judicial separations, of which there were about seven per 1,000 marriages in the rural areas in 1985. The combined urban/rural figures for North Karelia for that year show that the rate of divorce there was much lower, at about eight per 1,000 marriages, than that of the country as a whole, and the situation seems to be broadly similar in other more remote parts of the country. Separate rural figures are not available to me at this level, but it seems safe to assume that the rate for rural areas of the Province was in turn significantly lower than the total figure, which includes the population of Joensuu and other urban centres. It is interesting that figures for the country as a whole reveal an upward shift in the age at which people are divorcing. In the late 1960s the largest contingent of divorcing men and women were in the 25–9 age group, but by 1985 the largest group was that of 35–9-year-olds. This in turn may well reflect an increased number of unsuccessful remarriages.[22]

In Finland, as in many parts of Europe, including Britain, marriage with first cousins is technically possible, but it is frowned upon in practice. In my searches through the village records, and in discussions with villagers, I came across only one case of such marriage. This was early in the century, and I was told that the children of the marriage had extremely poor eyesight. The case was not spoken of with horror, but it was clearly felt that such marriages are neither desirable nor sensible.

Second-cousin marriage is a different matter, and there are several cases known to me. Such marriages are not particularly approved of, and they may even meet some opposition initially, but the general attitude towards them appears to be one of tolerant acceptance. Occasionally, a couple can trace links to each other through more than one route, and this reflects the more general density of some networks of relations in the area. Sometimes this arises where two siblings or first cousins marry another pair. An example of the complexities of linkage which develop in such cases is that of several marriages among the Siltavaara Honkanens and other families (see Figure 7). Two early members of the family, Antti (1) and Antti (2), were

---

[22] The figures in this section are derived from Central Statistical Office (1940, 1965, 1989).

patrilateral first cousins, and they married two sisters, Anni and Auno Kärkkäinen. One of Anni's daughters, Kaisa, married Yrjö Kärki, and their daughter Anni married Teuvo, the son of Viljo, who was in turn the son of Antti (2) and Auno. Anni and Teuvo are thus both second and third cousins to each other. The Honkanens have further complex links with the Karjalainens in the nearby Nurmes commune village of Kuohatti. Kaisa Honkanen's sister Taimi married Antti Karjalainen, and his sister Alma married Väinö, who was Teuvo's uncle. They had no children, and in fact their farm has passed to Teuvo and Anni, but it will be seen that if they had had children, the latter would again have been cousins three times over to Taimi and Antti Karjalainen's son. In addition, a further sister to Antti and Alma Karjalainen married Väinö's father's brother, Juho Honkanen, and a first cousin, Eino Karjalainen, married Taimi Honkanen's sister Jenny.

Another case is that of linkages centred upon the Kainulainen and Savelius families. These are shown in Figure 8. There are two second-cousin marriages, between Anna and Lauri Savelius in the grandparental generation, and more recently between Ilmari Turunen and Aino Kainulainen. It will also be seen that Aino and Leo Kainulainen are double second cousins, and Elma Savelius is both second and fourth cousin to both of them.

Such linkages within and between families form sporadic areas of density in the kinship and marriage networks of the villagers. Once again, I have no evidence that such dense areas reflect any sort of narrowly definable

Fig. 7 Some connections between the Honkanen and other families

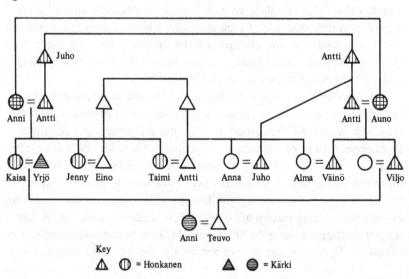

marriage strategy of alliance between certain families either for consolidation of land holdings or for other purposes. As far as I can tell, the
marriages in question mainly arose out of individual choices which were
constricted by the range of social contacts and potential spouses at
particular junctures in the relatively bounded social universe of those
concerned.

It is possible that a significant factor in the situation has been the pattern
of unequal inheritance between sons and daughters which has prevailed in
varying forms for much of the history of family farming in this area. I will
discuss this pattern in some detail later. For the moment, however, it will
suffice to bear in mind that especially in the past in eastern Finland women
did not typically inherit land as daughters, but received a dowry as a form of
pre-inheritance in movables. This relates historically to the division of
labour mentioned earlier, since some livestock was typically included in the
dowry. It has been noted sensibly by Voionmaa that the meaning of such

Fig. 8 Links between the Savelius and Kainulainen familes

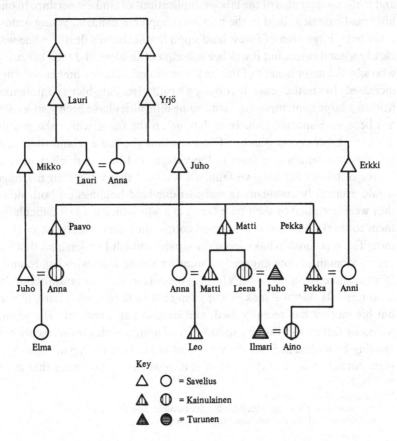

Key

△ ○ = Savelius

⒜ ⒤ = Kainulainen

⒜ ⬤ = Turunen

property division has changed over time, and largely in favour of men as land values have risen as against those of other property.[23] However this may be, the more general point holds that marriage in such circumstances would not typically entail the merging or other significant rearrangement of land holdings, and it is therefore less likely to have been the subject of strategic thinking in ways that have been described for areas where land is devolved through both sons and daughters.[24] It is true that in more recent decades several women have inherited parcels of land, and especially forest, which can form a useful adjunct to their husband's farm and to the property which their children will inherit. But such holdings seem unlikely to be large or regular enough to provide a basis for any consistent pattern of strategic marriages, and they have not, to my knowledge, done so.

At the same time, there can also be some complicating factors within situations in which individual strategies and tactics may appear at first sight to make sense. We have seen that women without brothers can be the inheritors of large areas of land, and this is also true occasionally of widows. Yet even such cases may need to be examined in the light of property values, and in the context also of the labour implications of land-ownership. In one historical case described in the previous chapter, a childless young widow inherited a large area of forest land upon her husband's death.[25] She was clearly a good catch, but it was her subsequent children and their offspring who saw the main benefit of this as the economic value of timber holdings increased. In another case, involving a brotherless daughter and potential heir on a large contemporary farm, some difficulties have been visible. She has been an important source of labour on the farm, which she mainly works with her ageing parents. For some time she had a relationship with the only son on another farm in the village, and he was similarly a vital source of labour for his own family. I was told that while their marriage would eventually amalgamate considerable land holdings on both sides, they were both tied to their own farms in a way which made it difficult for them to work together as a married couple on a joint enterprise of their own. The relationship has eventually lapsed, though I understand that the young woman is now engaged to another young man who has recently formally taken over his father's farm in the village. I am uncertain about the arrangements they will make – the young man's father is still fairly active, but his mother has recently died, and he also has a brother. The young woman's father will in turn soon retire. Though such arrangements can sensibly be looked at from the viewpoint of land-ownership and management considerations of this sort, it is also worth remembering that more

[23] Voionmaa (1915, p. 490).
[24] I am grateful to Dr Francis Pine for helpful comments on this issue.
[25] See discussion of the Kainulainen family in Chapter 3.

general issues are involved. Younger villagers who wish to remain in farming, and especially young men, do not in fact have a wide choice of spouses these days. They may wish to marry partly because husband and wife, and eventually their children, are accepted as the ideal farming unit. But they are also likely to want to do so as part of the more general fulfilment of their life potential within mainstream norms of their society.

Bachelors and spinsters

Although much of my discussion in the previous section focussed upon whom a person marries, it is clear that marrying at all is and has been a more salient question for some villagers. I noted in an earlier section that there was historically an interesting connection between the two ideas of 'unclehood' and 'bachelorhood', and I was struck during my field research by the numbers of unmarried people, and especially men, that I encountered. Both bachelors and spinsters are, and to a lesser extent have long been, common enough to create no great surprise in rural Finland, though celibacy is not typically seen as a desirable state. The ordinary words for bachelor (*vanhapoika*, literally 'old boy') and for spinster (*vanhapiika*, literally 'old maid') are not simply descriptive, for they often have a slightly amusing, and sometimes even a slightly derogatory air to them, with an implication that the person concerned has somehow failed to keep up with the main stream of life.

The broad outline of the situation in the village at the time of my research can be seen in Figure 9, which is based on Table 1. This reveals significant differences between the older and the younger members of the population. There are more women than men in the over-fifty age group, and a larger proportion of such women, and especially those above the age of sixty, are not married. Higher mortality of the men in this group, and accompanying high rates of widowhood, appear to be the most important factors here. In

Fig. 9 The population of Vieki, 1979

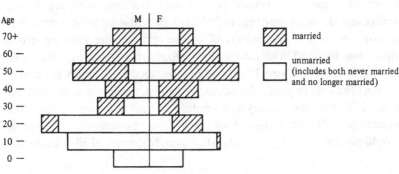

the 40–9 age group, there are still slightly fewer men than women, but there are proportionately more unmarried men than women in this cohort. Although the actual numbers are relatively small, it seems clear that there has been a sharp increase in the village's celibacy rates among such people since the turn of the century, since in 1900 there were only five unmarried men out of a total of 42 in the 45–50 age group, and only one unmarried woman out of 30 in that group.

Among 20–39-year-olds in 1979, and especially among 20–9-year-olds, one finds a much larger number of men in total and a smaller number of married men than married women. A major factor here is the tendency over recent decades for greater female emigration from the village, and this derives, as I have noted, from the relative attractiveness of urban over rural life for modern younger women, despite the fact that substantial numbers of both sexes have left the village to seek their fortunes elsewhere. This almost certainly accounts for a considerable proportion of male middle-aged celibacy, and it also means that a considerable number of young men cannot hope to find wives in the village.

At the same time, it is true that even with more balanced numbers, there has been a general tendency in Finland as a whole for men to marry at a later age than women. In 1930, for example, only 10.1 per cent of Finnish men in the 20–4 age group were married, as against 23.4 per cent of women, and in the 25–9 age group the figures were 39.5 and 49 per cent respectively. The figures for 30–4-year-olds were more even at 59 per cent for men and 60 per cent for women. Again in 1960, although the average marriage age had dropped, the general pattern was still much the same. About 1 per cent of Finnish men under the age of 20 were married, as against 5 per cent of women. In the 20–4 age group the figures were 24.8 per cent for men and 45.5 per cent for women, and among 25–9-year-olds they were 62.3 and 74 per cent. For 30–4-year-olds the figures were 76 per cent and 80 per cent respectively.[26]

I do not have exactly comparable figures for Vieki, but it is clear that the pattern there has been roughly similar, despite a clear tendency for the average age of men at marriage to be higher than that for the population of the country as a whole, which of course includes the growing urban population. In the 1938 *henkikirja* of the village, only 2 per cent of men aged 20–4 were married, as were 15 per cent of those aged 25–9, and 46 per cent of those in the 30–4 age group. In the case of women, the figures were more like those of 1930 for the country as a whole. Although there were no married women under 20 years of age, 24 per cent of 20–4-year-olds were married, as were 48 per cent of 25–9-year-olds. Moreover, in the case of 30–4-year-olds,

[26] Data drawn from Central Statistical Office (1940, 1965).

the Vieki figure was, at 77 per cent, much closer to the 1960 national figure. Again, in 1959–60, before really large-scale emigration from the village had begun, only 12 per cent of men in the 20–4 age group were married, as against 35 per cent of women in the group. In the 25–9 cohort, 42 per cent of men and 78 per cent of women were married, while for 30–4-year-olds, the figures were 59 and 90 per cent respectively. Two 19-year-old women were married out of 13 in that age group.[27]

Considerations of age and numbers do not, however, account for all cases of contemporary and past celibacy in the village. Personal characteristics which might make a person less attractive as a spouse or, in the case of shyness, less likely to meet one, have no doubt played their part, and some people may be simply less interested in marriage than others. It also seems likely that as total numbers get smaller, the availability of people who would actually like to marry each other will decrease, though a desire to marry as such may blunt individual sensitivities in this regard. Certainly the general picture I obtained was that many contemporary bachelor farmers would like to find suitable wives if they could. One interesting source of evidence for this in rural Finland generally is the regular advertisements for wives which have appeared in the farmers' weekly newspaper *Maaseudun Tulevaisuus* (literally *The Future of the Countryside*).

In addition to such personal and demographic factors, it seems likely that a range of social structural considerations has also been significant in varying degrees in this broad context. Goody has commented that what he calls 'preferential primogeniture' appears to contribute to rural celibacy, especially among men.[28] This point is of some interest in the Finnish case, where family strategies and state influence have often been directed at avoiding the excessive subdivision of farm holdings, though it is important to note that in such cases single heirs are often but by no means always eldest sons. There is some evidence to suggest that in the old days, Finnish men without a farm of their own may have found it hard to marry, and it seems likely that, other things being equal, a man with a good farm will appear to some women as a better catch than one without even today. On the other hand, it is also true that as the numbers of landless families increased during the nineteenth century, there appears to have been a growing supply of poor wives for poor men. Moreover, it is clear that even possession of a farm may be little solace in this context for modern rural bachelors, who stand much less chance of marrying than their age mates who have given up their claims to land and moved into the city.

In considering this question, I have also been struck by the possibility that some village men may have refrained from marriage partly in order to

---

[27] Data drawn from local census data in *henkikirjat*.   [28] See Goody (1976a, p. 58).

maintain the unity of family estates, even when these estates were large enough to be divided comfortably between them if they had so wished. I am thinking here particularly of the nineteenth-century bachelor brothers in the Turunen family whom I discussed in Chapter 3. This family certainly had enough land, on a number of separate farms, to provide relatively large holdings for each of those concerned. At the same time, it could also be argued that these men did not structurally require wives. As their wealth increased they became masters of a large household, in which most field and housework was performed by labourers and domestic servants, and it is not inconceivable that some sexual gratification was also available from such sources, though I have no indication of this.[29] Some labour was also provided by tenant crofters. In such a setting, the organisation of female farm and household labour could probably be managed just as well by one *emäntä* as by three. Individual qualities and quirks no doubt also played some part, however, since one of the men concerned had a strong local reputation for mysogyny.

Comparable structural arguments can perhaps be extended to take a wider range of cases into account. For in addition to creating conditions in which some individuals may find it hard to marry, such a system of inheritance and farm succession also seems to offer a solution to some of the problems of both involuntary and voluntary celibacy. For it guarantees in Finland, as in many other cases, that other children have negotiable rights to the property concerned. As I discuss in Chapter 5, such rights may be bought out from siblings who do not wish to remain on the farm. At the same time, it is clear that the system also provides some opportunity for an unmarried son or daughter to try to negotiate a place in the domestic circle of his or her married siblings. And this is especially so when farms are often capable of housing and supporting one or two additional adults who can contribute extra work, and possibly some income from a pension or outside earnings, for the family. I have come across some cases of this kind in the course of my research, such as that of the unmarried brother and sister living on the Lehtola farm, as I described in the previous chapter.

In the extreme case, moreover, this carrying capacity can be extended further to include bachelor farm labourers who may look to the farm family for non-sexual domestic services and food supplies. An interesting example in this context is that of Kalle K., who spent most of his life as a bachelor member of the Saarelainen and subsequent Kiiskinen household. It appears that after a difficult period in his younger days, he was taken in by the then owner of the farm, where he remained and became a much-loved permanent fixture in the economic and domestic life of the family until his death in

---

[29] In the next generation, one wealthy bachelor was jokingly described as 'naimaton, mutta paljon nainut' ('unwedded but much bedded').

the late 1970s. He does not seem to have wished to marry, and he is said to have spoken negatively sometimes about womenfolk in terms which suggested he had earlier been crossed in love. This is a special case, but it seems to fit with the capacity of farm family organisation to support some unmarried adults beyond the strict confines of a marriage-centred, nuclear family unit.

Marriage as a legal institution

I have already touched briefly on some features of the history of Finnish family law in my discussion of the nature of the *suku*. Marriage, as a core element in Finnish family structure, is a customary and personal relationship and a focus of religious interest, but it is also, of course, legally defined.[30] This is particularly significant in the context of the ownership and inheritance of property, including family farms, though the working of the rules may sometimes be importantly affected by local convention and individual choice. A form of conjugal joint ownership is recorded in the earliest written Swedish law, from which modern Finnish law has gradually emerged, and since that time the legal definition of relations between spouses has typically included some form of shared interests in property. The basic rules have differed, sometimes seriously, from one period to another, but they are often hedged around with complex limitations, and this has sometimes resulted in more continuity of practice than one might at first expect. I give here a brief outline of some of the main historical developments in this context.

In the middle ages there were different regulations between town and country law concerning spouses' property relations, and such distinctions were maintained in Finland until 1878. It was an important principle in early country law that real property (*kiinteistö*) should remain within the *suku*, and inherited family land (*perimysmaa*) was held to be a spouse's personal property to which the other spouse had no right. So too was rural land which a spouse had owned before his or her marriage. Since family land did not have the same significance in the towns, where on the contrary business activity was felt to demand more freedom of property disposal, the country law distinctions did not apply there, and all property was jointly held. In addition, a town wife had an equal share in joint property with her husband, whereas in the country the man's share was two-thirds and the woman's one-third of a joint estate or *pesä* (literally 'nest').

In the medieval social system, and again persisting well into the nineteenth century, a woman normally had to be represented in official contexts by a man, and in the case of a married woman this was typically her

---

[30] My main sources on marriage law are Andersson et al. (1973), Rautiala (1975) and Riihimäki (1970).

husband. None the less, a wife had acknowledged power of action in the internal affairs of the home, and an external symbol of this, here as elsewhere, was her carrying of the keys. This power included also the right to make purchases on credit to support the family.

Swedish law was comprehensively reformulated in 1734, but many of its basic principles remained unchanged, including those concerning property and the requirement for women to be represented by males in official contexts. The right of a spouse to part of a joint estate was called *naimaosa* (literally 'marriage portion'). The size of this share remained as before, and inherited or previously owned country realty was still classed as individual property. Not only land, but also livestock and field tools were counted as 'fixed' property for legal purposes, and this was only changed in 1889. The 1734 law contained provisions, which had previously existed customarily, for spouses to agree about the details of their respective *naimaosa* portions before marriage, and such an agreement was called an *avioehto* (literally 'marriage condition'). A person could lose entitlement to *naimaosa* in whole or in part by killing his or her spouse, committing a marital offence, rejecting his or her spouse or mishandling the inventory or division of inheritance after a spouse's death. Both the joint property of the spouses and the personal property of the wife was under the control of the husband, and this could not be changed by *avioehto* agreement until the new marriage law of 1889. On the other hand, the husband had no right to transfer or pawn his wife's fixed property without her agreement. Moreover, if a husband had absconded or was a lunatic, the wife had the right to look after the 'nest' alone, and the husband's control and representative rights were said to be 'resting'.

The 1734 law also contained regulations about customary marriage payments including dowry (*myötäjäiset*, literally 'what one takes with one') and *morgongåva* (Finnish *huomenlahja*, literally 'morning gift'). This last was given by the husband to the wife on the morning after the wedding, when the couple had spent the night together. The significance of the payment seems to have varied historically. Rautiala (1975, p. 43) notes that, though it may originally have been a recognition of the bride's virginity, the 1734 law decrees that the size of the payment was to be determined before marriage, and the husband had to give it to his wife 'whether maiden or widow'. Its function was, it seems, to help preserve the woman's position if her husband pre-deceased her, and it was abolished as a statutory require-ment in 1878, when new legislation was deemed to render it unnecessary. Dowry was, as I have mentioned, essentially a form of pre-inheritance, and it is significant that the same term, *myötäjäiset*, was used for the property which a son took with him if he left the farm to seek his fortune in the wider world. Like the 'morning gift', dowry ceased to be legally significant in the late nineteenth century. The only details of dowry which I have encountered from Vieki itself are monetary payments to daughters recorded in a will from the 1860s which I discuss in the context of inheritance in the next chapter. The payments are referred to there by the term *lepinko*, which appears to be a variant of the more common customary form *lepinto*. The latter form is used by Saloheimo in his discussion of earlier traditional payments in the neighbouring Nurmes area.[31] These were customarily in kind, and might consist of a cow or even simply of a sheep, though the content varied according to the wealth of the young woman's family, and it could be particularly valuable if a daughter had no brothers. Saloheimo reports one case from the 1790s in which the dowry of such a woman consisted of two cows, a heifer, a calf, a sheep, a horse, a quarter seine net, an axe, two scythes, a sickle, seven pounds of brass, a half share in a plough and a substantial sum of money.

The 1860s saw the beginning of many legal changes in Finnish society, including several which concerned marriage and the status of women. In a decree of 1864, women gained control of their own estates from the age of 15 onwards. They were free to marry at 21, and they became full legal adults at the age of 25. In 1878 the difference between town and country *naimaosa* was abolished and rural women became entitled to half shares. *Huomenlahja* was abolished in the same decree. In a decree of 1879 concerning occupations, wives were given the right to engage in trade or other subsistence activities, if the husband agreed and took responsibility for debts incurred for business purposes.

Modern marriages are governed by two separate bodies of legislation. Those entered into before 1 January 1930 are subject to the law of 1889 concerning the property and debt relations of spouses. Later marriages are subject to the marriage law of 1929. At the level of underlying principles, the two laws differ sharply from each other, but their practical consequences are often rather similar. This is especially the case if a marriage is not broken by divorce, and if questions of the legal liability of individual spouses for debts do not arise. I know of no divorce in the village until fairly recently, and even now it is quite rare in farming families. The issue of debts is more complicated. In theory, the 1929 law provides significantly increased protection against the use of one spouse's property to pay for the debts of the other, and this was felt to be especially valuable for women who brought property into a marriage. Although there was no shortage of bankruptcies in the Vieki area as elsewhere in Finland during the harsh years of the late nineteenth century and the 1930s depression, I do not have data on the practical effects of the legal changes involved. My assumption, however, is

[31] Saloheimo (1953, p. 339).

that informal arrangements between spouses will often have been made in cases of this sort, and that the degree of mutual support between husband and wife will not have differed radically between older and post-1930 marriages.

Like earlier legislation, the 1889 law was based on a principle of joint ownership of property, normally under the control and management of the husband. Joint ownership here means that each spouse's property is dissolved into the joint *pesä*, and each owns an ideal rather than a real half of this. This is similar to the *naimaosa* of 1734, and this term was retained in the 1889 law. The 'ideal' is only 'realised' after the marriage is dissolved, by divorce or death, and the property is divided. All the property of the spouses, in which the other spouse has *naimaosa*, belongs jointly to them. Neither spouse can say that he or she owns half of each or any object which belongs to the joint estate, but only half of the total joint estate. Only when the property is divided can one know which object or which part belongs to whom. If the spouses buy an estate in land together, they do not each own one half of it, but they have a right of undivided joint ownership in it, and this means that one of them cannot singly sell or pawn half of the property. The matter is different with the 1929 marriage law. If the spouses in a post-January 1930 marriage buy a property together they own half each, and subject to agreement each can sell or mortgage his or her own half.

Notwithstanding the principle of joint ownership, there are provisions for potentially important exceptions to it in the 1889 law, and some of these are based on earlier legislation and traditions. The spouses may have made a special prior agreement limiting the rights of one or the other to *naimaosa* in specific property, or they may have received property by gift or will on the condition that there is no *naimaosa* in it. A main exception to the general rule is any rural land holding which a spouse obtained before marrying, or which he or she inherited (the so-called *perimysmaa*) either before or during the marriage. Such property is called 'individual' or 'private' property (*yksityinen*), and it is not divided on the dissolution of the marriage. There is no *naimaosa* in it and, in the case of inherited land, *naimaosa* cannot be created in it by an *avioehto* agreement. In contrast, all the following are joint property unless otherwise declared through an *avioehto* agreement or a will, or in the terms of a gift: personal chattels or so-called 'loose' (*irtain*) property, rural real or so-called 'fixed' property (*kiinteistö*) bought during the marriage, and town *kiinteistö* inherited or bought before or after the marriage. If individually held property changes its character during a marriage – for example an inherited farm is sold and the proceeds are used to buy property in town – the replacement property (*surrogaatti*) is also individually owned. All the income from an individual property is joint, however, on the principle that even individual property should be used for the joint benefit of the couple.

Despite the rules concerning inherited family land (*perimysmaa*) in the 1889 legislation, it appears from material at my disposal that many nineteenth- and early twentieth-century farms in the Vieki area were effectively in joint ownership and subject to *naimaosa* provisions, even when they were passed down within a family. I do not possess sufficient details of the history of all such farms to clarify exactly why this was the case. Nevertheless it seems likely that the situation arose because some farms had been transferred *inter vivos* by purchase or gift, rather than inheritance, either at the time of or during the course of the marriage. The relatively recent origins of some farms as crown tenancies may also have been relevant in some cases. In any event, it is certain that some of the main provisions of prevailing law concerning family land were mitigated in such cases.

A number of examples of the workings of this early legislation emerge in the history of the Saarelainen family, who moved to Vieki from the nearby Nurmes village of Höljäkkä in the mid 1890s (see Figure 10). Mikko Saarelainen married Kaisa Nevalainen in 1859, and he is described in family documents as the recipient, with his brothers, of shares in the family farm as a gift (*lahjakirjan mukaan*) from his father, Mauno. Mikko died in 1872, when his father was already dead. In addition to his widow, Kaisa, he left four under-age children – two daughters, Anna (b. 1860) and Elli (b. 1863), and two sons, Mikko (b. 1866) and Mauno (b. 1870). At the division of inheritance the interests of the children were represented by their mother's brother, Mikko Nevalainen. The farm was formally described as

Fig. 10 The descendants of Mikko Saarelainen (d. 1872)

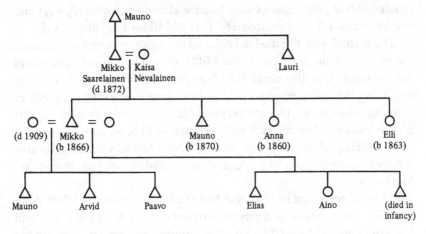

being in the joint control and ownership of the widow, Kaisa, and the deceased's brother Lauri. Another brother had sold his share of the holding to Lauri and Mikko in 1870. An inventory of the property was made, and it was then divided into two equal lots. One went to the brother Lauri, and the other to the widow and children. Their lot was then divided into three shares, of which the widow got one and the children two. A male neighbour was appointed to look after the continuing interests of the children in the property, but responsibility for this was transferred to the widow herself in 1885, when the neighbour moved away. By this time, the eldest daughter, Anna, was already twenty-five years old, and only the interests of the three younger children were involved in the arrangements.

Around 1895, the two sons Mikko and Mauno moved to Vieki. They bought a farm called Aputalo from Matti Mikkonen and his wife, Stiina Stahlman. Mikkonen is described as having bought this farm in 1888 from Olli Kärkkäinen, his wife Tiina and their son Olli. Mikko, who had married shortly before the move, bought up his as yet unmarried brother's share in 1904. Mikko's wife died in 1909, leaving him and their three sons to share the farm. Mikko retained one half, and the three sons, Mauno aged 13, Arvid, 11 and Paavo, 3, were each allocated one-sixth as their mother's heirs. Mikko remarried a couple of years later, and he and his second wife had three children, a boy who died in infancy, a daughter Aino (b. 1914) and a son Elias (b. 1915). Paavo, the youngest son from the previous marriage, died in 1917, and his share of the property was divided into two. One share went to his father, Mikko, who now had seven-twelfths of the farm ($\frac{1}{2}+\frac{1}{12}$), and the other went to the two remaining full brothers, who now had five-twenty-fourths each ($\frac{1}{6}+\frac{1}{24}$). In 1922, Mauno, the eldest of the three brothers, who left the area for a career in local government in northern Finland, sold half his share to his father and half to his full brother, Arvid. Their shares now became eleven-sixteenths ($\frac{7}{12}+\frac{5}{48}$) and five-sixteenths ($\frac{5}{24}+\frac{5}{48}$) respectively. Part of Mikko's holding was shared with his second wife. She died in 1927, and the property inventory prepared for inheritance purposes notes that Mikko owned half of the farm before the marriage. It is also noted that five-sixteenths belongs to Arvid. The remaining three-sixteenths is listed as belonging jointly to the couple, in addition to livestock and machinery and various domestic chattels. All this is once more divided into two parts between Mikko, on one side, and the two children, Aino and Elias, on the other. Mikko's holding became nineteen-thirty-seconds ($\frac{1}{2}+\frac{3}{32}$), and Aino and Elias had three-sixty-fourths each.

Mikko himself died in 1952, and he left all his property by will to Aino and Elias, who now owned eleven-thirty-seconds each ($\frac{19}{64}+\frac{3}{64}$). This will was not contested by Arvid, and a few months later Aino in fact sold her share in two equal parts to Elias and Arvid. These now ended up with thirty-three-sixty-fourths ($\frac{11}{32} + \frac{11}{64}$) and thirty-one-sixty-fourths ($\frac{5}{16} + \frac{11}{64}$) respectively. I should add that the history of this family and its property appears to have been very harmonious, and extremely good relations have persisted in more recent years between Elias and Arvid's children.

It will be noted that a number of the cases of farm transfer by inheritance in this summary account involve the recognition of a wife's rights to a half share in her husband's farm. In the case of the first Mikko's marriage to Kaisa Nevalainen, the fact that the land was received from the father Mauno as a gift seems to have been crucial. In the case of the son Mikko's first marriage, the purchase of the farm after the marriage was the determining factor. The chief exception to this pattern was the declaration, in accordance with the law, of Mikko's ownership of half the farm before his second marriage, though it is not clear to me why the one-twelfth share which he received on the .leath of his son, Paavo, was not also classed as 'inherited' and, as such, personal to him. In any event, it is interesting that the potential loss to the second wife's children, which this arrangement involved, was circumvented by the terms of Mikko's will, coupled with the sale of the daughter Aino's share to her full and half brothers. Comparable uses of wills to mitigate the effects of law in other circumstances are discussed in Chapter 5.

The large majority of modern marriages have been made since 1930, and as such they fall under the marriage law of 1929 and subsequent enactments. In contrast to the law of 1889, the basic principle of the 1929 legislation is that the two spouses each individually own their own property. One exception to this can arise if they have jointly obtained property together, and the general rule is also tempered by the fact that each has a 'marriage right' (*avio-oikeus*) in the other's property. This provides that on the dissolution of a marriage by death, all property which is liable to *avio-oikeus* is divided equally between the surviving spouse on the one side and the deceased's heirs, normally his or her children, on the other. There are also restrictions on the free use of certain types of property to which *avio-oikeus* applies, so that the agreement of the other spouse is necessary before a farm, for instance, could be transferred or mortgaged to a third party.

A spouse has *avio-oikeus* to all the other spouse's property, unless it falls within one of a number of excepted categories. These include property which a spouse has obtained by will or gift on condition that it remains free of such entailment, and also certain rights to lifetime benefit such as pension payments. There is also the possibility that the spouses can jointly arrange to exclude one or both of them from rights in the other's property by an *avioehto* agreement. Similarly, such an agreement can be made to reinstate such rights. Unlike the provisions of the 1889 law, the 1929 legislation permits the making of *avioehto* agreements during the course of the marriage.

As I have noted, the two sets of legislation in question start off from radically opposing principles, yet the differences between them are less sharp in practice than one might expect. The basic assumption of the 1889 law is the joint ownership of property by spouses, under the control of the husband. At the same time, the law provides certain safeguards for the individual spouses and their kin. These include the use of *avioehto* agreements between the parties in some contexts, and the protection of individual rights to land obtained at any time through inheritance (*perimys-maa*) and to land acquired in other ways before the marriage. Nevertheless, we have seen that such provisions may apply less commonly than one might at first assume, and their potential results may be circumvented by gifts, purchases and wills.

The 1929 law, in sharp contrast, asserts the fundamental principle of individual ownership and control of property by each spouse. It would be foolish to ignore the fact that we have here an expression of the develop-ment of ideological individualism in Finnish society, and with it of the equality of legal status between men and women. Yet the gulf between this and the principle of male-controlled joint property is narrowed by the recognition, in the *avio-oikeus* provisions, of strong rights of spouses in each other's property. All this is perhaps less surprising when one considers the peculiar nature of marriage as a 'union' of two distinct individuals which at a general level shares in the 'fictional' quality classically asserted by Maine and others for 'the corporation'. Such an institution is by definition 'neither one thing nor the other', and any legal definition of it which is based either on a unity of interests or on their plurality is liable to encounter many paradoxes.

The situation is encapsulated neatly in two texts on the laws in question. The first, which comes from a study of family law as part of Finnish culture, tells us that 'Although *naimaosa* and *avio-oikeus* are at first sight reminis-cent of each other, they differ from each other quite fundamentally.' The second is taken from a handbook on inheritance for the layman. It states that 'the end result of the former (sc. 1889) law was fundamentally similar to that of the marriage law (of 1929) despite differences in the property relations of the spouses in the marriage'.[32] This emerges clearly in a comparison of the basic inheritance rules under the two laws. As we have seen, under the old law a couple own property jointly until the marriage is dissolved. Then one half is ascribed to the deceased spouse and this is

[32] Rautiala (1975, p. 66) and Riihimäki (1970, p. 18).

inherited by his or her children. The other half is ascribed to and retained by the surviving spouse. In the case of the 1929 law, each spouse has his or her own property, but each also has *avio-oikeus* in the property of the other. If a spouse dies, half of his or her property goes to the surviving partner through *avio-oikeus*. The other half is inherited by the children. At the same time, however, half of the surviving spouse's property is ascribed by virtue of *avio-oikeus* to the deceased, and this too is inherited by the children. The end result is that the children inherit half of the property of each spouse on the death of one of them, and this amounts to one-half of the combined estate of the married couple. The other half remains with the surviving spouse.

As I discuss in the next chapter, it has until recently been possible for the children of a dead spouse to insist on the division of an inherited estate rather than to leave it undivided in the hands of the surviving spouse. This potentially threatened the position of a surviving spouse, and protection was sometimes provided by the use of wills or by provisions in a transfer between generations *inter vivos*. It should be said at once that such protection was by no means always necessary, since in many families the children themselves were keen to guarantee the security of a surviving parent. None the less, the rights of a surviving spouse to remain for his or her lifetime in the family home have now been protected by new legislation.

5

From generation to generation

Ageing and succession

It is a commonplace that humans are aware of ageing and mortality as their lot. This consciousness is closely linked to our facility for language, with its intrinsic qualities of abstraction and its formal recognition of time through tense and other mechanisms.[1] It is equally well known, however, that this universal area of experience and imagination can be given different cultural and social emphases. Formal groupings based on age and generation, for example, are quite rare, despite the widespread recognition of these principles of seniority in kinship systems.[2] Similarly, interest in the relations between generations, as one ages and another starts to replace it, varies considerably from one society to another. The existence of important property to be transmitted is clearly one of several elements which can significantly affect such variation.[3]

These matters were brought sharply to my notice during work in eastern Finland. My own focus on inter-generational relations and succession was essentially academic, developed in research in Africa and, more broadly, through my reading of a range of esoteric texts by writers such as Maine, Fortes and Goody.[4] It was therefore interesting to find a number of 'applied' Finnish studies, largely designed for farmers, of what villagers and academics alike there call *sukupolvenvaihdos* (literally 'change of generation'). One, published commercially, was readily available in the small country bookshop which served the rural area where I was working. Others

---

[1] See Leach (1972, p. 316).
[2] For discussion and analysis of formal age and generation groups in eastern Africa see Abrahams (1978a) and other papers in Baxter and Almagor (1978).
[3] J. Goody (1962 and 1983) discusses important aspects of the role of property in such contexts in both Africa and Europe.
[4] See Maine (1972), Fortes (1949 and 1961) and J. Goody (1962 and 1983 and 1976a). For a seminal discussion of succession in a rural European context see also Arensberg and Kimball (1961).

were produced by banks and agricultural research units, and there were also long newspaper articles on the subject.[5] While it was refreshing to find social theory so directly related to the real world of villagers' concerns, it was also slightly disconcerting that some of the more special contents of my professional toolkit were everyday common sense in the village.

The relation between the generations in the context of continuing connection between families and farm property has a long and complex history in this area. In addition to internal factors in the situation, it has been subject to a wide variety of important state and other outside influences. I have already described, for example, how education, industrialisation, and governmental agricultural policies have all contributed to a serious pruning of the farming sector and to out-migration from the countryside in recent decades, and this has obvious implications for succession. Closures have been common and, indeed, actively encouraged on small farms, and it has in any case been easier to attract young people to stay on and take over larger and more profitable holdings with good levels of machinery, and perhaps the chance to drive a decent family car. At the same time, government and others have been keen to avoid a complete collapse of agriculture, and have offered a variety of packages to support the continuity of more viable units. All this provides a crucially important context for my discussion of succession practices and strategies in this chapter. For my concentration on the process of succession should not lead us to forget that it is not always sought for or achieved.

Coupled with this, within the context of the family farm itself, it may be noted that much more is involved in succession than the actual transmission of wealth. A Finnish historian's comment on the medieval legal code is highly relevant here. 'The law', he writes, 'treated the inheritance of a farm as simply a question of property. But for the peasant farmer himself, keeping the farm under cultivation as the generations changed was often primarily a question of labour force.'[6] Beyond this, one might note that it also was a question of identity for both individual and family.

I have already discussed some of the basic factors operating on the inside of a family farm, and I will recall them only briefly here. Firstly, I noted the importance of the adaptive flexibility of families in coping with the problems farming poses. I also pointed out, however, that the connection between farm and family has intrinsic problems of its own, and that many of these are concerned with succession. Time and again one encounters the same basic difficulties. The continued viability of a farm does not always fit well with the rights, needs and availability of offspring. These may be too many or too few, or perhaps the only available heir is a daughter when sons are preferred.

[5] See Pokka et al. (1979) and Honkanen et al. (1975).
[6] Jutikkala (1958, p. 54).

In addition to attempting to cope with such issues, any satisfactory system of maintaining the connection between farm and family through the generations also has to deal successfully with the timing of the transfer. For a variety of reasons, post-mortem succession may not be the most favoured strategy. It either removes the matter out of the participants' control, or it tempts at least the junior generation to take it into their hands all too violently as they tire of waiting in uncertainty to come into their own. Moreover, any wishes of the older generation to remain in charge have to be balanced against increasing difficulties of coping with the physical and administrative work involved. As this implies, there may be mutual advantages in pre-mortem transfer, and in any case it would be mistaken to see the interests of the generations as purely self-centred. For parents and children are typically not entirely without sympathy for each other's problems.

In Finland, as in many other parts of Europe, a common solution to the problems of succession has been *inter vivos* agreements whereby an heir takes over the farm from one or both living parents. Like wills, which are much rarer, these agreements typically take the form of written documents, and they can pose some problems of interpretation. Goody has recently discussed comparable agreements from other areas, and he has remarked (1986, p. 146) that reading them, 'one is astonished to see the way that filial piety has to stand up and be counted, spelt out in exact quantities and decked out in lawyer's jargon'. In Finland also, such documents can seem to mark the full invasion of the family by both the form and spirit of legal rationality and capitalism. Maine's posited movement from status to contract has apparently been completed with the takeover of the family itself. The situation is, however, less straightforward than one might be tempted to assume.

I will deal with wills and with transactions *inter vivos* in more detail in the following sections, and I will refer to some of the main features of succession law in my discussion of them. With this in mind, a few preliminary comments on the role of law in contexts of farm transfer may be helpful here.

Much of the writing on succession pays attention to the distinction between 'partible' and 'impartible' systems, and the common presence in the latter case of rules prescribing primogeniture or ultimogeniture.[7] Such impartible systems are typically associated with a so-called 'stem family' pattern of household structure in which the parents and one married child, who will succeed them, live in the same household – though the incidence and detailed form of such co-residence can vary greatly from one period

[7] See Le Roy Ladurie (1976) and Segalen (1984).

and setting to another.[8] In recent years, though, scholars have become sharply aware of the need for caution in applying formal labels to succession rules and practices. As Berkner and Mendels have noted, there are many possibilities between strict impartibility and strict equal partibility. Moreover, since at least the time of Malinowski, anthropologists have stressed the significance of gaps between ideal and actual behaviour. Cole and Wolf have very neatly shown this for succession in their study of two Tyrolean communities. These operate with radically different legal 'ideologies' of succession, yet the prevailing practice is much the same in the two cases.[9] Elsewhere, Wolf has also observed that both single-heir and partible inheritance rules may reflect the political and economic interests of power-holding elites rather than the strategic preferences of the ordinary farmers on whom they are imposed.[10]

The laws of inheritance which have historically prevailed in Finland have for the most part stressed the equal rights of siblings, or at least of siblings of the same sex. As I have briefly mentioned, equality of rights between male and female heirs was legally established in the latter half of the last century. Beyond this, at different times, there have been various special regulations concerning such matters as crown tenancies and the conditions under which farms can be split. In attempting to make sense of the workings of the Finnish system, it is worth while to bear two main points in mind. Firstly, the legal rules do not always agree with local custom, and secondly, their character is often better thought of as permissive rather than as simply prescriptive. The law does not lay down as such, for instance, that estates in land should be divided. Rather it affirms that siblings have rights to an equal share in inheritance. This itself provides some room for manoeuvre in actual arrangements, if only because land is not the only form of property or measure of wealth. Farms can be passed on to one of a group of siblings by what might usefully be called 'preferential unigeniture', and the others may be compensated through cash payments or in other ways.[11] Flexibility in fact appears to be a general characteristic of succession practices in Nordic countries, notwithstanding legislative differences between them, and wills and documents of transfer *inter vivos* may usefully be viewed as instruments through which such flexibility is achieved.[12]

---

[8] See Berkner (1972, p. 145).

[9] See Berkner and Mendels (1978), Cole and Wolf (1974), especially Chapter 8). See also Shammas, Salmon and Dahlin (1987, p. 42) for a comparable comment on colonial American practices.

[10] Wolf (1966, pp. 73–7). See also Goldschmidt and Kunkel (1971, pp. 1065–70) and Wijeyewardene (1969).

[11] I follow J. Goody (1962, p. 323) in this use of the term 'unigeniture'. Although this sense of the word is not recognised by the *Oxford English Dictionary*, it valuably fills an awkward analytic gap in English inheritance vocabulary.

[12] See Löfgren (1974, pp. 34ff. and especially p. 38).

Wills

Wills are probably the most straightforward and the least important of succession documents in rural Finland, but their incidence and content provide useful clues to the nature of relations on a family farm. In considering the Finnish data, I have found some of Maine's comments on the early history of testamentary succession very helpful. His connection of wills to other forms of transaction, including sales and other transfers *inter vivos*, is especially pertinent, as too is his remark that early wills were not designed to alienate the members of a family from their property. His brief discussions of early German law and of the important role of the church in the promotion of the use of wills are also relevant to the origins of the Finnish system, and it is useful to recall his criticism of lawyers who think of wills as the norm and treat 'intestate' succession as a sort of oversight which the law is kind enough to provide for.[13]

In fact I came across few wills in my research, and I was told in the village that they are not a common instrument there for the transfer of farms. This fits well with the more general findings of an extensive 1975 survey of modern inter-generational succession to Finnish farms, where it was found that wills were used in only 3 per cent of the recorded cases.[14] It appears that rather more wills are made in rural areas than this implies, since other sources, including villagers, suggest that the most common form of modern will is a joint one drawn up between husband and wife to guarantee lifetime retention of their home by a surviving spouse. Figures available for registered wills during the 1960s indicate that about one in eight Finnish farmers make a will, and some further allowance needs to be made for those not registered.[15]

The low incidence of wills appears to have a long history in Finland, though there has no doubt been both temporal and local variation. One main reason has been the fact that early Swedish law, which was applied in Finland, and much of later Finnish law itself, were strongly protective of the rights of rural family members to inherit family land. The situation was a complicated one, but its main features involved a longstanding division between town and country law and also a distinction between movable (*irtaimisto*) and fixed property (*kiinteistö*), with the latter mainly divided between so-called 'inherited' and 'earned' land (*perimysmaa* and *ansiomaa*). Freedom of testation was restricted to movables and to earned fixed property, which appears to have reflected a principle that a person who gained land by inheritance, without the sweat of his own brow, had a duty to maintain it and eventually pass it on to his own rightful heirs. If the

---

[13] Maine (1972, pp. 102–4, 116). J. Goody (1976a, 1983 and 1984) has further explored some of the fundamental issues touched on here by Maine.
[14] Honkanen et al. (1975, p. 30).   [15] Aarnio (1975, p. 60).

owner of such land attempted to sell it or give it away or leave it by will to others, his heirs have had a right, which they have at least technically enjoyed in Finland into the middle years of the present century, to claim it back. This legal protection appears to reflect a victory, partly of state and partly of family interests, against the influence of the early church. In northern countries as elsewhere, the church strongly supported the use of wills, and was largely responsible for the institution's introduction and spread in the area. There are some medieval cases in both Sweden and Finland of peasant bequests to the church in order to have requiem masses held, but the situation does not appear to have developed in the church's favour to the same degree as in some countries further south.[16]

It seems clear that, historically, most of the land actually owned by Finnish farmers has been subject to these restrictions, but there is also the additional factor that many earlier farmers were tenants of one sort or another rather than land-owners. Thus, until the middle of the nineteenth century, most North Karelian farmers were crown tenants whose rights of testation were limited by this fact, though in most respects they were able to treat their land as their own and could pass it on to their heirs. Later, the number of private tenants became quite large in this and other areas of Finland, and it was only with the land reforms of the present century that full ownership of farms became the general rule. Although the old restrictions upon testamentary and other forms of alienation were finally removed by legislation in the 1930s and the early 1950s, they were replaced in part by the recognition of a minimal 'legal portion' (*lakiosa*) to which each direct heir is entitled. This is one half of the amount which a person would normally inherit in an intestate succession.

The historical situation which I have outlined is clearly not one in which wills might be expected to flourish as the expression of an individual's freedom to dispose of property to whomsoever he might wish. Nor is it surprising that when choices were made, they seem often to have been formulated within the framework of the family rather than in conflict with it. Voionmaa comments interestingly in this context on the patterns of succession to farms in some seventeenth-century eastern Finnish swidden areas. He mentions a number of wills in which one or more sons, to the exclusion of others, are nominated as successors to the farm. This might at first sight look like the exercise of individual freedom against family ties, but the situation is more complex. Unlike their brothers, the inheriting sons stay on the farm and look after their ageing parents till their death, and

---

[16] See Rautiala (1975, pp. 40–5), Blomstedt (1973), af Hällström (1934) and Jutikkala (1958, pp. 51ff. and 320–38). Mattila (1979) provides a useful discussion in French of modern Finnish inheritance legislation, and compares the situation there with that in Poland, Germany, Norway and Switzerland.

Voionmaa plausibly connects this with the fact that, in the swidden areas, only sons who stayed at home and worked a farm could customarily expect to inherit it. He appears to consider such provisions typical of wills of the period, and he also points out explicitly that their purpose was to gain formal legal support for local custom, rather than to overturn it.[17] For such custom was significantly different from the national law of intestate succession which gave an equal share to all male siblings irrespective of their whereabouts. Such use of 'formal-sector' institutional machinery for their own particular, but not necessarily individualistic, purposes is a recurring theme in Finnish villagers' relations with the state.

I have already referred briefly in an earlier chapter to some of the few wills which I encountered in the field. These appear to serve a range of functions. The earliest, from 1866, is the joint will of Olof Turunen and his wife Elin Nevalainen, which was made about two years before they died. I present it in full here because it is both short and illustrative of some interesting points.

We the undersigned, freely and deliberately, by this open letter, bequeath all our fixed and movable property to our sons Petter, Isak, and Johan Turunen, for their use and enjoyment after our death. To the fixed property belong the following redeemed heritable farms: Törmälä (No. 4) valued at 1,000 marks, Ollila (No. 21) valued at 2,000 marks, and half of farm No. 43 valued at 800 marks, all being in the village of Vieki in the parish of Pielisjärvi. To our daughters, Anna, Kaisa, and Sikke we have decided to pay an inheritance portion of 560 marks each along with the customary so-called *lepinko* [dowry]. As against this, Anna, who is married to Reittu Nevalainen, has already received 428 marks, and Kaisa, who is married to Henrik Hilonen, has received 400 marks, and both have already received their *lepinko*. All this is confirmed by the writing of our name and mark below in Pielisjärvi on 17 July 1866.

The will was witnessed by three men, one of whom actually wrote it.[18] The other two worked for the Turunens.

A number of points seem to be relevant here. Firstly, as I noted earlier, the Turunens were at this time 'accumulators' and were becoming one of the village's most wealthy families. As such, the amount of property, both fixed and movable, to be disposed of was unusually large. At least some of the holdings seem likely to have been classed as 'earned' land (*ansiomaa*) since they had been bought from other farmers, and it is possible that other land the freehold of which had been acquired from the state was also in a special class. In any case, the will was not likely to be contested on the

[17] Voionmaa (1915, pp. 373–4).
[18] The testators signed the will with their initials only. It is also interesting that Swedish forms of their own and their children's Christian names are used in the will though they would not have been used in everyday life. Swedish forms still tended to be used in official documents of the period, including census lists.

grounds that it disposed of 'inherited land' when the named legatees were the couple's children, and the will's provisions were in keeping both with local custom of the period and with the likely wishes of the sons. It may be recalled here that only the youngest of the three sons was married and the other two were on their way to becoming confirmed bachelors. This had positive implications for the peaceful maintenance of the farms in an undivided state under joint control, since the two bachelor brothers would not be structurally drawn into segmentary domestic politics arising out of separate family interests.

With regard to custom, quite the most important point concerns the daughters. Although the will specified monetary payments to them in addition to the customary *lepinko*, the provisions for them were substantially below those specified in Finnish law. This shortfall was in accord with eastern Finnish custom (itself said to derive from early Russian law), whereby only a small dowry in the form of movables was given to daughters while the main estate, and especially land, was reserved for sons.[19] The formal legal provision for daughters in rural Finland had been fixed for many centuries at one-half of that for sons, irrespective of the nature of the property. Moreover, new developments were looming which were even more removed from local practice. Women in Sweden had already been granted equal rights to men as heirs in 1845, and the issue was apparently already in the air in Finland by the middle 1860s following the granting of full majority status in 1864 to unmarried women from the age of twenty-five. A formal proposal of equal inheritance rights was put to the Finnish Diet in 1872 with the support of the three upper estates, and it became law in 1878. The change, predictably enough, was strongly opposed by representatives of the eastern Finnish farming sector. In this context the will in question seems broadly comparable to the earlier ones noted by Voionmaa, since it appears to involve the use of a legal instrument as a reinforcement of local custom against national law, rather than an emphasis upon the freedom of individuals to distribute their property however they might wish.[20]

A later case from 1904 is more problematic in this context. It is the will of

[19] See Blomstedt (1973, p. 33) and also Jutikkala (1958, pp. 320–38).

[20] Jutikkala (1958, p. 338); Voionmaa (1915, pp. 373–4). It is interesting that recent studies of modern English and American wills suggests that they too are only rarely used to free individuals from their ties to spouse and family. See Horsman (1978), and also Smith, Kish and Crawford (1987). I am grateful to Dr P. Wells of Goldsmiths' College for this last reference. For a study of comparable American practice with regard to wills, see Shammas, Salmon and Dahlin (1987, pp. 42ff.). I am much indebted to Professor John Langbein for drawing my attention to this work on the history of American inheritance. His own studies of modern American practice, e.g. Langbein (1984 and 1988), bring out very clearly the effects on such practices of modern legal, economic, educational and demographic developments.

Petter Turunen, who was one of the two bachelor sons of Olof. The will was made in old age and it left the large majority of his substantial wealth in both fixed and movable property only to men. His bachelor brother Isak was to hold and enjoy the property for his lifetime, and after his death the estate was to be divided into four equal parts. These were to be inherited by sons and grandsons of the third brother, who was himself by-passed in the will. It is not clear why this was done, and it may in fact have happened with that brother's knowledge and approval. More significant is that there were no female beneficiaries of the will, despite the fact that Petter had a living sister and also a number of sister's daughters, brother's daughters and great-nieces. When the will was submitted for probate in 1907, one of the witnesses to the document said that he had asked the deceased why he had left nothing to his brother's daughters or their offspring (one great-niece) and he had answered that his brother had property of his own which he could give to them.

It appears from comments I have heard that Petter was at least as much an old misogynist as a traditionalist. None the less, it is interesting that his brother Isak, who pre-deceased him in 1906, also left a will in which the bulk of his estate went to his brother Johan's children with the proviso that the daughters' portions should be half the size of those given to the sons. The two wills were actually dealt with at the same time along with a division of Johan's landed property which he had arranged to sell in equal portions to his children. The end result was that the land of the three brothers was divided among Johan's children and his two sons' sons as I have described in Chapter 3. Out of a total of 180 shares, each of his unmarried sons received thirty-seven, his two married sons each received twenty-two, the two sets of sons of these last, but not their daughters, received fifteen each, and each of his two daughters received sixteen. Had the three brothers died intestate, part of their estate would have gone to their surviving sister and their dead sister's children, and the remainder would have been divided equally among Johan's sons and daughters.

Another case, from the turn of the century, is still more closely reminiscent of those cited by Voionmaa. Here a will was used to guarantee succession to an in-marrying son-in-law and his wife. The owner of the farm, Olli Mustonen, had no sons and several daughters. Most of the daughters were married out, but one remained at home after her marriage to Markus Ryynänen, a man from a well-established family in another village. The will specified that she and her husband would inherit the farm, and that her sisters would each receive a payment of 1,000 marks to be paid without interest over a period of six years. It is clear that the relative value of this provision was substantially eroded by inflation by the time the farm owner and his wife died in 1904, and the matter was complicated by the fact that the son-in-law Ryynänen had himself already died in 1903. The will was contested by some of the other sisters and their husbands, but the court ruled in favour of Ryynänen's widow and children 'in accordance with modern law', and his descendants have held the farm since then. My understanding of the case is that the original intention of this will was to protect the rights of Ryynänen and his wife as the couple living on and running the farm, and there was most probably an agreement between him and the ageing Olli Mustonen to this effect. The interjection of 'modern law' was apparently an accidental element in the situation which arose through the unforeseen contingency of Ryynänen's pre-decease of his father-in-law.

In some cases, the use of wills seems to have been connected with increasing complexities of property ownership, and particularly the existence of substantial amounts of personal property in addition to land. Sometimes, too, the disposal of pieces of land and other property outside the immediate family is involved, for example in some legacies to the local church (built in 1915) and other charities, and occasionally to personal friends. Substantial sums were in fact left to charity by the two bachelor Turunen brothers in addition to their bequests to their brother's sons and grandsons. One of these sons, who died childless after a late marriage, left his property to his wife for her lifetime with the provision that she should not transfer its ownership to another party. After her death everything was to go to the local parish to form a charitable trust in his memory.

Such bequests fit much more clearly with our common preconception of a will as a clear recognition of the rights of individuals to hold property for themselves and distribute it as they wish. Certainly it would be hard to deny the presence and significance of such 'modern' developments in Finland over at least the last two centuries. But this is only a small part of the total picture. Except in carefully defined special circumstances, modern Finnish law still prevents the total disinheritance of children, who are entitled to at least half of what they would have got from an intestate inheritance. Again, as I noted earlier, many and possibly most relatively modern wills have been designed mainly to shield a bereaved spouse from the division and perhaps sale of house and property by children or other heirs. Before 1966, any such heirs could insist if they wished on the immediate division of the estate so as to obtain their share of the inheritance, but legislation in that year gave protection to a bereaved spouse against such action by all except the deceased's children. As a result, the number of such wills seems to have decreased, though some protection against children has sometimes been sought through them. More recently (1983), additional protection for the rights of a surviving spouse has been incorporated into the inheritance law, and it is possible that the incidence of such wills will decrease still further. Nevertheless, it is apparent that we are dealing once more in such cases with the use of wills within a family setting in order to offset the law's unwelcome implications for family structure and development.[21]

In addition to this influence on content, it is reasonable to assume more generally that the law has also been partly responsible for the rather limited use of wills through the restrictions which it has historically placed on them. On the other hand, it can also fairly readily be seen that the handing on of family farms might not in itself fit very comfortably with the use of wills. Even when there is a wish to avoid fragmentation or to protect the rights of a particular successor, there is strong evidence of preference for other mechanisms, and particularly for pre-mortem arrangements, to handle the transmission of a farm between generations. The combination of issues of labour, farm organisation, and differing needs and interests of the members of a family, which are all involved in such a transfer, tends to make the process longer and more complex than that usually encompassed in the framework of a will. The earlier-quoted comment on the medieval Swedish national code and the significance of the connection between farm property and farm labour 'for the peasant farmer himself' is still relevant today and, as its author also notes, the same connection can be seen quite clearly in the various farm pension agreements to which I now turn.[22]

Heating, lighting and a decent funeral

As I have noted, the Finnish material supports the comments of writers such as Maine and Goody on the need to treat a wide range of institutional arrangements as a set when looking at succession. In Finland, as at least elsewhere in northern Europe, pension agreements and associated transfers of farms *inter vivos* constitute a major member of this set. As such, it is no accident that Jutikkala's main chapter on succession in his history of the Finnish peasantry is entitled 'Pension and Inheritance'.[23]

Two main types of transactions are important in the transfer of a farm from living parents to one or more of their children. Firstly, and most directly, there are the retirement agreements between holders and successors which may include some monetary payment for the property along with various arrangements for housing and maintaining the retiring owners. Such pension payments and provisions for the senior generation were traditionally known as *syytinki*.[24] Secondly, there are often related arrangements – which we have already encountered in the discussion of wills – which deal with the rights of a successor's siblings. This usually

---

[21] See Santala (1983).   [22] Jutikkala (1958, p. 54).   [23] Jutikkala (1958, pp. 320–8).
[24] The standard term for pension is *eläke*. *Syytinki* is an old word apparently derived from Swedish *sytning*, which is said to come from a dialect verb *syta* meaning 'to nurse' or 'care for' (see Gaunt 1983, p. 252). The term is mainly used today to refer to old pension agreements, but it is also sometimes used to stress the traditional background of comparable modern arrangements.

involves the buying out of their shares in the property, but it may include the reservation of some limited rights for them in the farm and its amenities. Both inter- and intragenerational arrangements may be included in a single document. The need for both arises from the fact that a farmer's children all have equal rights of inheritance, but it is commonly thought desirable to keep the farm intact by passing it on to one successor while at the same time trying to do justice to the others.

It is clear from the literature that there is a very long history of such arrangements in Finland.[25] Not surprisingly, they involve quite fundamental aspects of family relations and farm management. It is easy to see that both joint and potentially differing individual interests are likely to be present in the situation, and that the resolution of any problems which arise will depend to a considerable extent upon the range of opportunities available to those concerned. The ability of the young to become their own masters on a farm is likely to depend on the careers and attitudes of their siblings and on the willingness of their parents to retire. This last in turn depends partly on the parents' perceptions of their ability to keep up the farm as they grow older, and partly on their ability to guarantee a reasonable living in retirement for themselves. At the same time, the young successor typically has to take on the burden of parental support and also compensate those siblings who are willing to forgo their own share of the holding. It is in these contexts that one can encounter the sorts of documents that roused Goody's earlier-mentioned curiosity, with their apparent implications of legalism and commercialism within the family.

Most of the transfer documents which I myself saw in the village are quite recent, and the earliest dates from the beginning of the century. One example involves a document of transfer of a farm from the farmer, O.K., and his wife to their son T. The document is from the early 1970s and it is formally laid out, signed and witnessed. It is entitled 'Document of Sale', (*kauppakirja*) and it begins as follows:

> By this document of sale I, the undersigned farmer O.K. with the agreement of my wife . . . sell and transfer my farm holdings . . . along with all buildings on them and other presently or future attached benefits and rights plus all movables, livestock, machinery and fittings to our son T. for a price formed as follows.

The document then specifies the price (70,000 marks) and its component parts, and it notes that just under a third of this is covered by the successor's taking on the repayment of loan debts. A further reduction of 3,000 marks for a brother, and 2,000 and 1,500 marks respectively for two sisters, is noted. This sum is to be paid to the siblings without interest as soon as a

---

[25] For an English-language discussion of the history of such agreements in Finland and other northern countries see Gaunt (1983). See also Jutikkala (1958, pp. 320–8).

loan to cover this has been received or within a year, whichever is the shorter. The payment to the parents is to be further reduced by a sum of 9,000 marks. This is because the buyer is to provide his parents with dwelling space, lighting and heating on the farm during their lifetime, and he is to provide similar facilities for his two under-age sisters until they reach their majority. The remaining money (just over 30,000 marks) is to be paid to the parents within eighteen months and without interest. Some further details, about tax liability, electricity and the absence of other agreements, are then specified and the document is signed by the parties and witnessed by a public notary who drew up the agreement.

In another case, from the 1960s and 1970s, a retiring farmer and his wife first sold their land to their daughter and her husband, and they later made a comparable arrangement concerning other property, including livestock and machinery, on the farm. In the document marking this second transaction the buyers are contracted to give the sellers subsistence for their lifetime, a dwelling with heating and lighting included, and cleaning when the sellers cannot do this for themselves. On their death they are to give them a decent funeral in accordance with local custom. The sellers are bound to use their state pensions for clothing and for medical and other personal expenses, and the buyers are responsible for sharing in such expense only when the state pensions are insufficient or if medical insurance does not cover them. No payments were set out for the siblings of the succeeding daughter.

My deeper understanding of such documents began when I was shown one dealing with a transfer in the 1960s. In this case, land was being sold by adult children to their father, rather than vice versa, but the principles involved were of more general relevance. The mother and the father had been joint owners of the farm, and when she died each child inherited a portion of one-half of the farm through her. The other half stayed in the father's hands, and the document set out the terms of the sale whereby he reacquired part of the children's share. I spent some time translating the document which one of the children (a son) had been kind enough to show me, and I later began to discuss it with him. I was then somewhat surprised to learn that 'No money actually changed hands.'

It appears that this document of sale was a fiction the main purpose of which was to avoid liability to gift tax for the father. Spurred on to pursue the matter further with regard to other transfers, I discovered that there were quite often fictional elements in them also. In discussing some of the land transfers from parents to children and some of the related documents of sibling compensation, I was told how parents and, perhaps less often, siblings had not insisted on receiving their legally contracted payments, and it appears that they had never envisaged otherwise.[26] I was told that succeeding couples would often have been unable to survive if they had had to make the payments. I was also told that the willingness of siblings to forgo their due commonly depended on whether they had already established themselves elsewhere, and especially in an urban setting. It appears that urban siblings often appreciate the willingness of the successor to take on the maintenance of the farm and the main responsibility for looking after the retired generation. More generally it began to emerge that a main function of such documents was to provide evidence which would entitle the successors to cheap loans originally designed to ease the burden of such payments. Once obtained, the loan could then be used for other purposes such as developing the farm's buildings and equipment. I am not at all sure how widespread this sort of practice was, but at least one man who drew up such documents was aware of it, and he is said to have given some people helpful advice about the optimum values and prices to be specified in deeds of transfer.

The need to treat farm transfer documents with caution is, it seems, by no means new, and the fictive element in them has taken diverse forms. In many cases, varying in detail from one area and period to another, the value placed on a farm in the records of transactions between close kin has been different from the going open-market price for comparable farms. Jutikkala makes this clear, and he also notes another way in which the letter of such documents has historically differed from their spirit. This is particularly relevant to Goody's query. For Jutikkala describes some early cases, albeit from north Sweden, in which the onerous and detailed terms of pension agreements between parents and children were not in fact expected to be honoured by a succeeding child, but were designed mainly as an encumbrance on the farm to be observed if the successor sold it to a stranger.[27] There would be less reason to expect good will and commitment to the parents from such a new owner, and in any case the aim was as much to discourage such a purchase as to protect against its consequences.

---

[26] Parental help partly turns on residence arrangements. In both the cases discussed, as in most others I have come across, accommodation was to be on the farm, though in the second a separate adjoining cottage was involved rather than rooms in the same house. Continued residence on the farm was normal for most old agreements also, sometimes with an assumption of taking food together. If the retiring parents plan to move to town, they may need money for the move, and this may naturally affect the form of the transactions.

[27] Jutikkala (1958, p. 332). Generally, but not always, the stated price was lower than the market price. Jutikkala also describes cases where an increase of pension is stipulated if the farm is sold to strangers. Macfarlane (1978, p. 138) interestingly discusses some comparable problems in the interpretation of English transfer documents, though he suggests that contingency clauses (about separate residence) may have been a good index of actual practice in this case. John Barnes (personal communication) tells me that there may also have been fictional elements involved in some Norwegian transfers.

This last point draws attention to another issue, which I have already briefly noted. So far I have mainly discussed joint and more or less converging individual interests in succession. This is reasonable enough since most families have joint interests in the maintenance of a viable farm across the generations, and the pattern of succession involved in its transmission by agreement *inter vivos* often has advantages for all the parties. This is especially the case nowadays, when there is state and other formal-sector financial support for such moves. More generally than this, however, such transfer allows the parental generation to avoid the spectre of an increasingly burdensome physical and mental responsibility for keeping the farm going as they age, and it is important to remember here that we are dealing with farms which are normally worked only by the family members. The chosen successor in turn has a chance to feel secure in the knowledge that the efforts he puts in are firmly grounded in farm-ownership, and it is also not uncommon, now and in some periods in the past, for siblings to be quite relieved that one of their number is willing to take on the task. In many cases, the retiring couple lend a hand upon the farm as long as they are fit to do so, and urban siblings relish the opportunity to take summer holidays there and help out in haymaking.

Yet it would, of course, be quite unrealistic to convey a picture of rural familial harmony without, at times, bitter conflict. Siblings can feel badly done by and some successors, especially in the harder periods of the nineteenth century, have found the upkeep of their parents an unpleasant burden, especially if they have retired early.[28] On the other hand, some parents may retire later than suits their successors, and some may not wish to retire at all. In addition, it seems clear that the sons and daughters who succeed to a farm cannot simply be viewed as individuals in relation to their siblings and their parents. Successors to a farm are often, though by no means always, married. This is more than a statistical phenomenon, since a married couple is, as I have said, the basic structural unit of farm labour.

---

[28] Jutikkala (1958, p. 127) discusses this point in some detail. There was a lively and largely critical discussion of the issue in the press and in parliamentary committee. Jutikkala notes that such discussion was somewhat one-sided. A similar point is well made by Gaunt (1983, p. 260) when he comments that there was an element of cultural conflict in the negative reports which came largely from priests and other members of non-peasant estates who came in contact with the peasantry. One such commentator even goes as far as to blame the high toll of the 1860s famines upon the retirement system (quoted in Gaunt, pp. 274–5). The dire results of these famines seem more straightforwardly explicable in terms of the national and international politico-economic circumstances which led to their unchecked development, as Soininen (1974, pp. 402–10, 458–9) makes clear. More generally, and despite his caveats, Gaunt gives slightly more weight to the elements of inter-generational conflict and economic dysfunction than I myself am tempted to do on the basis of my own data. Nevertheless, it is true that the modern situation is marked by positive attitudes and practical support from the formal sector, not least in the form of state pensions and other welfare facilities. For some comparable discussion of German and American examples see Spiegel (1939) and Wehrwein (1932).

Despite many cases to the contrary, the unhappy position of in-marrying daughters-in-law is a commonplace of rural Finnish ideas about farming families, and it is clear that here, as elsewhere, they face and create structural problems. This is perhaps especially so in a monogamous system where – since there are no co-wives – such a newcomer is likely to be the main source of competition for power which the mother-in-law has had to face since her own younger days. Whereas the intrinsic tensions between parent and child are to some degree alleviated by the other pole of their ambivalent relationship, there is no such mitigating element of love intrinsic to the interaction between daughter-in-law and husband's parents.[29] All too easily she can appear as an outsider who is liable to alienate a son from his parents through her legitimate close connection with him. It is possibly of interest in this regard that Finnish terminology does not try to create a quasi-kinship tie between such affines since, unlike English 'in-law' terms, the Finnish ones have no connection with kinship nomenclature. Of course, the personalities of the parties and their willingness to adapt to each other can help overcome the difficulties of the situation, and the birth of children helps to create a new sort of relationship with the parental generation, though there is room for conflict and diverging interests here also. I might add that the position of in-marrying sons-in-law in some degree appears to pose a comparable set of problems for a wife's father. Though considerably rarer than their female counterparts, such men are a regular feature of the Finnish farming-family scene, and it is perhaps significant that two cases which I describe in more detail in the next section involved succession problems. In one the father-in-law refused formally to retire or even make a will in his daughter's and her husband's favour, despite the fact that the husband was living and working hard on the farm. In the second, the father first suggested that the couple could *de facto* take responsibility for the farm and that he would leave it to them in a will. The son-in-law refused this offer, however, and insisted on a sale. The matter was in this case dealt with amicably. It seems possible that the transfer of a farm to a son-in-law in these and other cases makes retirement harder for a farmer, when he passes on responsibility to a younger 'stranger' whose different surname may also throw the implications of succession into sharper relief.

In addition to the factors which I noted earlier, the 'insidious stranger in the camp' role of in-marrying affines may go some way to explain the

---

[29] See the poem 'Hiihtävä Surma' (literally 'skiing death', but glossed as 'Death on the Prowl') in Kuusi, Bosley and Branch (1977, pp. 351 and 352) for a traditional folk reference to what the editors (p. 560) refer to as the 'harsh and lonely fate of daughters in law'. See also Tanttu's well-known folk-saw-based cartoon (1974, p. 14), in which a harsh old woman offers some scraps with the words 'Syöpik minijä vai annetoak kissal!' ('Will daughter-in-law eat it or shall I give it to the cat?').

legalistic spelling out of pension rights for the retiring generation. There is always, of course, the possibility that a succeeding son or daughter might turn against them in any case if the burden of support begins to chafe, and the documents no doubt also take this into account. But this likelihood is heightened when a spouse's influence also needs to be considered, and when there is a further possibility that the succeeding child might pre-decease both spouse and parents and leave the latter to the spouse's tender mercies.

It is clear that though some of the difficulties I have outlined relate very closely to the issue of pre-mortem transfer, many of them also derive from more general and ultimately irresolvable structural contradictions. As I have noted elsewhere, the fit over time between a family and a farm is not an easy one, and a farming couple are always likely to be faced with mutually inconsistent wishes and demands. Their wish to see their children receive equal shares of their estate runs contrary to their wish to see the farm which they have built and worked continue viably into the future.[30] Their same attachment to this farm and their ambivalent attitudes to growing old may also jeopardise the chances of the younger generation to enjoy an independent adulthood themselves. Cases are known to me where parents have caused serious frustrations and anxieties in their adult children through their reluctance or refusal to hand on responsibility and ownership to them, and occasionally this even appears to have led to homicide. In such circumstances, and given the advantages that I have described above, it is not surprising that pre-mortem succession to a farm seems to be, at least in Finnish eyes, the overall best though by no means perfect strategy for its inter-generational transmission. This is well illustrated by a recent extensive survey of Finnish farms to which the present holder had succeeded. As Table 3 shows, it was found that at least one parent was alive at the time of transfer in 95 per cent of cases investigated, and both parents were alive in 60 per cent of the cases.

In-marrying sons-in-law
My account of the origins and backgrounds of some farming families includes reference to cases where a farm passed to a daughter and her husband, and I have also briefly discussed transfers of this sort in the previous section. I want now to explore their nature and significance a little further. For apart from the intrinsic interest which they hold, such arrangements also throw useful light on some more general basic features of succession.

In a paper published in 1964, Dorrian Apple Sweetser discusses the patterns of residence and inheritance on Finnish farms. She notes that in

---

[30] See Chapter 4 above. See also Barnes (1957, p. 54 and passim) and J. Goody (1976b, p. 5 quoting Cole and Wolf, 1974, p. 176).

Table 3 *Patterns of succession on Finnish farms*

Situation at time of succession	
Both parents alive	60%
Both parents dead	5%
Former farmer's widow alive	25%
Former farmer alive as widower	10%

Note:
N = 485
Source: Honkanen et al., 1975

several countries married couples live more often with one or both of the wife's parents than with those of the husband. She also notes that while this is true of Finland, when the total population is considered, the situation among *farmers* runs against the trend. She analyses Finnish data on this subject drawn from survey material collected in 1959–60 by the Social Research Bureau of the Ministry of Social Affairs, and she pays particular attention to variation between different regions of the country. In the north and east, there is a heavy preponderance of husband's over wife's parents in the sample families where such parents are co-resident with their married children, whereas in parts of the south and south-west, cases of co-resident wife's parents are in a majority. In more central and north-central areas, households with one or more husband's parents are more common, constituting about two-thirds of the relevant cases. These residential data, she suggests, may provide evidence that the previously strong customary pattern of what she calls 'patrilineal' succession to Finnish farms is changing or breaking down in some parts of the country.

Sweetser's paper raises a number of interesting questions both about her data and about her framework of interpretation. For example, in the course of her discussion she examines the relationship between the residence patterns in question and some other features of the different regions, and she finds a positive correlation between them. Areas with a relatively high proportion of wife's parent households are also those with more urban settlement and with a relatively large proportion of women in the rural population. This suggests among other things that more men go to town in these areas, and more women are left to inherit farms. At the same time, however, Sweetser notes that the data at her disposal do not permit a detailed explanation of the regional differences in question, and my own examination of some of the relevant statistical material shows the situation to have been extremely complex. Population figures for the southern and south-western urban zones, for instance, reveal the presence of even higher concentrations of women there than in the nearby rural areas. This suggests that, although migration seems to be a factor as Sweetser assumes, a full analysis needs to include population movement to the south and south-west from more distant parts of Finland, and a tendency for such movement to involve more women than men. Similarly emigration to Sweden and elsewhere from southern and other areas of Finland is a further element in the situation. In addition, in a comment upon Sweetser's paper, Goody has suggested (1976a, pp. 93–4) that the contrast between southern and eastern Finnish figures might be partly a result of regional differences in birth rates and mortality.[31] It is difficult to test this from available statistics, but some evidence suggests that influence of this sort may have been at work. Live birth rates in the 1920s and 1930s, when many of the heirs in Sweetser's sample will have been born, were somewhat lower in the south and south-west than in eastern Finland. In 1930, for example, the relevant figures for rural Uusimaa in the south and Kuopio (including modern North Karelia) in the east can be estimated at around 18 and 26 per thousand of the population respectively. This difference was probably narrowed by slightly higher rates of infant mortality in the east, and the difference between Kuopio and other south-western areas such as Turku and Pori was in any case somewhat smaller. On the other hand, it is also possible that male mortality resulting from the war with Russia caused more inheritance problems in the south and south-west areas with their lower birth rates. Whether this is so or not, a more general point which Goody makes also seems likely to be relevant. In proportions which vary with birth and mortality rates, there are always likely to be some families which have only daughters as potential heirs. Son-in-law succession makes sense as one possible solution to this problem, in addition to the possibility of its deployment in situations where a son is available but is unwilling or unsuitable to take on the inheritance of a farm.

In her interpretation of the data, Sweetser tells us that she uses the term 'patrilineal' simply to denote connections between a married couple and the husband's parents. This is a slightly unfortunate usage of the term, which is more commonly reserved for lines of connection through males over a number of generations, and especially for rules of agnatic descent and groups based on them.[32] Coupled with this, and more important, it is not wholly clear what she means by 'custom' and by its change or breakdown, though she does include both statistical and normative elements in her analysis, and she appears to assume that there were fairly strict rules of

---

[31] J. Goody (1976a, pp. 93–4). See also Tarvert (1952) for comparable comments on American data.

[32] For problems in the use of the terms 'patrilineal' see J. Goody (1983, Appendix 1) and also Abrahams (1978b).

father–son succession in the past. This leads back to the question whether flexibility of residence and inheritance patterns is likely to be a normal rather than a deviant feature of a family-farm system. Goody's arguments, which I have noted, about varying birth rates and sex ratios in families suggest that this will often be the case; and we have already begun to see some evidence of flexible adaptability in Finnish families, and not least in North Karelia, despite the rather rigid patterns which Sweetser's data tempt her to posit for that area.

Uxorilocal residence and subsequent takeover of a farm by a daughter of the house and her husband have been reported as a secondary pattern of succession in a range of European settings from Ireland to Greece, and they have a long history in Finnish society.[33] Records of such arrangements date back to at least the seventeenth century, and many modern cases can also be found. Certainly there are many examples spread throughout the documented history of North Karelian villages such as Vieki where I have worked, though it would be mistaken to see the practice as other than a regularly recurring secondary form. This view is supported by earlier writings, including the work of Väinö Voionmaa, who devotes attention to the subject in his remarkable study of Finland's Karelian people.[34] Statistics which he provides from two eastern parishes for the year 1654 suggest that about 7 per cent of households in that area contained uxorilocally married men. He further interestingly argues that the practice was historically most common in the east and north-east of the country, and least so in the west. This, of course, is in broad contrast to the distribution which appears to emerge from Sweetser's more recent data, though such a shift seems quite possible when one properly understands the nature of the practice.

Voionmaa's discussion places the matter squarely within the context of family-farm organisation in general and swidden cultivation in particular. The historical importance of swidden in the east of Finland is a central theme of his book. He considers that in swidden systems the main issue tends to be availability of labour rather than of land, and he makes much of the contrast between this sort of system and that of field agriculture, which predominated in the west of Finland. An important aspect of this is the way in which traditional Karelian inheritance seems to have depended upon the heir or heirs remaining as part of the resident labour force of the family. Moving away was tantamount to abdication from one's rights of ownership. At a more general level also, Voionmaa is keenly aware of the crucial importance of labour supply on a family farm. Thus he notes that ideally a farming family should be able to maintain its work strength in continuous

---

[33] See Arensberg and Kimball (1961, p. 114), Collomp (1984, p. 159) and Friedl (1962, p. 65).
[34] Voionmaa (1915, pp. 402, 432–4).

equilibrium with its needs and its material resources, but it is rarely capable of doing this. Sometimes the group grows beyond the carrying capacity of its holdings, and new holdings need to be obtained to match this growth, or members of the family have to move away. Sometimes the work strength of the group declines, however, and supplementary labour has to be sought from outside. In such contexts, different strategies are possible. Hiring labour is one, and taking partners or adopting children is another. Voionmaa argues that, historically, in-marrying sons-in-law are to be understood as such additional supplies of labour in the east of Finland. Sometimes they appear to be like labourers, though working for a share in the farm rather than for wages. Sometimes they are taken in as partners, and sometimes 'as a son' to the extent that they are guaranteed a son's share of inheritance. In the west of Finland, however, he suggests that hiring labour by the year was a more common practice, and he links this to the differences between swidden and fixed agriculture. In the west it was quite easy to become landless and to need whatever source of sustenance might be available from others. In the east, landlessness was scarcely a problem, at least in the early days of the seventeenth and eighteenth century, and more dignified and attractive offers were needed to tempt labour in from outside.[35]

I have already noted how Jutikkala makes a similar point more generally about property and labour on a family farm, and he interestingly discusses in-marrying sons-in-law in this context.[36] Unlike Voionmaa, though, he tends to stress the similarities rather than the contrasts between them and hired labour. In this regard, there is probably much sense in Voionmaa's own recognition that such arrangements have meant different things not only at different times and in different places, but also to different people at the same time and in the same area. Nor does it seem necessary to treat labour and property issues as exclusive of each other. The main point is that the presence of daughters and their husbands as part of a farm's resident labour force tends to have inheritance implications, just as the inheritance of a farm by such people often turns upon their prior labour input. This can be seen in modern North Karelian cases where the practice continues long after the end of swidden and the development of field agriculture, with all its property implications, in the area.

As I have implied, in-marrying sons-in-law are regular if not very frequent features of Vieki's social landscape. I myself know of at least six contemporary cases, and many past ones, and there are no doubt others which have not come to my notice. Though it is fair to say that father–son inheritance and virilocal residence are the ideal, such uxorilocal husbands

[35] *Ibid.*, pp. 431–2.   [36] Jutikkala (1958, pp. 54ff.).

create no particular surprise, and they are usually said simply to have come 'as sons-in-law' (*vävyksi*). The old term *kotivävy* (literally 'home son-in-law'), by which Voionmaa refers to them, is also sometimes used both by the men concerned and by others. This may draw the tiniest traces of a smile to people's lips, with its slightly archaic specificity and its ambiguous though gentle nuances of male domesticity and encroachment, but it would be wrong to see it as implying even the mild criticism which Friedl reports for such cases in Vasilika.[37]

A couple of examples from my field material, which I have already mentioned briefly in the course of earlier discussion, may help to illustrate some main features of the situation. The first is that of Veikko Kiiskinen, a member of a longstanding Vieki family which has occupied the whole or part of the village's farm No. 12 since the early nineteenth century. I have described some of the background to this case in Chapter 3, and it will be recalled that Veikko's ancestor, Johan, came himself as *kotivävy* to this farm early in the nineteenth century.

Veikko was born on a No. 12 farm holding, but there was not enough land there for him and his wife, Helka Saarelainen, and they eventually moved to her parents' farm. Helka had several sisters and one brother, but none of them wished to take up farming. Most of the sisters have married urban husbands, and the brother has also moved to an urban industrial area where he works.

When Veikko and Helka moved to Saarela, her father and mother were still alive. Veikko was a bit uncertain of their future there, and eventually arrangements were made for him and Helka to buy the farm from her parents. The father had first offered to draw up a will in her and Veikko's favour, but Veikko refused. Wills could be changed, he said, whereas a sale is final. Helka's siblings did not ask for a share in the proceeds, and they have never done so since, for instance when the father died. This stance has been based on the understanding that the main burden of looking after the place and Helka's ageing parents would fall on her and Veikko, and there was in fact a formal agreement, included in the documents of sale, which specified the residence and pension rights of the old couple. As I have mentioned, Veikko and Helka have now formally transferred the farm to one of their own sons, though they remain resident and working on it, and a comparable agreement has been drawn up in their case also. The farm has also started to be known as Kiiskilä, though one or two older people still occasionally refer to it as Saarela.

Relations with Helka's kin have remained good throughout the years. Her father's brother owns the next-door farm – both were divisions of a larger single unit – and he has always been helpful and co-operative. Her brother and sisters like to visit in the summer with their families, and they may give some useful help with urgent work like haymaking. They enjoy getting together with each other and with Helka's family, though it is clear that until her recent death their mother was the major social focus for them. They spent a lot of time with her, and it was noticeable on one Mid-summer's Eve that she and two of her daughters and their families formed a slightly separate group from Helka and Veikko and their immediate family as they sat by the traditional bonfire. Each group had brought its own sausages to grill on the fire. It is also true that the other siblings still retain rights to their mother's estate, which includes the old three-roomed timber cottage in which they grew up and which their parents continued to occupy in old age; and the fact that they have not been formally bought out might give them a basis for creating difficulties if they were not made welcome on the place. But there is more to the situation than simply exercising rights and avoiding friction. For Veikko and Helka and their children go well beyond the demands of such considerations in their efforts to look after their guests, even occasionally vacating their own house and sleeping in an outbuilding or a tent when they have very many summer visitors.

A second case is rather different in some ways. At the time of my research V.M. and his wife held part of a farm which had been M. family land for many generations. V. was in his seventies, and his wife in her late sixties, and they had a son and a daughter. The son had a professional career in Helsinki, but the daughter stayed at home where she lived with her husband, a good-natured and hardworking young man from a neighbour-ing village. They had one young child. The daughter worked in the Vieki bank and her husband was assistant churchwarden, but both of them also helped a great deal with the running of the farm.

The situation on the farm was of considerable interest to local villagers. Many people felt that V. should clarify the young couple's position by formally transferring the farm to them. He seems to have refused to do this since, despite his age, he was reluctant to let control of the place pass out of his hands. Nor, apparently, was he willing to make over the property to them in a will. This left the couple in considerable doubt over their future, since the Helsinki son in theory still retained rights to half of the farm in due course if he wished to exercise them. In the end, V. died and his wife died shortly afterwards, and I am told that the farm has now in fact gone formally to the daughter and her husband. I do not have details of the actual arrangements which this involved, but the main feature of the case I wish to stress here is the moral right to inheritance which the young couple's efforts on the farm were widely deemed to merit.

The legal situation is itself quite interesting in this context. Largely in line with Voionmaa's and Jutikkala's comments, the law has long treated inheritance as purely a matter of property rights, and such rights have not been legally affected by issues of residence and work input. More recently, however, new legislation has been drafted and is expected to modify such situations substantially. The spur to this appears to have been the fact that siblings who have left the rural areas have often been better educated than those who have stayed, and they have commonly been able to establish themselves well in an urban environment, while their village siblings have stayed on in more arduous and economically less favourable conditions to look after their parents and the family farm. Of course, the situation in the past was often very different, and many of those for whom there was no room at home fared badly. The new legislation is expected to take more account of this shift of fortunes, and to ensure that siblings who remain at home in such circumstances receive proper recognition for their labours in inheritance arrangements. This will be much more in accord with popular opinion not only at village level but also among many townsfolk who have left farm and parents in the hands of a brother or sister and his or her spouse. Indeed, the voluntary forgoing of inheritance rights, as by Helka Kiiskinen's siblings, is not uncommon in such cases.

We can now begin to gain a clearer picture of the main features of such cases. Firstly, Voionmaa's comments about the close links between residence, labour and inheritance still apply in modern times, though not with the same force and in exactly the same way as in the days of swidden. Even the law, which has tended to pay scant attention to this point, is now moving towards a sympathetic recognition of its cogency. Of course, the modern situation has its special features such as an unprecedented high level of movement away from farms by younger people, but even this is not as special as appears at first sight. Saloheimo, for example, in his history of the Pielisjärvi area to which Vieki belongs, notes that fathers commonly found it difficult to keep their sons at home at the end of the seventeenth century. In that case the attraction was not so much the towns as the possibility of opening up new settlements as farmers independent of the senior generation. Fathers found themselves threatened with a miserable and impoverished old age as their ability to cope with the farming workload waned. They would seek younger partners (*yhtiömiehet*) to help them carry the strain in return for a promise of inheritance in due course. *Kotivävyt* were occasionally found to take on this role, but they too were rare, given the opportunities for setting up on their own, and even unrelated men were sometimes recruited into partnership.[38]

[38] Saloheimo (1954, pp. 186–7).

Secondly, it is clear that inheritance custom has always been fairly flexible and that the relationship between son and daughter-in-law inheritance and that by sons-in-law and daughters has always had a statistical as well as a normative component. It is true that the ideal is father–son succession and that daughters were often given dowry as a form of pre-inheritance, but the possibility of succession to farm ownership by a daughter and her husband seems to have been open for at least four centuries. This possibility is best viewed as a strategy which individuals or families adopt out of a customary repertoire to solve their problems. In part the practice may be thought of as a 'strategy of heirship', to use Goody's phrase, but it can be misleading to think of it as only that since, as Goody himself recognises, more than the transmission of property is involved.[39] One needs also to take into account the fact that such arrangements involve different parties with different perspectives which are in part structurally determined. This is especially noticeable with regard to the element of time. For the senior generation, however anxious they might be to have their farm persist beyond their lifetime, the main consideration none the less seems likely to be the present and the shorter-term future. For them, coping with the running of the farm and managing a reasonably comfortable passage through their final years seem to be the pressing problems. For the younger generation, the issue is a longer-term one in which the labour input in the shorter term is in some degree the price of ownership and independence later. This is not to say that the two parties cannot see and even sympathise with each other's problems, or that they necessarily act simply in their own interests. None the less it seems fair to say that labour and inheritance have different meanings for them, and that it is thus difficult if not impossible to allocate an objective primacy to either of these vital factors in the situation.

Returning now to Sweetser's paper, two further points may be noted. As she herself acknowledges, the material she analyses is on residence rather than inheritance itself. It is interesting in this regard that she also quotes some figures for parent–child farm transfers in a footnote. These actually show a general tendency to father–son succession upon Finnish farms, without sharp differences between eastern and western regions, though it is true that the tendency is slightly less marked in the west. None the less, although her data on residence are thus not simply transformable into inheritance statistics, a degree of connection between the two is still highly plausible in the light of my discussion. Certainly, inheritance by a daughter and her husband seems likely to be preceded by their residence on the farm.

---

[39] J. Goody (1976a, pp. 86–98).

At the same time, it may also be that a number of the cases which she deals with, and especially those of co-residence with a wife's widowed mother, arise from the movement of such widows to a daughter's home when there is no son to support them.

The second point is that, despite the detailed framing of her argument in terms of change in, and the breaking down, of custom, Sweetser was at least right to assume that inheritance practices were liable to change statistically with changing circumstances. Such circumstances seem likely to include the nature of opportunities for the younger generation both within and outside rural areas, and the opportunities for the senior generation to retire with or without giving up their farms. State and wider society more generally have played a strong role in determining the nature of such opportunities, but the farming community also has its own flexible ways of responding to the problems which arise. One of these is the pattern of in-marrying sons-in-law that I have discussed here. The fact that the need for such a flexible package can arise even in relatively stable political and economic conditions is an important guarantee of its persistence. For, as Voionmaa stressed, there are always likely to be families which find it hard to balance the account between labour supply and its demand from one farming generation to another.[40]

Retirement and the interlocking of the generations

It will be clear from my discussion that the devolution of farms commonly involves some form of retirement for the senior generation. It is also clear that the ageing process has a vital social structural component. Farmers and their wives do not age simply as biological individuals. For apart from their connection to each other, their life course is inescapably interlocked with that of their children, and many of its details are substantially determined by their interaction with wider society and the state.

We have already seen that the lives of farmers have been seriously affected over the centuries by a variety of legislative and other developments. A modern example is the series of packages in recent years designed to tempt farmers into early retirement. Some are aimed at closing down the farms concerned, while others are directed towards making succession by a son or other member of the younger generation more attractive. A main aim is to reduce the average age of farmers, which has risen steadily since 1950 to its 1980 level of about fifty-five. Younger farmers are thought to be more receptive than their older counterparts to new ideas, and the combination of early retirement and new blood is aimed at the production

[40] Voionmaa (1915, pp. 429–30).

of a trimmer, more efficient system.[41] The early retirement schemes accompanied by farm closures offer farmers an attractive pension package, and those involving transfer to a suitable successor offer the incentive of cheap loans to help him buy the farm and pay off his siblings. The schemes have been promoted through pamphlets, newspapers and local meetings. They have had considerable success, and I know of many farm owners who have felt they constitute an offer which it would be foolish to refuse.

Despite such powerful external influence, it would be misleading to portray farmers and their successors as simply lacking choices and space for manoeuvre in a situation totally dictated for them by developments outside their control. I have already shown how some of the detailed arrangements which they make about retirement and succession may involve considerable room for choice and the expression of preference. There are also several further contexts in which options can be exercised, though one must not forget, here as elsewhere, that illness and death can easily disrupt the best-laid schemes, including those which outside pressure may push people into. One such area of choice is that of residential arrangements. As I have mentioned, the agreements between heir and holder commonly stipulate the latter's right to shelter after transfer of the farm. Various arrangements are found. Occasionally, a retiring couple or individual may move into a flat

[41] The problem and the solutions offered are not unlike the pattern in British universities, where early retirement and 'new-blood' schemes have been introduced as the teaching population ages.

Plate 7 Father and son at work

in town, or they may simply be given a room in the house, but it is more usual for them to be provided with their own at least partially self-contained quarters if this is possible. In some cases this involves the allocation to them of their own part of the house, and this will ideally have its own cooking facilities and television. There is also a growing tendency to build new accommodation on the farm for those retiring. In some cases an existing house is extended, while in others a new house with separate accommodation for the two families is provided. Sometimes a separate dwelling is built absolutely adjacent to the existing farm-house, but the new place has its own entrance and facilities. Such developments have been facilitated by new credit arrangements introduced in 1980. It is commonly expected that the younger generation and their children will be able to make good use of the house when the retiring generation die, or if they become so infirm that they need to go to an old people's home or be hospitalised.

Such separate residential arrangements are usually, in my experience, best understood as mechanisms for avoiding conflict and maintaining good relations in the process. The former holders and their heirs may quite often get together, in the evening for example, and they may co-operate significantly in other ways, as will be seen. Grandchildren particularly may form a vital link as they flit in and out of the two zones.

A commonly recurring element in the situation, which I have already noted, is the problem posed by the position of a young daughter-in-law in a house, and the eventual transfer of domestic authority to her from her

Plate 8 Holder and heir. House extensions for a transfer between generations

husband's mother. Husband's sisters too can sometimes be a source of friction, since for them the farm is still their natal home, and they may tend to see their brother's wife as an outsider. The relationship demands great tact since, even without ill will, their very familiarity with the place may lead such women to behave as if it is their own establishment, and this can breed resentment. In addition, the position of sons (and, of course, of in-marrying sons-in-law, as we have seen) is not without its problems. As elsewhere, fathers do not always age gracefully, and some widowed mothers seem to be as critical of their sons as of their wives. The capacity for hard work and organisation of a dead father is recalled and invidiously compared with the son's behaviour, and this can create tension in a joint household even into the son's middle age.

Beyond all this, however, people seem more generally quite conscious of the need to respect each other's freedom, and also to respect the differences of taste and interest which are common between the younger and older generations today. At some risk of over-simplification, it may be said that members of the older generation – at least in eastern Finland – tend much more to religious pietism than their juniors, and they are less interested in many modern technical developments such as photographic and tape- and record-playing equipment which younger people are keen to have. For some older people, any music other than church music seems to be suspect if not actually sinful, and although their tastes have recently been extending in some cases to classical and 'serious' modern music, they do not usually embrace the pop and rock which younger people like. Again, younger people often find church matters dull and unattractive, and while they may peacefully tolerate a gathering at home of older neighbours for a session of hymn-singing, it is not their ideal way of passing an evening. Another, and partially related, point of difference between the generations is that rural younger people are in general better educated than their seniors, if only because they have had the benefit of more modern syllabuses. Many of them learn at least some biology at school and take aspects of science such as evolutionary theory for granted. The contrast between this and the fundamentalist 'creationism' of their parents is also sometimes one small extra element of discomfort between them.

I turn now to the question of what retirement as farm-owner and the process leading to it entail in practice, especially when the retiring individual or couple are still relatively fit, as often happens with an early transfer. There is considerable variation on this issue, but it is clear that the point which I made earlier concerning property and labour applies in various ways here. Firstly, one sees that such a transfer helps to guarantee the continuity of labour on the farm, and in some cases to enhance its productivity as the young successor responds to the incentives and advantages which the establishment of his ownership provides. At the same time, however, there is also often a tendency for the radical change in legal property relations to be complemented by at least a short-term maintenance of the *status quo* in labour input. Many families carry on their previous arrangements more or less unchanged for several years, and the technically retired parent(s) may continue to play a vital role in working the farm and, importantly, in planning and organisation. Health and good relations permitting, their handing over in these contexts to the younger generation often takes place gradually.

Here too, as in other contexts, a significant variable is whether the succeeding son has married. There are many sides to this. Parents in rural Finland as elsewhere are extremely keen to see their children marry. Partly this is simply a matter of wishing to see them follow a 'normal' life-cycle, and there is, of course, a common wish for grandchildren. In addition, a daughter-in-law should make a significant contribution to farm labour, which should help to relieve the burden of the older generation as they age. Moreover, transfer of a farm to an unmarried son may partly help to make him 'a better catch'. It is true that there is a shortage of young rural women these days, and that this is in no small part due to their desire to escape from the drudgery of agriculture. At the same time, however, as I noted in the previous chapter, there seems to be some trace left of older considerations in which the idea of marrying a farm-owner is more attractive than simply marrying a farmer's son whose future on the farm may be uncertain.

But a son's marriage may be intimately related to the transfer of a farm in other ways. For as we have already seen, a daughter-in-law is also a sort of wedge between him and his parents. She and the family they will found together provide him with concerns which give him a legitimate identity beyond his ties to parents and to siblings. If she is there before a transfer, she may well accelerate its occurrence through exhortation, criticism and her very presence, and later she may well push him faster than he might otherwise be tempted to go towards taking over the control of the farm in addition to owning it as a sort of formality. This is, of course, an old story, which in its general outline goes well beyond the present ethnographic setting. A classical account of the kinds of problem involved is provided by Arensberg and Kimball in their study of Irish farming families. Their account shows that, as in Finland, the people themselves are very conscious of the potential for conflict in such situations and of the need to exercise great tact and restraint if such potential is not to be realised. Similarly, Alain Collomp has described a comparable range of tensions for Haute Provence, and he notes the existence of a rich folk-lore on the subject.[42] It is

---

[42] Arensberg and Kimball (1961, p. 128 and passim) and Collomp (1984, p. 153). Friedl (1962, p. 55) reports the normal status of some friction in the rather different system of Vasilika. One might expect more regular discussion of this issue in the literature on family farming, but conflicts involving men are more commonly discussed.

clearly an important way in which the life-cycles of adjacent generations are tied to each other, and it is especially significant in the stem-family pattern of succession, which typically involves a period of co-residence between holder and successor couples.

6

Co-operation between farming families

Finnish farmers are often characterised as fierce individualists, with a deep suspicion of anything which smacks of the *kolkhoz*, though they sometimes use this term in joke for collaboration among themselves. The well-known Finnish literary image of a man, a hoe and a swamp captures dramatically the idea of the farmer as an individual who relies on his own determination and capacity for long, hard work as he tames nature and transforms it to his will.[1] These much-admired qualities are encapsulated in one of the most important Finnish key words, *sisu*, literally what is 'inside' a person, his 'guts' and inner strength. This image of the farmer takes for granted that he works within the context of a family in which his marriage is the pivotal relationship, but it tends to ignore or at least play down the idea of dependence on relationships beyond this narrow circle. Farmers often stress how their desire for independence makes it difficult for them to engage in fruitful co-operation with each other, and although they may express regret at this, they also clearly take a certain pride in such self-portraits.

Not surprisingly, the link between such images and the real world of historical and modern social interaction is quite complex. The images are not merely a reflection of that world, nor are they simply its negation. They are part truths in the sense that they both reflect and deny aspects of reality, and in the further sense that they can also influence its form.

---

[1] I refer here especially to Linna's (1959) well-known novel, *Täällä Pohjantähden alla* (*Here under the North Star*), which opens with the line 'Alussa olivat suo, kuokka – ja Jussi' ('In the beginning there was a swamp, a hoe – and Jussi'). Variations on the theme also occur, however, in several earlier poetry and prose contexts. Cf. the Runeberg poem about the Saarijärvi peasant Paavo (quoted in translation in Fox (1926, p. 51) and Juhani Aho's story 'Pioneers' (quoted in translation in Tompuri (1947)). For a more stratified version, in which the hero has workmen to perform the task of reclamation, see the close of Linnankoski's novel *Laulu tulipunaisesta kukasta* (*Song of the Flame-Red Flower*), which is also quoted in translation in Fox (1926, pp. 42–3).

It would demand a detailed study of its own to trace the roots and the development of such values and ideas in Finnish culture and society.[2] Ecological, religious and political factors have all probably played their part. One source seems likely to have been the long history in Finland of tough backwoods pioneering in an inhospitable climate, and evangelical Lutheranism has undoubtedly contributed to the strong work ethic and the emphasis on individual responsibility. Land-use and land-tenure policies in already settled areas have also been of some significance. The eighteenth- and nineteenth-century programmes of farm enclosure and consolidation (*isojako* and *uusijako*) encouraged an attachment to ideals of individual land-ownership and farm management; and such sentiments were rein- forced by the land-reform programmes of the 1920s, with their aim, after the civil war and independence, of pacifying a potentially dangerous landless section of the rural population by turning them into small but none the less land-owning farmers. Looming as a background to such measures was Russian Communism and the fear of more radical reform. In its own way too, the war with Russia also served to emphasise these features of the Finnish character. The tough, independent, individual Finn was writ large in the small independent nation daring to stand up for itself and go it alone, not wholly unsuccessfully, against a giant enemy.

Change is implicit in this sketch of factors which appear to have influenced the formation and development of farmers' values, but it is difficult to know just how much is involved. The most straightforward reading would be one of a transition from traditional forms of village community life to modern individualism, but this is much too simple. Certainly, there is evidence from the seventeenth century and before of many early forms of organised co-operation among Finnish villagers in such activities as swidden cultivation, net fishing, hunting and milling; and linguistic evidence suggests that mutual aid with heavy and urgent tasks (*talkoot*) is of quite ancient origin.[3] There is, however, also later evidence of such collaboration, and several new forms have developed in more recent periods, so that the apparent sharp shift of emphasis in values does not appear to have been matched by quite as clear a change at the level of behaviour.

Indeed, like their predecessors, modern Finnish farmers regularly colla- borate a great deal with each other, though the extent to which they do so varies both within and between regions. Regional variation in itself is nothing new, though it has differed in its details from one period to another.[4] Not surprisingly, self-sufficiency in labour and equipment is

---

[2] For a useful discussion of this subject see Köppä (1979). Roberts (1989) also interestingly brings out a range of comparable points.
[3] See Talve (1979, pp. 167–73).   [4] *Ibid.*, Köppä (1979, pp. 58ff., 182).

relatively common nowadays in areas, such as the south-west, where there are many large and prosperous farms. Such farms are more likely to be able to support a full complement of machinery and possibly a regular, if small, hired workforce, though they still make use of more formal, large-scale co-operative marketing and banking facilities. It is also interesting that, over a long period, inter-farm collaboration has been well developed in some areas of compact village settlement, like Pohjanmaa in the north-west. In North Karelia, although settlement is relatively scattered, there are many small and medium-sized farms for which collaboration makes good sense. Farmers in Vieki and other villages of the region participate in a wide range of co-operative activity including, sometimes, even the joint ownership of farm machinery. The paradox which such activity presents, when juxtaposed with the stereotype of tough individualism, can at least partly be resolved if one looks closely at the forms collaboration takes. A crucial point – especially at the inter-personal level – is that co-operation should be seen to be an act of will, arising from the exercise of choice and, thus, enhancing rather than detracting from the individual identity of those involved.

Patterns of co-operation in Vieki: formal structures
The analysis of collaborative activity in face-to-face communities has been a longstanding area of interest in social anthropology. Some of the main issues involved were first clearly signposted by Mauss (1954) in his classic study of the closely related field of gift exchange. In addition to noting the problems of identifying individuals as the relevant actors in some systems of exchange, Mauss also drew attention to the diffuseness (to use a more recent term) of what he called 'prestations' as a class of 'total social facts'.[5] Clearly, where such diffuseness is a characteristic of relationships and institutions, the application of analysis is likely to create a range of artificial boundaries which are more than simply a set of arbitrary constructs. For they also run directly against the grain of the phenomena in question. In such circumstances, the more we multiply and refine our analytic terminology, the worse the situation gets. We sharpen our chisels when we should perhaps be reaching for the glue.

Of course, language is the chief resource we have at our disposal for handling such problems, and academic language tends to be analytical in nature. Attempts to move into other less exact and more symbolic literary modes of discourse may solve some problems but are likely to have other costs, and I suspect that the best we can achieve is an awareness of the problem and of the limitations of our toolkit. We can sensibly continue to

---

[5] Mauss (1954, pp. 1, 4). The idea of diffuseness as the opposite of specificity is developed by Parsons (1951, p. 66 and passim).

attempt to document varieties of collaborative and comparable activities within communities. But we need to remain conscious of the ability of our material to disobey the law of the impossible middle, for it *can* be different things at once, and it is frequently involved in shifts of emphasis and in a process of becoming. Because of this, in the following discussion I apply some distinctions, such as that between 'formal' and 'informal' patterns of co-operation, with some caution. I should also add that I use the two generic terms 'collaboration' and 'co-operation' interchangeably in order to avoid excessive repetition. 'Co-operation' is a slightly problematic term because it has been usurped to some extent by the formal 'co-operative' sector, but I hope that differences of context will resolve potential ambiguities in this regard.

It makes reasonable sense in many contexts to distinguish between formal and informal structures of co-operation among farmers. In the former category one would include such institutions as co-operative dairies and banks, while in the latter zone one finds more personal networks of collaboration and support. As I have implied, though, the boundary between the two sectors is not always absolutely clear. Thus, although the structure and organisation of the more formal institutions in the area were based on models generated outside the community, I have noted in Chapter 2 how their successful establishment in the village, around the turn of the century, depended upon the collaboration of a relatively small number of active villagers who knew each other well and who mainly had local concerns in mind. It appears also that a combination of externally derived formality and neighbourly collaboration was no new experience for these men or for many of their predecessors. In 1861, for instance, eighteen of the village's main land-owning farmers came together at the home of Olof Turunen for a meeting which appears to have been called within the then prevailing framework of parish organisation, prior to the establishment of the modern *kunta* (commune) system.[6] Formal notice of the meeting had been given in the parish church in Lieksa eight days before, and its purpose was the allocation of responsibility for fencing lake-side meadows. Each farmer was assigned a length of fencing to be built, and a roster of responsibilities for maintenance was drawn up. The agreed allocations were written up by a notary in an officially stamped document entitled *Reklementti*. This was signed with the identifying 'marks' (*puumerkki*, literally 'tree mark') and the initials of the participants, and endorsed by two witnesses. I need scarcely add that as local land-owning farmers these men already had many connections of kinship, marriage and neighbourhood with each other which ante-dated and outlasted the formalities of such a contract.

[6] See Saloheimo (1953, pp. 531ff.).

Banks and other formal institutions, with their bureaucratic trappings, were used to bring the benefits of the wider world into the village, but in doing this they were not simply agencies of change and transformation of the village into a scaled-down version of that world. This is part of a more general pattern which is visible in a range of contexts, including the succession and inheritance practices described in Chapter 5. It would also be wrong, however, to ignore the special character of the formal sector, or to claim that it has made no mark on the patterns of collaboration among villagers. The institutions concerned, with their strict rules and their officers and committees, handle large quantities of business and have many members. And their lasting success at the local level has at least partly depended upon their ability to combine a manifest concern for the community with a reputation for bureaucratic efficiency, due process and impartiality.

The element of concern for the community also entails some blurring of boundaries within the formal sector itself. Some turn-of-the-century developments, like the Co-operative Bank, the credit grain-store and the 'Rural Association' (*Maalaisseura*) were relatively 'technical' in orientation, but they had their cultural and social side as well, and they were part of the same general movement which produced youth associations and women's groups, and which brought the influence of church and school more strongly and directly than ever before into village life. As I have discussed in Chapter 2, this last point was exceptionally clear in the roles played by the teacher, Alen, and the pastor, Kolkki, in the organisation of the many institutions concerned.

By the time of my fieldwork, several of the village's earlier more formal institutions and associations had either disappeared or been absorbed into a wider framework, though one, the Youth Association, was re-established during my visit. The credit grain-store ceased to function in the 1950s when farmers began to have enough money at their disposal simply to purchase grain from commercial suppliers. In the late 1940s a village electricity supply company was set up on co-operative lines, but it was soon drawn into the wider supply system. The Vieki dairy was incorporated into and eventually displaced by the Lieksa and, ultimately, the regional Joensuu Co-operative Dairy, which is the largest in the northern countries. This is mainly used by farmers in the central and southern parts of the village, while those in northern areas, such as Siltavaara, and a few further south have found it more convenient to be affiliated to the Nurmes dairy, even though they live in Lieksa Commune. This division was a source of conflict at one time in the village, but it appears to cause no problems at the present time. Villagers are encouraged to play a part in these large-scale co-operatives, and a number of them have sat on their governing committees.

The proximity and smaller scale of the Nurmes dairy has helped to maintain a particularly keen sense of personal involvement among many of its members.

The village bank has been the most persistently successful of the institutions concerned. It has maintained a considerable degree of autonomy, in spite of its incorporation into the wider co-operative bank (*osuuspankki*) system and its formally dependent status, in some contexts, as a sub-branch of the larger bank in Lieksa. Its staff and committee members and officers have always been local and, with the exception of Alen and Kolkki in the initial phase, most of them have come from farming families in the village. At its peak in 1962, the number of members stood at 496 (as compared with the initial figure of forty-four), and in 1979, the last year for which I have detailed information, it was 285. Deposits at the end of 1979 were at a record high point of over 6 million marks, after a good year for agriculture and timber trading. Loans of some 5 million marks were made in the year, the majority being for agricultural and forestry purposes. Since 1927 the bank has had its own premises on its own plot of land in the central *kirkonkylä* area of the village, and a series of substantial improvements to the buildings provides clearly visible evidence of continuing prosperity. The bank still sees itself as mainly serving the community, and villagers appreciate having a banking facility which is genuinely their own. It is noticeable that even in more recent years, members of several of the families which were involved in the venture at its outset have been elected to the committee or as local auditors. There is, however, quite a wide range of members who become involved in such activities, including some of the Karelian settlers of the 1950s, and grumbles about representation do not seem to be very common. It is clear that trustworthiness and respectability are the key elements which people look for in those they elect, and it is not surprising in a small community of this sort if the perception of such qualities is tied in to some degree with family reputation and informal networks of relationship.[7]

Village committees and the new 'agricultural village'
The co-operative banking movement, to which the Vieki bank is affiliated, has been supportive of a relatively new collaborative development in rural Finland. This is the initiation of 'village action' (*kylätoiminta*) through the establishment of village committees (*kylätoimikunta*), which have spread rapidly throughout the country in recent years. Their development has been considerably influenced by a group of academic geographers, and one of these, Lauri Hautamäki, has published a guide to their operation in his 1976

[7] Information on the Vieki bank was provided by a variety of villagers. Valuable written sources include Mikkonen (1975) and official annual reports and accounts.

book *Elävä Kylä* (literally *The Living Village*). While encouraging the establishment of these committees, the co-operative banks have been anxious to allow them to retain their separate identity, and in Vieki support has involved little more than some help with the relatively small overheads of holding meetings. The banks have an understandably keen interest in the viability and prosperity of rural communities, where many of their members live, and they are natural allies in this context of the Centre Party, which was formerly the Agrarian League and which derives a substantial amount of its support from farmers. It is important for both banks and party to keep their distance, however, since it is a fundamental element in the concept of the committees that they are independent grass-roots institutions, representing the needs of their communities and quite explicitly divorced from party politics.

Committee members are typically elected at a general meeting of the people of the area concerned. They meet quite often to discuss a range of local problems and their possible solutions, and they sometimes make valuable representations on local issues to local government and other bodies such as transport companies. In the Vieki area they have been concerned with issues such as school closures, the state of local roads and the possibility of changes to bus timetables, and they have had some success in influencing decisions on such matters. Each committee normally works alone, but committees in the Vieki area also have a good record of collaboration with each other.

A committee was established for the whole of Vieki in the late 1970s, but after a couple of years farmers in the northern areas of Loukku and Siltavaara felt that they had enough distinct problems to merit the establishment of a committee of their own. This was created without any overt conflict with the rest of Vieki, and the two groups have in fact worked very well together on a number of occasions. One of the main difficulties which the people of Loukku–Siltavaara faced was the threatened closure of Loukku school, which served both areas after the closure of the Siltavaara school some years before. It is not easy to reopen such a school once it has been closed. The minimum number of prospective pupils is twenty-four for a reopening, whereas only twelve are needed to keep one open, and of course the lack of school facilities discourages people with young families from moving into such an area. Much of the Loukku–Siltavaara committee's energies were devoted in 1980–1 to an ultimately unsuccessful attempt to prevent closure of the school. Nevertheless their efforts were not completely unrewarded. They managed to prevent the selling off of the school buildings, which has happened in many other cases, and they obtained a promise that the buildings could be used for local community needs, including courses, meetings and other events. This was a valuable concession, and the buildings have been the focus of a variety of activities including the establishment of a new form of co-operative enterprise in the area, a *maatalouskylä* or 'agricultural village'.[8]

Unlike the Vieki committee, which draws its members from a variety of occupations and a wide political spectrum, the Loukku–Siltavaara committee has consisted solely of farmers. This reflects the more differentiated occupational structure of Vieki, particularly in its central area, and the almost wholly agricultural emphasis in Loukku–Siltavaara. This emphasis has also been apparent in the fact that there has been a very close degree of overlap between membership of the village committee and the group of farmers who have formed the *maatalouskylä*, with a major role in both enterprises being played by individuals such as Matti Kärki, Inkeri Hn, and Leo O. I am not aware of anything sinister about this overlap, or about the fact that the main local activists have been the more successful farmers in the area. These are for the most part the people with the longest-term stakes in the area, both from the standpoint of capital and labour investment, and in hopes for the future. They are also, almost by definition, some of the more dynamic and hardworking individuals in the area.

The *maatalouskylä* concept was, I understand, initially developed in the North Karelian region. The introduction of the scheme into Lieksa was due in no small measure to the interest and influence of the Lieksa Agricultural Adviser, Jaakko P., who had previously worked in Ilomantsi and had experience of a successful *maatalouskylä* there in the village of Hakovaara. This had been the first such unit to be set up (in 1975), and it was followed by the establishment of four more in other North Karelian communes. Jaakko P. was keen to start up such an arrangement in Lieksa, and he was able to persuade the Commune Council to agree to the foundation of a single unit there. Partly through informal contacts, but also through the medium of local 'farmers' society' (*maamiesseura*) meetings, he then brought this possibility to the attention of farmers in different parts of the Commune, including Loukku–Siltavaara. This is an area which he himself knows well, since he comes from very near there.

The idea of the *maatalouskylä* is that a group of neighbouring farms, which should ideally number between 8 and 20, are linked together in a variety of activities designed to aid their advancement and development. Ideally also, the owners of the farms should be relatively young, and they should if possible have potential successors. When I met him, Jaakko P. explained the emphasis on age to me in terms of the tendency, which he believed existed, for older farmers to be unreceptive to new ideas. The farms should be reasonably well equipped with machinery, and their buildings

---

[8] See Abrahams (1988) for a fuller discussion of this development in Loukka–Siltavaara.

should be in decent condition, though improvements in these respects, and in others such as drainage, are among anticipated benefits for participants. The state and commune both assist the scheme financially. Included in the scheme are the making of a 'village plan', computer analyses of each farm with an accompanying review of the best direction for its future development; arrangements for the joint purchase of materials and, if desired, of equipment; and the provision of courses for improving farmers' understanding of modern techniques along with the organisation of trips to see new developments elsewhere. A team-leader (*vetäjä*) is chosen from among the participating farmers, and in the case of Loukku–Siltavaara, Matti Kärki was chosen. The provision of special support for the 'village' is expected to last for five years.

The existence of schemes of this sort was first mentioned to me in Siltavaara by Matti Kärki when I visited him in 1981. We were talking about machinery and mutual aid, and he commented that he had heard about a village in Ilomantsi where a great deal of joint activity had been organised. Like many others whom I subsequently spoke to, he went on to note that such schemes were not likely to arouse great interest, given the Finnish farmer's tendency to value his freedom of choice and action so strongly. None the less, he said, the Ilomantsi village was by all accounts doing quite well. It seems clear that Jaakko P. was at least one of the sources of Matti's information, and that plans were already at that time afoot to try to introduce the scheme into Lieksa commune. When this eventually happened, there was in fact a very positive response from the Loukku–Siltavaara area. An application was put in from there along with five others from different parts of Lieksa, including one from another part of Vieki.

As I have implied, Loukku–Siltavaara was chosen as the site of the new venture, and it began to operate in 1982. There were eventually eleven farms in the scheme, and although they differed somewhat from each other, they fitted the overall parameters of the system quite well. The average field area was officially described as 19.3 hectares, average forest holdings were 69 hectares, and the average age of collaborating farmers was thirty-seven, though they covered a considerable range.[9] The fact that the overall level of available machinery was good was in the application's favour. I have received brief reports about the progress of the scheme on subsequent short visits to the area. In general there appears to have been substantial satisfaction among the farmers concerned, and it is hard to imagine why this should not be so when they have mainly received help to do things

[9] The figure of 19.3 hectares for average field holdings is higher than I would have expected from the data available to me on some of the individual farms. I am not sure why this should be, but it may include some rented holdings. It is not surprising that the figure is higher than the one quoted in Chapter 3 for Vieki as a whole, since this contains a much wider range of farms.

which many if not all of them were already keen to do. Anni, the *emäntä* (mistress) of the Repola farm, which was included in the scheme, was particularly enthusiastic about things when I saw her in 1982. The 'village' plan which the participants had drawn up with expert advice had included the establishment of a machine repair and service workshop on their farm, and this would remain theirs after the scheme had run its course. The fact that one of her sons was a trained mechanic had clearly been an important consideration in the matter. It may be noted that there is a small potential for conflict here, since one or two of Repola's neighbours also engage in machine repair work but are not included in the scheme. Anni, however, expressed the view that there would be plenty of work to go round for all concerned.

A number of points about this new development are worth discussion here in the light of my introductory comments. Firstly, there is the fact that in spite of expressed protestations about the uncooperative nature of the Finnish farmer's character, six applications were made for participation in the scheme, and similar arrangements had already been successfully established elsewhere in the region. It is also fairly clear to me from conversations with some farmers that more of them were interested in such a scheme than actually put in applications, though they expressed little overt interest in it. One aspect of the situation is that such postures and protestations commonly appear to involve an element of self-protective bluff. The farmers concerned were keen not to show their hand too early in case they found themselves embarrased later. Some were not sure they could get an attractive enough application together, and some too probably worried that they might express an interest only to find themselves not invited by their neighbours to participate. At the same time it is also true that Finnish farmers do not enter lightly into such arrangements, and most cases of joint ownership of machinery and other equipment occur between people who have known and come to trust each other over many years.

It is no accident that there were already close relations between several of the Loukku–Siltavaara farms prior to their application for the *maatalous-kylä* project, and here again one sees a blurring of the boundary between the formal and informal sectors of activity. Anni from Repola and Matti Kärki are siblings, and Anni's husband is her second cousin. Matti's wife is a Tn from the original Loukku farm, and another participant, Inkeri Hn, is her sister's daughter. Another member, Leo O., came to Loukku in 1966 at the age of twenty-two. He called on an older, well-established neighbour, Onni Mn, because he knew that Onni's wife was distantly related to his mother. He and Onni got to know and like each other. Onni needed labour on the farm and Leo did a lot of work for him. Onni, in turn, had machinery which he lent to Leo until he managed to obtain his own. This somewhat asymmetrical relationship gradually grew more equal, and the two men began to own machinery in common. Onni was also one of those who planned to join the scheme, though he did not do so in the end. I am not sure what led to this decision, but the fact that he did not have any obvious successor to his farm appears to have been a factor.

This last case is instructive with regard to the significance of kinship in such situations. Leo O. himself sensibly sees the kinship tie to Onni's wife as the seed from which a fruitful co-operative relationship developed, rather than an automatic basis of collaboration between the two farms. The same is also true to some extent of the closer kinship ties involved in the other cases I have mentioned. There are several examples known to me of siblings and other kin who cannot get on well with each other, and it is in such situations, as much as anywhere, that the divisive features of the structured individualism of Finnish family farming can be seen. Kinship is intrinsically a propitious base for active co-operation between farming families, but its equally intrinsic potential for conflict can easily counter this, and some farmers in fact seem to prefer to collaborate with good friends and neighbours.

Informal collaboration

In this section I mainly discuss some of the collaborative activities which farmers enter into among themselves without the 'umbrella' of a wider, bureaucratic structure. As I have said, though, it is not always straightforward to mark off the formal and informal in this way. Holiday arrangements are a relatively unproblematic example of this, inasmuch as formal and informal ways of dealing with them exist side by side. Some farming families simply turn to a neighbour for help when they want to go on holiday or need to take a few days off, while others engage in more formal 'holiday rings' in which a number of families jointly arrange to share the services of a holiday stand-in (*lomittaja*) along guidelines provided by the agricultural services. There is also the further fact that just as more formal patterns of co-operation can be partially dependent on less formal links between the parties, so too one can encounter some impingement of the norms and values of the formal sector into personal relations. This point was made classically by Durkheim (1893) in his analysis of legal and other wider societal influence upon apparently free contracts between individuals, and I have already examined several aspects of the interplay between the public and the private in my discussion of inheritance practice. As there, I have been conscious in the present context of the role of banks and other financial institutions as sources of credit within a general framework of legal rules about property ownership and individual responsibility.

An example from the history of the Saarelainen and Kiiskinen families, which I outlined earlier, brings out some aspects of the situation. The case is one where the two zones of inheritance and subsequent collaboration meet. As I have described in Chapter 4, the two brothers Mikko and Mauno Saarelainen bought a farm in Vieki in 1894, and Mikko bought his brother's share in 1904. He married twice and was a widower for many years until his death in 1952. Through a complex series of transactions, Mikko's farm was passed down to two of his sons. Arvid, a son from the first marriage, received very slightly under half the farm, and Elias, a son from the second marriage, had the remainder. Both men were married and were active farmers, but they never formally divided off their separate holdings. They made their own personal agreements about which fields they used, and they informally divided the proceeds of forest sales between them. They also gave each other help with farming tasks from time to time. In 1963 Arvid and his wife transferred their farm to their daughter Helka and her husband Veikko Kiiskinen, and formal boundaries were drawn up and registered the next year between this farm and Elias's holdings. It appears that Veikko himself was more generally in favour of such clarification, though he stresses that relations between the parties have always been excellent. His philosophy is of the 'good fences make good neighbours' variety, and he likes the combination this implies of friendly co-operation on the one hand and being clearly one's own master on the other. It is also possible that his views on such matters may have been influenced by his position as an in-marrying son-in-law. Still, the key factor in the situation was apparently his need for credit from the bank and other sources. In this context a clear allocation of property and, with it, of responsibility, was necessary to meet the requirements of the lending institutions. Afterwards, friendly collaboration between the two farms continued as before, but their separate identities were now quite clearly established.

Here, as in inheritance affairs more generally, one sees a complex and variable mixture of *gemeinschaft* ideals and the demands of the wider socio-economic system. Comparable situations can also arise in other contexts of property-owning, such as the sharing of machinery between friends and neighbours. At the same time, it is clear that many farmers like to keep the formal side of such arrangements to a minimum.

There are a number of cases in the village of farmers who own some machinery in common. Often the machinery in question is expensive – a combine harvester, for instance – and joint ownership makes sense more generally if a machine is not likely to be in continual use on a single farm. In the cases I know of, relations between the farmers concerned are quite longstanding, and participants have stressed that it is crucial for them to feel confident about each other. More is involved here than simple honesty and reliability, though these are, of course, important qualities. There are also issues of general temperament and compatibility, since joint ownership can otherwise quite easily lead to dissatisfaction and quarrels about sharing arrangements and responsibility for wear or accidental damage. A farmer who worries unduly about whether a machine was already damaged before it broke down on his farm, or who is nagged by suspicions that his fellow owner is misusing the machinery in some way, is unlikely to make a good partner. In this regard it also makes sense if the farms involved are of much the same size, so that their needs are fairly similar, but even in such cases there is room for discord if the machine is also hired out to others. One farmer may be keener on this kind of work than his co-owner, and may be eager to gain extra income through driving the machine – for which he is paid personally – in addition to the shared hiring charges. In such circumstances, the mutually best balance between their individual interests, and also between income and the costs in wear and tear, may easily be differently perceived by those concerned. Overall, it seems clear that successful co-ownership typically provides a further strengthening of already-existing good relations between farmers, which may be based initially on a wide range of foundations such as friendship and collaboration in village and church activities. It is particularly interesting that often no written agreements and contracts exist between co-owners, beyond the formal documentation for credit, guarantee and insurance purposes of ownership itself. One finds here the antithesis of Sam Goldwyn's well-known quip that 'a verbal agreement isn't worth the paper it is written on'. For one detects a strong feeling in such cases that arrangements would be doomed to failure if written contractual agreements about use and liability for damage were needed, since only patience, trust and good will can ultimately solve the variety of problems which are likely to arise.

Because differences of temperament can seriously affect a farmer's attractiveness as a partner and also his own interest in sharing, it is clear that a simple structural explanation of joint ownership in terms of size of farm or age of farmer will not suffice. It is true that large farms are more likely to have a full range of their own equipment, and small farms are less likely to demand the use of large complex machines or to generate the capital required for their joint purchase. But within the range of medium-sized farms one still finds a variety of patterns.[10] One farmer may own everything he has individually, and engage in varying forms of reciprocal borrowing and lending to make up any shortfall in his requirements. Another may engage in such activities, and also be quite keen on the joint

---

[10] Köppä (1979, Chapter 5, pp. 76–8 and passim) provides a detailed discussion of the structural factors, including farm size, affecting co-operation. His large-scale survey data suggest that age is also a factor of some significance, but I have not found noticeable evidence of this in the small number of local cases known to me.

ownership of some equipment. Not surprisingly, the equipment in question is commonly additional to a farm's most basic requirements. Thus, as was seen in Chapter 4, Ilmari Turunen had a large stock of his own machinery, and engaged in an exchange of services with others, but he also participated in a wide range of joint-ownership arrangements. He shared the ownership of a set of field rolls with four others, a fertiliser drill with one other, a crop sprayer with four others, a potato harvester with six others, a combine harvester with one other, a slurry tank with one other, a winch with two others, and a ditching disc with one other. There is some overlap in the membership of these different groups, which involved a total of thirteen people including Ilmari himself. It is no accident that he was more generally a very popular man in the village, well known for his cheerful character and for his readiness to give help to individuals and in community affairs. He was often asked to participate in such joint-ownership groups (*porukka* is the colloquialism usually used to describe these and other informal groupings), and he himself sometimes initiated the arrangements.

As I have implied, the borrowing and lending of equipment is more common than joint ownership. One farmer may have a particular type of harrow which another borrows, and the second farmer may in turn lend him a ploughing attachment or a buck-rake. Interestingly, it is not only the more modern types of equipment which are in demand in such arrangements. At the time of my fieldwork, many farmers still liked to use a horse and horse-plough for potato planting and subsequent tillage, and horses were by then as rare as tractors used to be. One farmer in the village, with a relatively small farm of his own, did a great deal of this kind of work for his neighbours, often in exchange for the use of tractors and auxiliary equipment which he himself did not possess. In one case where he did such work, the farmer he had helped asked, as is customary, how much he owed him. The man replied, not unexpectedly, that they should not discuss that at the moment. 'I'll let you know if I've got anything to complain about', he said. This was taken to mean that he wanted help in due course with a tractor for his mowing and would ask for it when the time came, as indeed he did.

My discussion so far has mainly concentrated on the ownership and use of agricultural equipment, but it is already clear that this sometimes includes a labour element. The owner of a horse and plough or a machine may have to work it for the hirer or borrower, and this is normally taken into account, especially if payment is made. Occasionally, a farmer may need help from others for some manual task, and he is likely to ask one or two neighbours with whom he has good working relations to provide this. During my stay at Kiiskilä, for instance, a neighbouring farmer, Pekka K., asked Veikko Kiiskinen and another neighbour to come to help him put a large load of fodder into his silo. Pekka had more or less retired, but he kept a horse and a small number of other livestock. He lived alone with his wife, who was not in very good health, and their grown-up children had moved away. The work in question lasted all day, and was quite arduous, but it was clear from my own observations and from subsequent discussion that strong efforts were made to ensure that, in spite of payment, the situation differed sharply from that of simply employing a hired hand. Breaks in the work were called at frequent intervals by Pekka, as the 'host', and they lasted longer than was strictly necessary. Refreshments and food were relatively lavishly provided, and Pekka also insisted on paying very generously for the work. The workers would have been upset if they had felt in any way exploited and demeaned by their neighbour, and he himself would have been unhappy if he was thought to have acted in this way. Such dangers were successfully avoided, with the result that both sides were amply satisfied and the way was kept open for future fruitful collaboration. Villagers take a keen interest in behaviour in such contexts, and I have heard adverse comments made about the meanness of some individuals. In one case, I was told by a farmer who had an excellent reputation for hard work that he used to give some help to a particular neighbour, but he eventually gave up because the man kept an oppressively close watch on the work in his anxiety to make sure he got his money's worth. Another farmer is said to have been forced eventually to give up farming altogether, since he was unable to get help when he needed it because he had acquired a reputation for being too tight-fisted. On the other hand, a man who knows how to treat his helpers well, and who is ready to give a hand himself when others are in need, is unlikely to be denied support if he is temporarily short-handed.

Not surprisingly, handing over money for some service between neighbours can be a delicate and long-drawn-out affair. In some cases, such as the hiring out of combine harvesters, the matter is usually fairly straightforward. There are nationally recognised rates of payment for the use of these and other machines which are set out, among other places, in the farmer's diaries produced by the Pellervo Society and the Farmers' Union. The machines are much less common than tractors, and the range of people who may want to hire them is quite wide. Their owners are, moreover, relatively prosperous farmers who are not likely to be looking for some comparable help from those they serve. As such there tends to be much less of an element of 'doing the odd favour' for a friend or neighbour in providing such machines for others' use, though people are keen to establish an informal understanding with a particular owner in order to guarantee that they will have the use of a machine during the brief period in which they need to get their crops in.

The situation is more complicated in the type of case described above when a farmer helps out a good neighbour in a tight spot as part of an ongoing relationship between them. I did not witness the actual payment in that instance, but I was present on another occasion when the same two farmers were involved. Pekka had asked Veikko for a lift to a party to which both couples were invited, and Veikko was happy to provide this. On their return, when Veikko had taken Pekka and his wife to their own place down the road, Pekka began to insist on paying something for the petrol and the trouble involved. A long argument ensured and Pekka eventually firmly placed a couple of notes on the floor of the car and left. I understand that some arguments of this sort may go on until both sides appear to be quite outraged, and the person who wants to pay slams money down on the table and marches off. Pride on both sides has to be satisfied. Neither party must be allowed to feel dependent on or done down by the other. There is clearly a ritual element to such arguments, but it would be mistaken to treat them as pure 'play-acting' in which the emotions of participants were not genuinely involved.

If more formal co-operative arrangements must be understood within the context of interpersonal relations in the village, this is true *a fortiori* of informal ones. Informal patterns of collaboration and reciprocity are in fact best seen as part of the more general fabric of interaction between villagers. Help with some task on the farm does not seem to be distinguished sharply by the people from help in other contexts, though there are some

Plate 9 A co-operative task at the planning stage

pressures towards this. When the car of a farmer I was travelling with got stuck in deep snow, he got one of his neighbours to haul him out with a tractor. This was seen by both of them as part of the give and take of a broader long-term relationship, rather than a one-off piece of help, though there are problems which can occasionally arise in such a case. Like their counterparts elsewhere, Finnish farmers are entitled to buy cheap fuel for their agricultural work, and technically a tractor-owner who goes out to tow a friend out of a ditch should drain his tank and put in ordinary fuel. If he is caught using the cheaper, specially coloured variety, he is liable to a fine. Common sense often, of course, prevails and the risk is taken, but this is one further case, if only a small one, where the demands of the formal institutions of the outside world for clear-cut categories create problems for the more diffuse arrangements of the local community.

Payment was neither offered nor required in this last case, as opposed to the two just discussed where the recipient of help insisted upon paying generously. It is possible that here too there is individual variation, since some individuals are particularly self-conscious about the need to be 'in credit' in their links to others. There is, however, the further factor that in the first two cases, Pekka, who is relatively old and does not own a car, was not really in a position to reciprocate in kind at some time in the future. In the second case, the two farmers concerned were very comparable to each other in their ages, and in their ownership of vehicles and working farms with a good range of machinery, and there was a much more realistic basis

Plate 10 Helping out a neighbour

to the idea of an ongoing flow of help in both directions than in the first case.

Two other areas of village life are worth discussion in this context, both in themselves as forms of interaction, and also for the further light which they may throw on aspects of co-operation in other contexts, including agriculture. The first is visiting and hospitality. This can sometimes be a relatively formal matter, for instance when people are invited for some special occasion or when a meeting is held at a particular house. Sometimes there might be a family celebration such as the *lakkiaiset* to celebrate a child's success in the final school examinations, or it may be that there is a gathering for prayer and hymn-singing of the so-called Tuesday 'sewing group' (*ompeluseura*), or a Martta meeting, at a member's home. On such occasions, the 'ceremony' of drinking coffee, as Roberts (1989) interestingly calls it, takes place in a quite formal manner. But even in less restrained circumstances, when friends are simply visiting each other, taking coffee is *de rigueur* and subject to relatively strict rules of etiquette. Buns (*pulla*) and a variety of more elaborate baked confections are often served, and people have to help themselves to these in the right order (buns first), and also take their coffee in a carefully orchestrated way. Roberts (1978, 1989) has sensitively described some of these patterns. The hostess may have to announce several times that coffee is served, before she manages to persuade her apparently reluctant guests to come forward to take coffee from the table. A main problem is to get someone to break the ice and be the first to take one of the cups, and later it may be difficult to persuade people to take seconds. The guests are anxious not to appear greedy, and also not to seem to place their own requirements over those of others. Self-discipline is the order of the day.

It seems clear that the etiquette and hesitation which mark such occasions both reflect and encourage a positively valued mixture of respect for oneself and others. It would be a serious mistake to under-estimate the pressures to conform to the norms in question, but there is some reason also to suspect that attitudes towards the 'ceremonial' are more complex and ambivalent than this implies. The hesitation to be the first to take and the polite refusals to have second cups of coffee and further helpings of cake are often described by the Finnish verb *kursailla* and related words. This word apparently derives from the Swedish noun *krus*, which means 'ceremony' in the sense of 'fuss', and it is commonly translated into English as 'to stand on ceremony'. There is typically an element of criticism in its use and, along with the more positive attitudes towards the displays of self-control, one detects some impatience with the pretensions to refinement which appear to be implicit in the etiquette and ceremonial. People seem in this, as in some other contexts, to be trapped in a value system derived from urban bourgeois culture which they both approve and yet hold slightly suspect. One side of them demands conformity to the stylistic niceties involved, while the other harks back to the idea of a simple life uncluttered by such fuss and bother. Another side of the same issue comes out in one of the famous Erkki Tanttu cartoons, which are based on rural sayings and witticisms. A peasant is listening hard to a prim and proper, soft-spoken official and asks him 'Did you say something, or was it just the wind moving your lips?'

The coffee hostess herself is keen to provide a good and varied spread, which may include high-quality shop-bought gâteaus as well as the usual mixture of home-baked products. This is part of a more general emphasis, which it would be very hard to over-estimate, upon generous hospitality towards guests. Women like to have good things in stock in case of a sudden visit, and many find home freezers very valuable these days for this. Buns can be quickly thawed in the oven, and ice-cream also makes a useful standby. All this can also have its side-effects upon research, when the number of household visits and surveys one can cope with is subject to the constraints of what might be called 'the *pulla* [bun] factor'. Of course, as visitors from outside, my family and I were often given extra special treatment, but this was just an extreme statement of a general imperative that visitors to a house should be made welcome beyond the demands of practical considerations of their need for sustenance. On many occasions we visited someone's home and were given coffee, and then found when about to take our leave that food was now ready and the table reset for a meal which it would be churlish to refuse.[11] Here again one sees the pattern visible in the behaviour of Pekka K. that no one should be allowed to think or say that they received short rations at their host's home and table.

In addition to visits to each other's homes, people also sometimes meet together elsewhere. The church is an important centre for some people, and there is also a chapel for funeral services at the nearby cemetery. The parish also owns a pretty lake-side log house which some parishioners occasionally use on summer evenings, and there is a parish hall (*seurakuntatalo*) where meetings and celebrations sometimes take place. Such gatherings may also be held in the school and other civic buildings. At many such public get-togethers, coffee and food are provided as at home, and there is a parish *emäntä* who is in charge of providing these at *seurakuntalo* occasions, usually with the help of other local women. Individual reputations for generous hospitality are naturally not at stake on such occasions, but the *emäntä* and her helpers are still keen to make a good impression with their catering, and the same patterns of coffee 'ceremonial' are followed as at someone's home.

Not surprisingly, visits and other sorts of gathering form one of the main

---

[11] Roberts (1989) quotes an interesting passage from Boholm's (1983) study of Swedish kinship in which a Swedish schoolteacher who drops in on a Finnish family living in Sweden is perplexed by an irrefusable invitation to stay to dinner.

ways in which relations between villagers are developed and maintained. The patterns of multiplex relationships which Gluckman has described as typical of small communities are also found in Vieki, and people who collaborate with each other economically usually also meet in a variety of other contexts. Two farmers who collaborate as co-owners of machinery may also meet as fellow members of the church choir or at 'sewing evenings', or they may simply exchange visits from time to time. There are no hard and fast rules about this, and there is considerable variation in the extent to which families engage in these and other joint activities, such as going out on day trips with each other. This variation mostly reflects what are seen as legitimate differences of temperament and situation, for example if a family has a very heavy workload or other personal commitments. There are, however, a few families which tend to keep very closely to themselves, and this may arouse some critical gossip. Usually it appears to result from eccentricity, and I suspect that this may be a 'pathological' variant of the self-reliance fostered and encouraged by the social system. For the pattern of dispersed settlement, with each family occupying its own small kingdom, seems to permit individuals to keep to themselves and develop their own quirks of character more easily than would be the case in more compact communal settings. However this may be, such eccentricity is not as bad as any signs of a stand-offishness which might be ascribed to a desire to set oneself apart as better than one's fellow villagers. This tends to manifest itself, if at all, at the level of relations between particular families, for example if a family which often used to get together with one or more others ceases to do so. This may be interpreted by the neglected parties as stemming from an undue uppishness on the part of the others, but such judgments are not easy to assess since they can of course easily mask other tensions, even if there is a grain of truth in them.

The second pattern of activity I mentioned is the collections which people make for villagers to mark each other's special birthdays and comparable occasions. This requires a point of focus and co-ordination which is usually provided by one of the village shopkeepers. She keeps a note of imminent major birthdays (fiftieth, sixtieth, seventieth etc.) and acts as the collector of money for a joint present for the individual concerned. She keeps a list of contributors, and also provides a separate small card for each one. These are presented in a neatly tied bundle for the 'birthday heroine or hero' (*syntymäpäiväsankari*). It is clear that some individuals give more gener-ously than others on such occasions, and it is also true that people who are popular tend to receive more from more people. It would be misleading to give the impression that any serious tally of such matters was kept. This would be disruptive of relations between villagers, and would almost certainly damage the efficacy of the collection system. None the less the system offers people an opportunity to express their regard for each other, and it is a further small testament to the role of temperament and popularity in collaborative activity. It was interesting in this regard that one villager who gave a party on his fiftieth birthday and sent out invitations for it was the subject of some critical comment for doing so. It is true that the man had already created some stir in the village in another context, and this may have tempted people to be more critical than they might otherwise have been. But the point they made appears to have been a valid one. It is customary to invite people to wedding and funeral parties, and to examination celebrations, but such birthday parties should, it seems, be open-house affairs which people should feel free to come to *if they wish* to congratulate the person concerned.

Conclusion

It will, I hope, be clear from the material I have presented in this chapter that Finnish farmers interact co-operatively with each other in a wide variety of interlocking ways. As I noted at the start of my discussion, this presents a paradox when it is juxtaposed with the typical picture of the farmer as a fiercely individualistic and self-reliant figure. As I have hinted, the resolution of this problem lies largely in the idea of choice and, with it, the distinction between co-operation and enforced collectivism. Also important is the further point, which has so far remained implicit in my account, that agricultural co-operation does not impinge upon the individual relation between a farming family and the income from the product of their own farm. Indeed one commentator (Köppä, 1979, pp. 56–7) has noted that even the use of shared equipment tends to be limited to mobile machinery rather than to relatively permanent and fixed resources such as shared cowsheds, which are very rare.

Finnish farmers are not, of course, alone in their desire to maintain their individual identity and that of their farm, and in fact this seems to be a widespread trait of farmers both within and outside Europe.[12] It is, moreover, arguable more generally that one will always find some element of tension between a person's consciousness of his identity and the demands which arise from his relationship to others. This is implicit in the very concepts of the social person and society, and it typically involves opposing tendencies within the cultural and social system, rather than being simply a conflict between society and the 'individual' as some sort of given psycho-biological entity. It would take me too far afield to discuss this point in detail here, but the sorts of tensions in question are well illustrated in many kinship institutions, such as levirate (see Abrahams, 1973), which are

---

[12] See the discussions of this issue in Abrahams (1981 and 1985) for some African evidence.

predicated at one and the same time on the social and cultural definition of both the equivalence and the separate identity of siblings and other kin.

Even so, it would still be hard to find a group who were more self-conscious and more explicit than Finnish farmers about their wish for independence, at the same time as they develop and maintain their links with others. The result is predictably a delicate compromise. People are extremely jealous of their freedom and of their individual reputations for hard work and honest dealing, while they also value in themselves and others a willingness to participate in the community and to lend a ready hand to others when needed. But sociability and co-operation must not be allowed to impinge noticeably upon people's sense of their own privacy and independence.

One should, for instance, take an interest in the welfare of one's neighbours, but this should none the less be kept within strict limits, and it should never in the slightest smack of nosiness. Thus one woman told me how her children used to visit a neighbouring house when they were young. The *emäntä* there used to chat with the children, but their mother became quite indignant when she learned that they were asked what they had had for breakfast or for lunch. This was seen as an unwarranted infringement of the privacy of her home, and as a potential source of tally-keeping of her reputation as farm-wife and mother. She therefore told the children they were not to go there any more. It is not surprising, in this regard, that most people are quite wary of asking direct questions of each other, and it is fortunate for an anthropologist that research is a respected occupation which excuses what would otherwise often be a serious breach of good manners. Once again, of course, there is individual variation in such matters. One farmer, who was well known for his jovial directness, greeted me one day with the question 'Well, have you been keeping faithful to your wife?' Even though this was a joke rather than a genuine question expecting an answer, I know of no one else in the community who would have asked it. People partly explain away such sallies by reference to the man's Karelian origins, and beyond this they respect and like him as a hardworking and co-operative neighbour. None the less they recognise that such behaviour is unusual. At the other extreme, I have watched as a farmer has shuffled uncomfortably on his chair before asking my wife if he could ask her a 'personal question'. Given permission, he then went on to ask 'Was your father a mining engineer or a railway engineer?'! While such a high degree of diffidence is also exceptional, most people operate well towards the more hesitant and tactful end of the continuum between extremes of caution and directness, and they generally prefer to err in that direction if they are at all uncertain of the outcome.

Similarly, it is good to shine, but only within limits, and one should certainly not show off and appear to wish to assert social superiority over others. In general people are anxious to appear as good as the next family, and to stress the importance of personal qualities rather than other sources of worth. In the old days, it is clear that a major social gap developed between the landed and the landless sectors of the population, and although it was less salient in the North Karelian region than in western areas of Finland, the idea of 'gentry' (*herrasväki*) was to some extent important here as elsewhere. This type of class distinction has largely if not wholly passed away from modern villages, and as far as I can tell most people are quite glad to see the back of it and welcome its replacement by the more egalitarian ethic which tends to prevail these days. The good reputation of a family is still of vital interest, but it is felt to be based directly on personal qualities. Of course, this is more complicated than it seems, since in this context as elsewhere, individuals may easily be held largely to blame for problems which to some degree have structural roots, and it is arguable that this is especially likely in a society like the one under consideration where a protestant ethic of personal responsibility is strongly developed. Thus one can hear criticism from time to time of families, especially in the backwoods areas outside the main village, whose members are said to live off welfare rather than hard work and to drink more than they should, as well as sometimes getting on the wrong side of the law, perhaps through keeping an unlicensed car. Character flaws are clearly often involved in such cases, but it seems plausible also that such problems are more likely to develop in the depressed conditions of more remote rural areas. I may also add that even among the more general run of respectable families, differences of relative esteem occasionally emerge from contexts in which character may play a lesser role than good fortune in one guise or another. How well children have performed in the school-leaving examinations, for example, and their subsequent careers and status in the outside world, can be a source of pride to some and a minor irritant to others.

Here once again the presence of opposing trends becomes apparent. It would be in quite poor taste for someone to appear to gloat over such differences, but this does not, of course, prevent their being registered and thought about. At the same time, their significance does not stem simply from their divisive potential within the community. For they are also reminders for villagers of the problematic future of their community and the family farms within it, and of the further fact that these exist within a wider society whose powerful urban, industrial and bureaucratic trends and values are not wholly consonant with their own. We have seen that many village families manage to participate to quite a high degree in both these worlds, though this can be at the cost of knowing that their farming enterprise will cease when the present *isäntä* and *emäntä* retire. But such participation can only mitigate rather than eradicate the contrasts in question and the mixed attitudes of villagers towards them. I remember being touched by the slightly regretful and almost apologetic tone of one successful farmer – who was in general firmly committed to the values of village life – when he informed me that he had never been to Helsinki. My response that few Helsinki people had been to Vieki seemed to amuse and warm him, but such thoughts cannot do much to redress the uneven balance between centre and periphery.

7

Farming families in a changing world

As I noted in my introductory chapter, it is probable that a majority of the world's working population still engages in agricultural production upon family farms. Of course, both the numbers and the regional distribution of such farms have changed dramatically in the last century or so, as too has the extent to which farming families are dependent on the produce of their holdings for their livelihood. These changes have arisen partly through commercial and industrial expansion in Europe and elsewhere, and also – at least temporarily – in the wake of collectivisation and other economic experiments in countries such as China, the USSR and Tanzania. If reports of the demise of Socialism in the late 1980s have not been, as Mark Twain put it of his own case, 'an exaggeration', it is probable that forms of family farming will arise again out of the ashes of the *kolkhoz* and of *ujamaa*. At the same time it is possible that the development of 'green' consciousness in some of the more industrialised areas of Europe may do something to regenerate the family farm there also, if only on a minor scale.

However this may be, anthropological research into such farming within modern Europe may easily appear to be an odd if not a self-indulgent exercise. Family farms have become such a small part of the total economic system of countries such as Britain, France, Germany, Sweden and Finland, as well as many countries of the 'Eastern Bloc', that one might be tempted to consider them as at best a 'dying art form', as a Finnish businessman without strong rural ties once put it to me, and a marginal curiosity which scarcely deserves serious study. They are, however, worth an anthropologist's attention for a number of related reasons besides the deceptively simple fact that, like the mountaineer's mountains, 'they are there'. Such farms and the rural communities to which they belong often occupy a much more prominent place in a society's value system than their numbers and their quantitative contribution to the national economy might seem to merit. Partly this reflects the way a country wishes to define and represent its national character, and partly too it relates to deep-seated feelings of the need to maintain some degree of self-sufficiency in food supplies. Again, despite some protestations to the contrary, such farms and the communities they compose can also provide actor and observer alike with an instructive contrast to the industrial and commercial urban world to which they seem to be appended.[1] As this point implies, similarities and differences between such farms, at varying times both within and outside Europe, may also be a matter of some wider interest.

It will be clear from the material I have presented that the presence and future of family farms in modern Finland is a problematic issue. For such farms do not 'simply exist'. They are the result of a complex history of social, political and economic change, in which families have had to try to adapt to changing circumstances as best they can. Since the beginning of the century, the proportion of the economically active population engaged in agriculture and forestry has fallen sharply from around 80 per cent to slightly over 10 per cent, and a substantial part of this decline has taken place during the lifetime of present farmers. Many of the forces at work in these changes have been quite beyond the control of those tossed about by them, but this does not mean that survival has been purely random. Chance has entered into it in a variety of ways, but so too have determination, work and the ability to adapt to new demands. As I have tried to show, the resilience and flexibility of response which a farming family can display, as both moral community and workforce, is impressive, and what such a family temporarily lacks in its own resources can often be made good through collaboration between kin and neighbours. Of course, the relatively small scale of family farms can appear wasteful of time, labour and equipment, but there is no shortage of cases of unsuccessful development plans and state interventions to show that large-scale, 'rational', agricultural enterprises are often less effective and adaptive than *a priori* argument might lead their supporters to assume.[2]

The place of agriculture in a nation's value system is extremely difficult to assess since it commonly involves a complex combination of strong sentiments and vested political and economic interests. As writers like

[1] See Mendras (1970, Chapter 6). See Newby (1977, p. 100 and passim) for arguments, based on large-scale farming in East Anglia, that modern rural society does not differ fundamentally from other areas of modern industrial society. In a later publication (1980, pp. 34, 41, 66, 81 and passim), Newby takes a more positive approach towards some forms of 'rural' sociology, while remaining justifiably critical of simplistic and idealistic dichotomies.
[2] For an interesting critique of large-scale state intervention in a third-world context see Hart (1982, pp. 89, 93–4). Rappaport (1978, pp. 49–71) raises general issues of the maladaptation of large-scale centralised systems for performing such tasks. See Warriner (1964, Chapter 8 and passim) for a balanced comparison of family farming and collective systems.

Howard Newby and Raymond Williams have shown, this is a well-known fertile zone for myth to flourish.[3] Country areas may be idealised, especially in industrial societies, as the last outposts of a slower, better life unpolluted by the smoke and other effluents of the city. In Britain such ideas are long established, and many a Victorian painting was devoted to the peaceful cottages and landscapes, and the cheerful villagers of this rural world. More recently, television series like *All Creatures Great and Small* have helped almost despite themselves to perpetuate this vision. The programmes are set in the past, but advertising literature for the Yorkshire Dales stresses the continuity with the present. Moreover, though the Dales are, indeed, exceptionally beautiful and peaceful, this is in many ways a result of the very industrial revolution to which one tends to contrast their qualities. Much of the contemporary economy of the area depends on tourism by those anxious to escape the city and the crowded main arterial roads, whereas in the past it was clearly extremely hard to make a living there, and many people left to seek their fortunes in the towns. Indeed, until the end of the nineteenth century, many of the most beautiful modern sites were scarred by working lead-mines, whose remains are now passed off, not wholly convincingly, as a tourist attraction in themselves, and these seem to have provided a vital supplement to the meagre incomes which many people could expect to get from farming.[4]

In a country like Britain, where industrialisation and urbanisation have occurred on a grand scale relatively early, conceptions and misconceptions about rural life have commonly provided little more than a welcome sense that not all is lost. It is true that public concern for the environment has significantly increased in recent years, and politicians feel compelled to express their awareness of pollution problems. But the time when agriculture was the mainstay of our economic life is too far past for Kipling's sentimental verses about Sussex yeomen, or even Blake's genuinely emotive visions of a 'green and pleasant land', to provide an effective basis for most Britons' sense of their identity, except perhaps in time of crisis. And farmers are themselves now often blamed for water pollution and other forms of ecological deterioration.

The situation in Finland is somewhat different, since the growth of industry and towns is much more recent there. Very many urban Finns – though by no means all – have relatively recent rural origins, and they maintain good connections with the villages from which they or their parents have migrated. Many of them own areas of forest or other land

[3] Newby (1977, pp. 10–22); Williams (1973, p. 96 and passim).
[4] For an interesting discussion of Dales tourism see Alan Bennett's article in the *Guardian* (16 December 1989).

there, and they tend to make regular visits for winter ski breaks or for summer holidays. They have grown up on farms, and they retain a genuine nostalgia for the peaceful spaciousness of rural life, the berries, and of course the forests and the lakes. This point was made clear to me on a number of occasions, but never more sharply than when I accompanied a young engineering student on an evening fishing trip. He had just returned home to the village for a few days' break from his industrial training course, and it was impossible not to notice the sheer pleasure which he took simply in breathing and in seeing, and in treading well-known paths down to the lake. All this does not imply that those who leave the countryside would readily give up the salaries and creature comforts that urban life can offer them, or that they forget the drudgery and other hardship which farming can impose. But it does mean that rural life is a more deeply engrained and immediate experience for them than for most Britains, and that the idea of a fundamentally agrarian Finnish spirit is a much more realistic one, despite industrial development and settlement patterns, than would be the case for Britain.

This said, it must also be admitted that there are elements of ideological commitment and political persuasion in views of this sort. As I have discussed, the fostering of the idea of Finland as a country of independent farming villagers has been connected with the long history of struggles to achieve and maintain the country's independence from external domination. It appears to have been part of the early development of a national self-consciousness, and later it became a weapon in the political struggles of non-Communists to keep the country free of Soviet influence and control. This aspect of the situation emerged in its most extreme form in the participation of farmers in the Lapua movement of the early 1930s. There sentiments of close attachment to the land and farming took on strong right-wing overtones, as they were pumped up and harnessed to express the violent hostility of the movement's members to those on the left, who were portrayed as a threat to farmers' rights to own and manage their farms for themselves. In more recent and more peaceful years, more moderate feelings of attachment and commitment to farming and the land have helped many Finnish farmers to survive in agriculture under the demanding conditions of the modern Finnish economy, and the idea of a fundamentally rural Finland has also sometimes been exploited in the debates over fiscal support for agriculture and the division of the national cake between town and country. Although they can involve strong disagreements, it seems likely that such debates are somewhat tempered for the present by the close ties between town and country dwellers I have mentioned, and they may well grow more serious as generations pass and such ties become more tenuous and lose their force.

Continuity and change

Although one can readily distinguish on an abstract level between concepts such as growth, continuity and change, it can be much more difficult to choose between them when attempting to delineate real social processes.[5] In Finland, as elsewhere, the comparability of modern family farms to earlier patterns, and indeed to present forms in other countries, is thus predictably not wholly a straightforward matter. As I have shown, many Vieki farming families are descended from long lines of farming ancestors who farmed some of the same land in their own day. Like such ancestors, many of these modern families produce milk and vegetables for their own use, and many farm-wives bake their own rye bread, sometimes with flour from their home-grown rye. They also often weave their own floor coverings. In general, the labour of running a Vieki farm is, as it was two hundred years ago, almost wholly provided by members of the immediate farm family.

It is easy in such circumstances to think in terms of continuities from the past, but such a view is clearly quite misleading in a number of important ways. Modern family farms are the result of a long history of change and adaptation to new opportunities and pressures, rather than a simple replication of past forms. Since the beginning of the nineteenth century there have been large numbers of quite influential new developments. The growth of a money and market economy and of farmers' involvement in it, the steady rise and later fall of village populations, the creation and dispersion of a large landless class, political independence, industrialisation and the availability of tractors and other new technology are but some of the main factors which have shaped the modern face of family farming in the area. Thus, if modern farming families largely provide their own labour force on their own farms as their ancestors once did, they do so in a vastly different economic and political context, and in response to various opportunities provided by contemporary industrial development, rather than as a simple survival of some earlier 'domestic mode of production'. Moreover, the persistence of the present farming families in the area has been only one result of a process in which many earlier families were doomed to agricultural inviability, if not worse, irrespective of whatever they might try to do about it.

Finnish farmers are themselves, of course, quite well aware that life is very different now from what it was even a few decades ago; and they mostly welcome the material improvements in living standards which have become increasingly available to them from the industrial world in the form of cars,

---

[5] See Abrahams (1967, Chapter 6) for a discussion of such problems with regard to political office.

freezers, televisions and modern plumbing. Nor are they opposed to improvements in social and welfare facilities, and they are naturally anxious to preserve these against erosion as village populations decline. Farmers are part of the modern world, and they are keen to be so. And yet, when all this has been said, it is also true that rural life and family farming do have genuinely special and somewhat old-fashioned qualities, which are attractive to the actors and consciously pursued by them.

A major element here is the opportunity for independent choice and action, and responsibility for one's own affairs, which farming offers and which farmers much appreciate, despite the fact that choices are made and actions undertaken under changing political and economic constraints over which they have had little control. This last problem is, however, not at all confined to farming; and farmers value highly the fact that they at least have their own family enterprise and do not need to 'clock on' and 'clock off' at set hours in someone else's factory or business. Closely coupled with this emphasis on responsibility and independence, which I need scarcely say can also serve to mask the force and influence of structural constraints, there is also a strong faith that, although good fortune helps, organisational ability and the capacity for sustained hard work (*sisu*) on behalf of oneself and one's family are essential and can bring just rewards to those possessing them. Hard work in particular is deeply respected, even though people are aware that it can leave its scars in later life if it is done to excess by some individuals who are described with a mixture of admiration, awe and occasionally critical regret as 'work-mad' (*työhullu*). Certainly, even such excess is much preferred to laziness and 'slowness to turn round', as one man put it pithily. And it is a substantial compliment to describe someone as energetic, strong and not afraid of work, which are qualities encapsulated in the single short word *riski*. Nor are such qualities seen simply as vital for survival in a minimal sense. For farming is perceived as a creative occupation, not merely because farmers grow things, but because they also mould and modify their often unpromising natural environment through stone-clearing, draining and other soil-improvement techniques. Farmers and their families often take considerable pride in the work they have put into such improvements either directly or through creating in other contexts the wherewithal to hire specialised contractors for the work.

A further aspect of the situation can be seen in the development of farm mechanisation. As I have described, the ability of modern farmers to maintain and improve their farms is firmly based on access to machinery which is capable of far more than the mere replacement of a dwindling labour force. Yet, although farmers have become thoroughly dependent on machines, Finnish farming has not typically moved away from older organisational patterns in which the machine remains an extension of the person rather than vice versa; and it is clear, as Mendras has discussed for France, that the central role of families in agriculture helps to guarantee this.[6] Farming is still imbued with family morality, in which concern for the welfare of family members and their reputation in the wider community are key elements, and it still retains a vital domestic quality in spite of its deep involvement in the market economy and the state. Farmers are becoming more and more like businessmen, but at least in North Karelia and, as far as I can see, most other parts of Finland, they are also typically at the same time, and more importantly in the same context, family members.

This familial and domestic quality of modern farming is expressed in a variety of ways. For example, although milk production has become increasingly commercialised, dairy herds still tend to be treated in a relatively personalised way as collections of individually named and known animals with which the life of an *emäntä*, and often nowadays her husband, is inextricably bound up. I might add here that despite the very different circumstances of cattle-keeping in East Africa, I have been struck by the similarity of comments made to me in this regard by Tanzanian herders and by Finnish dairy farmers. Both stress the unceasingly demanding nature of a herd which sometimes seems to own and to exploit the farmer rather than vice versa, and both have left me with the impression that it is only by establishing a personal relation to a herd that farmers can cope with the constant pressures which the animal impose.

Certain attitudes to bread and rye are also interesting in this context, and perhaps especially because rye does not constitute a major source of local income for Vieki farmers. Rye bread is a major staple in the Finnish diet, and in the past each family liked to produce its bread from its own grain. Most modern farm-wives still prefer to bake their own rye bread, which varies in flavour from *emäntä* to *emäntä*, and from oven to oven, and such bread is often an acceptable, and on some occasions a customary, personal gift from one household to another. Rather fewer people grow their own rye these days in this area, however, since it is not always a reliable crop and its production cannot easily compete with that of other economically more valuable food and fodder. Most people buy the flour from commercial suppliers, but home-grown rye is still very highly valued by those who grow it, and it is much appreciated by others to whom it may be given. In 1982 I was present when one farmer harvested a good rye crop grown in a small field without artificial fertilisers. I was deeply impressed by the pleasure and excitement which this generated in his own family and among some friends to whom he gave some of the grain. It was plain that the element of self-provisioning involved, and the potential for reciprocity with relatives and

[6] Mendras (1970, pp. 83–7).

friends who shared his sentiments, both contributed to the high symbolic value of the crop and bread baked from it, which far outstripped any commercial value they might have. It is not, I think, too fanciful to see here the assertion of fundamental values about farming as an occupation and a way of life, in which human beings can ideally look after themselves and their families and collaborate with others without losing their identity and integrity as productive individuals. At the same time, of course, it is also clear from the same data that the forces of alienation and commercialisation are by no means wholly absent from the farmer's world.

My line of argument so far suggests that legitimate comparison is possible between contemporary and older forms of family farming in this area, despite the complex history of modern farming and its location in a political and economic setting very different from that of the eighteenth and early nineteenth centuries. At some risk of caricature, we can note that this modern wider world is typically marked by high levels of impersonality and formal rationality, and by sharp differences both between work place and home and between the owners of an enterprise and its workforce. Past and present family farms, both individually and in collaboration, have clearly tended to operate on very different principles. I should stress that I have no wish to deny either the existence of the personal and informal in many areas of urban interaction or the very powerful influence of the wider world on modern farming.[7] I have indeed already noted several ways in which this influence can be detected even in some of the most apparently 'traditional' aspects of farm life. Nor do I wish to suggest that when we compare such modern farms with earlier ones or, for that matter, with contemporary farms in less 'developed' societies, we are dealing simply with the presence in the one case and the absence in the others of vitally important wider institutions.

One need only mention the long history of feudal institutions to dispel at once the idea that one might find any form of 'natural' domestic economy in most of Europe since at least the middle ages. In such systems, and especially in the more oppressive forms of eastern European serfdom, the demand for 'rent' has sometimes even seriously impaired the capacity of families to support themselves by farming.[8] It is also well known, though sometimes forgotten, that familial systems of succession (and with them the life histories of members of the families concerned) have typically been interesting to a much wider range of parties than those most immediately involved as family members. Goody (1983) and others have taught us, for example, how the history of testamentary succession in Europe is intimately

[7] See Newby (1980, pp. 23–6).
[8] See Kula (1976, pp. 65–6), Plakans (1973) and Raun (1987, pp. 30, 43).

connected with the history of the church.[9] Similarly, there is strong evidence suggesting that systems of primogeniture are very often the result of direct political influence upon peasant families from above, and it seems clear that, more generally, the formal patterns of inheritance of many peasant families in Europe owed more to the strategies and interests of their masters than to their own calculations and perceptions.[10] Again, as Plakans has noted, the size and structure of some peasant households, and the domestic architecture of their dwellings, probably resulted from the heavy demands of estate-owners for produce and labour, and from their control over building materials.[11]

Compared with their unfortunate counterparts in many other areas of Europe, including the south Baltic littoral, earlier generations of Finnish farmers were for the most part not excessively oppressed by such demands and constraints from above. None the less, they were significant sources of food, labour and taxation for the state and other sections of the population, and they were sometimes the victims of predatory violence from officials such as Simo Affleck, whose activities I discussed in Chapter 2. It has also been quite clear to villagers themselves and others that the size and structure of the families resident on farms were relevant to the ways in which they could avoid or satisfy the demands made upon them. Peasants have at times been tempted to avoid tax by creating, through partition, numerous small units which fell below the threshold of taxable size and productivity; or they have sometimes tried to avoid partition if the tax burden of a single large farm was smaller than that of two lesser ones.[12] Governments are naturally likely to be keen to make such strategies more difficult, or perhaps to exploit the fear of taxation in order to promote certain types of structure over others.

In the eighteenth century, when some of the main groundwork for the creation of present-day agricultural communities in eastern Finland took place, problems of labour and food supply loomed specially large.[13] Finland was still part of the Swedish kingdom, which ceded its possession of important southern Baltic shorelands to Peter the Great's Russia in the early years of the century. These Baltic lands had been the 'granary' of the kingdom, and there was much anxious discussion about possibilities of making up their loss in other ways. 'Demographic politics', to use Witold Kula's apt phrase, were the order of the day, and several proposals were

[9] J. Goody (1983, Chapter 6). See also Maine (1972, p. 102) and Jutikkala (1958, p. 51).
[10] See Wolf (1966, p. 76) and Goldschmidt and Kunkel (1971, p. 1070 and passim).
[11] See also McArdle (1974) for a comparison between Plakans's (1973) material and Tuscan conditions.
[12] See Löfgren (1974, pp. 23, 47) and also Voionmaa (1915, pp. 247–8).
[13] My source for this discussion of eighteenth-century debates is Jutikkala (1958, pp. 234ff.).

focussed upon strategies for increasing the supply of peasant labourers on aristocratic estates, so that food production on these could be raised to make up the shortfall.[14] Indeed it seems likely that the estate-owners in question looked with envy on the powers which landlords could exercise over their serfs in some of the lost lands. The Swedish Diet heard suggestions that peasants should be pushed to marry earlier under the threat of conscription into the army if they failed to do so. It was hoped that early marriage would lead to a higher peasant birth rate and a resulting increased labour supply. Other proposals involved tightening already-existing regulations upon the number of people who could legally stay on a farm, since tighter rules would drive more people off the farms and, it was hoped, on to the estates as labourers. Some realised, however, that rules of this sort would make it harder for such dispossessed peasant men to marry, since a man needed a farm in order to attract a wife. In the end, for reasons which seem to have been partly philosophical and partly political, but not especially concerned with the well-being of the peasantry itself, the king decided to promote a policy of agricultural expansion through further smallholding in outlying areas of which eastern Finland was one.

The question of possible similarities between modern European institutions and those of so-called traditional societies in other continents is more thorny, and comparisons across cultural and historical boundaries of this magnitude are often thought to be quite hazardous. In fact there has been a common tendency to depict stark contrasts between modern western and traditional 'other' cultural and social systems, such as those of Africa or Melanesia, and most anthropologists of course go well beyond this to explore the differences between such traditional systems themselves.[15] Such contrasts between modern 'west' and 'rest' have developed from the classic work of earlier writers such as Maine, Morgan, Durkheim and Tönnies, and they also have a modern grounding in some of the sensitive analyses of ethnographic data more recently collected at first hand. I need scarcely remark that such detailed ethnographic studies constitute one of anthropology's most vital contributions to our understanding of ourselves and others. Yet such work also has to bear relation to our need to generalise, and an anthropology which seeks to take its stand on one or other side of a divide between the general and the particular must suffer from a self-imposed impoverishment. I realise that for many writers a more general contrast between 'us' and 'them' provides a sort of bridge between the two

---

[14]   Kula (1976, pp. 46–7). See Vuorela (1987, pp. 26–31, 33) for a discussion of some aspects of such politics in a modern third-world setting and also references to French historical material. I am told that political concern is rising in Estonia about low Estonian, as compared to Russian, birth rates in the country, so that slogans are now heard encouraging people to 'fill Estonia with Estonians'.

[15]   For a recent example of such macro-level and micro-level contrasts see Strathern (1989).

sides of this argument, since it permits comparison and contrast among 'other' cultures and societies within a posited broad range of similarities, which in turn serve to mark them off from 'us'. This is what Gluckman, for example, tried to do in his critique of Bohannan's so-called 'tivnocentric' viewpoint, claiming that law and dispute settlement among the Tiv of Nigeria were similar to many other traditional forms, including certain early English ones, which in turn could jointly be distinguished from our own modern patterns.[16] Yet it is also possible that other societies are, in some respects at least, considerably more like those of modern Europe than such arguments suggest. In addition, there is arguably some danger that simplistic views of modern Europe, which are often used as a contrastive backdrop to our investigations of 'the other', are by no means as well grounded as our fieldwork-based analyses in other continents.

There is no simple, general answer to these problems of comparison. An example of some of the issues involved in the field of kinship, marriage and the family is interestingly provided once again by Gluckman (1950) in his well-known study of the Lozi, in what is now western Zambia, and the Zulu of Natal. Gluckman contrasts the patrilineal emphasis in Zulu kinship with the equilateral tendencies of the Lozi system, and he asserts a connection between these two contrasting features and the patterns of marital stability in the two societies. He argues that a low divorce rate is predictable in patrilineal systems like that of the Zulu, whereas in the Lozi and similar systems marriage is likely to be much less stable. At the same time he suggests, however, that such a correlation is only to be posited for tribal social systems lacking the complexities of large-scale, modern society.[17] Here he probably had in mind the influence of powerful institutions like the Christian church upon divorce, and such an argument can easily be expanded to encompass a wide range of similar phenomena, as my earlier discussion of inheritance suggests. Put simply, the issue is the implications of the contrast, at least at the level of ideal types, between simpler societies where kinship and marriage are, so to speak, 'do it yourself' systems, and more complex ones in which major decisions on such matters may be made not by the people themselves but by those in power, and at times even against the interests and wishes of those on whom they are imposed.

I have already given some examples of such external legislation in the Finnish context. On the other hand, I have also shown that in this case, as elsewhere, the complexity of the situation, and with it the nature of the contrast itself, does not simply stop there. If it did so, then the study of family systems in European societies would tend simply to be a sub-branch of the study of law and the state, and of their interaction with religious and

---

[16] Bohannan (1957); Gluckman (1965, pp. 209–13). See also Epstein (1967, pp. 212–14).
[17] Gluckman (1950, p. 206).

economic tendencies and forces. It is arguable, though, that the problems posed by such a study are compounded, and at the same time partly by-passed, by the fact that European villagers and other 'ordinary people' are not simply the passive recipients of rules from above. For, as we have seen, they are typically adaptive and manipulative in their reactions to the varied influences which impinge upon them.[18]

At the same time, it should be remembered that, even in African and other 'traditional' societies, families and households also operate in wider settings which can influence their form and economic viability. In their immediate vicinity, there are typically other units with which they collaborate, and beyond this level there lies one or other form of polity. It is interesting here that Esther Goody has suggested that the cognatic kinship system of the Zambian Lozi, like that of the Ghanaian Gonja whom she herself has studied, fits well with their patterns of state organisation; and it seems clear that, along with ecological constraints, these two related elements of kinship and the state have together strongly influenced household and village structures in these two societies.[19]

An example from my own research in Tanzania may further illustrate some African connections between farming households and the wider society. The Nyamwezi have been mixed farmers, cultivating grain and other crops and keeping livestock, for at least two centuries and probably much longer. Prior to independence, they lived in villages under the control of chiefs and headmen. Traditionally, the chiefs were said to be the 'owners of the land'. Most generally this meant that those who lived on chiefdom land were the chief's subjects, but it also involved some claims to rights of control over the inheritance of plots by villagers. In pre-colonial times of peace, the population seems to have been fairly mobile. In times of fighting, between chiefdoms or with enemies from outside the area, mobility was restricted, and extended families farmed fields in the vicinity of compact village settlements where they enjoyed a higher level of security than more scattered forms of residence could offer. The area was placed under German colonial rule in 1890. Some early pockets of resistance were forcibly repressed, and the subsequent peace was then disrupted by the First World War. All these events seriously affected family life and economic activities for many villagers. Later, with 'Pax Britannica', the people began to move out to more scattered settlements in which married men and their dependants built their homesteads in their own fields. These settlements passed through successive phases of growth, saturation and decline as people first moved into them and then, when soils deteriorated, individual families were impelled to seek new land elsewhere. At this time, with the

---

[18] Berkner and Mendels (1978).
[19] E. N. Goody (1973, pp. 3076–8). See also Abrahams (1978b, pp. 79–85).

main exception of the colonial government's enforced resettlement of villagers from tsetse areas, villagers were relatively free to adapt to changing family and environmental circumstances by movement from one village and one chiefdom to another. Chiefs were keen to gain new subjects, and the chiefdom and village system provided an organisational framework into which newcomers could readily move and farm in a well-ordered social setting. Many of a family's neighbours were not related to them by kinship, and forms of neighbourhood collaboration in farming, building and other activities including dispute settlement were highly developed. After independence, Socialist policies of *ujamaa* and subsequent 'villagisation' programmes led to the emergence of new forms of collective farming, and to the compulsory resettlement of most people into specially created compact villages. Elementary families were now allocated one-acre plots in these new villages, and they were also given access to both communal and individually held land in the surrounding area. More recently, as these policies have been relaxed, people are beginning to drift back to their former holdings and their associated patterns of more scattered settlement. I have dealt with most of these changing patterns in some detail elsewhere, and I need not elaborate further on them here.[20] It will be clear, however, that the people in question have a long history of settlement and farming in conditions whose ground rules were largely laid down for them by the various political regimes under which they lived. These regimes at different times, in peace and war, encouraged or restricted the mobility of villagers, and they also seriously affected their domestic settlement and land-use patterns. At the same time, it is also clear that the people themselves have a long history of adaptation to such pressures.

Comparable though contextually varying arguments can be adduced for other so-called simpler societies, where the embeddedness of households within systems of lineage or age-group organisation can be shown to exercise an influence upon the patterns of domestic life, including agricultural and other economic activities.[21] Yet where does all this lead us? Part of my discussion highlights the existence of a gulf between the past and present forms of Finnish family farming. On the other hand, I have also tried to argue that there are none the less real elements of comparability between the two, and in addition that comparison is also possible between them both and family farming in a range of other socio-political environments. What form can such comparison take?

It may be useful here to recall that the same kind of problem of a mixed bag of similarities and differences recurs in a variety of forms in the

---

[20] See Abrahams (1967 and 1981) for a more detailed treatment of the material discussed here. For post-villagisation settlement in the same area see Wily (1988).
[21] See J. Goody (1958) and Abrahams (1978a).

literature on rural social systems. Some writers, for example, ask in what circumstances African villagers can usefully be called peasants, while others wonder when the term is and is not applicable to European farmers. Similarly, many scholars have debated where and when feudalism begins and ends.[22] There is no clear agreement on these issues, and more generally there is no guarantee that different writers will use terms like 'feudal' or 'peasant' in exactly the same way. Indeed, the divergent origins and root meanings of the words for 'peasant' in such languages as English, German, Swahili and Finnish suggest that, in that case at least, full cross-cultural convergence is unlikely.[23]

It would take me too far astray here to engage in a detailed review of these concepts, and I will only comment briefly on some issues which may be enlightening in the present context. In any case, the literature on them is already vast and the choices of approach and definition available are relatively clear. One can attempt to define 'peasants' in a range of different ways – by what they do and how and where they do it, for example – or one can concentrate on the broader notions of a 'peasant society' in which elements such as town and country, land-owner and tenant, high and low culture, constitute a series of more or less related pairs of opposites. The identification of such approaches and associated variables seems more valuable for comparative purposes than at least some attempts to make a set of rigid categories of peasant and non-peasant farms and systems. Certainly, peasants as family farmers, however else we might define them, seem to share important qualities with other family farmers whom we might wish for other reasons to exclude from the category of peasantry. Again, in the case of feudalism, one may emphasise the lord–vassal dyad, or pursue the more inclusive setting of a 'feudal system' where the stress may be placed to a greater or lesser extent on the political or economic structure, and the extent to which land constitutes a scarce resource. Such a system characteristically exhibits many major differences from later forms of capitalist and Socialist societies, with their elements of choice, individualism and impersonality, on the one side, and state planning and state ownership of major resources on the other. Yet the rigidity of such apparently obvious distinctions may also occasionally mask similarities across their boundaries. A feudal estate and a modern village collective

[22] See Saul and Woods (1971), Fallers (1961), Hann (1985, pp. 9–11), Shanin (1971), J. Goody (1971, Chapter 1) and Beattie (1964).

[23] 'Peasant' itself and related terms, like French *paysan*, focus on the rural basis of the concept, and with this they appear to imply the opposition between town and country and, perhaps, the contrast with such terms as 'urbane' and even 'civilised'. German, however, uses what is in principle an occupational term, *Bauer*, and similar usage in Swahili, i.e. *mkulima* (literally 'cultivator'), appears to have no special connotations of inferiority of culture or of social status in Tanzania. Finnish *talonpoika* (literally 'son of the house') is different again with its special intimations of the domestic nature of the role.

farm run by an elite committee in the Soviet Union or in Tanzania might, for instance, seem more similar to those working on them than ideal delineations of them would suggest.[24]

Several issues are combined in such a case. In addition to the possibility of overlap between the categories in question, there are problems of the link between the ideal and the real and between the general and particular. An interesting attempt to deal directly with this latter problem has been made by Witold Kula in the course of his analysis of the Polish feudal system.[25] In part, Kula can be said to have rediscovered Merton's concept of the 'theory of the middle range'.[26] He asserts with disarming simplicity that one can develop models of greater or lesser degrees of abstraction of a phenomemon like feudalism. The more abstract the model, the more it will embrace, and the less close it will come to an explanation of reality in all its detail. The less abstract a model, the more specifically it will cope with the complexities of some phenomena while excluding many others from its purview. This calls to mind the zoom lens of a camera, which makes it possible to home in on different combinations of breadth and detail and to choose the one which seems most suitable for the task in hand. All this implies, perhaps over-optimistically, that such different levels of analysis genuinely correspond to levels of reality, and it tends to ignore the distinction between simple abstraction and the more selective and exaggerated model-building of Max Weber, where no simple fit between the model and reality is expected. None the less, the general point seems plausible enough, that different frames and levels of abstraction and generalisation may be complementary to each other rather than mutually exclusive.

This, however, still leaves open several questions of the kind of link one might hope to establish between different levels of abstraction in the case of family farming. Berkner and Mendels (1978) have thrown interesting light upon this issue in a study of eighteenth- and nineteenth-century European family structures and inheritance. They note that European systems of land inheritance can be classified into three basic types. Two of these are polar categories of 'strict impartibility' and its opposite, 'strictly equal partibility'. Between these two poles there is a third, middle zone – which would include the Finnish patterns I have discussed – in which various forms of preference are exercised in farm-inheritance arrangements. In such preferential systems, some farms may pass to a single heir, while others may be divided between two or more, and other children may be given their share of

[24] See Thiele (1985, p. 85 and passim) for an account of *ujamaa* villages as 'landlords'. See also n. 28 below.

[25] Kula is not formally an anthropologist, but his sensitivity to the rationale of a different social system from his own is in the best anthropological traditions. Mendras (1970) displays a comparable sensitivity when exploring peasant values and priorities.

[26] Merton (1968, pp. 39–72).

inheritance in cash or other ways. The authors show that even in societies where one of the two extreme forms is encountered, its effects on other patterns, such as those of household structure and demographic processes, are by no means easy to predict. The case of strict impartibility is said to be the more straightforward of the two, but even here other factors, including economic opportunities outside agriculture, may complicate the situation. When one turns to 'preferential' systems, the authors note their very great complexity, which stems from the interaction between their built-in flexibility and the nature of the particular demographic, ecological, political and economic circumstances in which they operate. The contrast here is somewhat similar to the classical distinction drawn by Lévi-Strauss (1949) and others between 'elementary' prescriptive and 'complex' statistical forms of marriage system. Even in the elementary systems, actual patterns of intermarriage can be rather less predictable than one might be tempted to assume. In the complex systems, however, we move into a zone in which choice is intrinsic, and the rules can tell us relatively little about who does what.

In such fundamentally optative settings, the comparison between areas or epochs may also be reminiscent of that between collections of chess games which are played within the loose constraints of different opening systems. Such opening systems are comparable in several ways. They all operate within the same main structural parameters, and they may also have the same broad aims, such as control of the board's central area. But they may pursue these aims in different ways. Broad similarities and contrasts can be recognised, such as those between open and closed formations, and immediate or deferred engagement in the centre; and more narrowly defined patterns can be recognised, such as those of the Queen's or the King's gambit. But it is hard to compare these patterns beyond pointing to the different ways in which they deal with similar problems. And when one gets down to the level of real games, a range of immediate pressures and opportunities as well as differences of skill and temperament may seriously affect the choice and the significance of moves.

This metaphor appears to have some, albeit limited, applicability to the world of farming families. On the one hand we can try, like Goody, Berkner and Mendels, and others, to identify the main features of the 'game' which such families try to play. This involves a recognition of the social and material resources and limitations of those who engage in it, and of the varying relation between these. Various strategic possibilities and potentialities, to use Goody's (1984) terminology, can be recognised, such as those of daughter and son-in-law succession and pre-mortem inheritance, and the relative degrees of freedom and constraint can be explored. On the other hand, we can examine the ways in which particular sets of people organise their lives in their own temporal and local context. Systematic and enlightening comparison, through the use of rigorously constructed formal models, is, however, difficult if not impossible with material of this sort, and the best one can hope for seems likely to be to conduct one's discourse in a language which makes sense to those familiar with the 'game' in question.

At the same time, one has to recognise that living a way of life, like that of farming villagers, is not sensibly reducible to playing games, and that in any case it certainly involves much more than any single game. It is much less clear than in chess what 'winning' might mean for the members of a Vieki farming family. Material advantage may be perceived in different ways by different actors, and moral values may compete with such perceptions and also with each other. Individual identity, the future of a family and the future of a farm are all at stake, and choices may have to be made between these as well as within the context of the opportunities and constraints which they separately offer and impose.

I shall discuss some further aspects of these questions in the following section. Returning more directly to the point at issue here, one can suggest that family farming at all times and everywhere is likely to display certain qualities. I have already tried to highlight some of these in Chapter 4 and other parts of my account, and I have noted my indebtedness to others in this context. I have mentioned the well-established fact that the family is always a dynamic social unit whose development through time can involve substantial changes in both size and structure associated with the changing phases of the life course of its members. I also noted that there is an inherent contradiction between this aspect of a family and the static characteristics of a piece of land. Family farming must involve some coming to terms between these static and dynamic elements. The ways in which this can happen will vary in their detail, depending on such factors as the heritability of holdings and the practices adopted for inheritance, and also on the possibility of extending holdings through expansion or, artificially, through technological developments which permit more intensive production on existing land. Despite such more or less detailed variations, certain general patterns of adjustment are extremely common. The most common problem faced by farming families is the failure of fit between the size of a holding and the number of potential heirs. It is, of course, in this context that rules of partibility and impartibility emerge in part as opposite solutions to a single puzzle, and that flexible responses in between these two extremes are often found in actual behaviour. It is also in this context that the recurring theme of the family farm as at once a moral and an economic unit, which is capable of great adaptive flexibility both in its internal arrangements and in its interaction with like units, is extremely clear. Beyond this level there is, as I have said, always an influential wider political and economic setting.

Here, variants of capitalism, feudalism and Socialism are some of the main external forms encountered, but I have noted that other centralised and non-centralised political structures may also play a comparable role.

Within Europe, however, variations of the three first-mentioned forms of wider setting naturally tend to be the most important. I may also add in passing that their temporal and spatial distribution appears to offer useful scope for a reasonably controlled comparative discussion and analysis of Finnish farming with that found elsewhere in the Baltic area. It would be interesting, for example, to compare family organisation and the development of social and economic differentiation among the relatively free Finnish peasantry of the eighteenth and nineteenth century with patterns and conditions prevailing among tied serfs and their successors at that time in the culturally and linguistically closely related area of Estonia. Later, and especially in the period between the two world wars, there was clearly much more common ground between the agricultural systems of the two countries, when in both cases we find important land reforms aimed at a wider distribution of land-ownership by farming families. Then the Soviet period in Estonia, and the accompanying development of *kolkhoz* and *sovkhoz* farming, marks a second sharp break between them, though both societies have seen a scaling down of agriculture as people have moved away from rural areas, and other zones of the economy have developed. Estonians are now, it seems, beginning to set up private farming once again, though it has in any case persisted in the Socialist period to a limited extent on the personal holdings of state and collective farm workers. Meanwhile the viability of Finnish family farming under capitalism has been far from unproblematic during recent decades, as I have described.

I cannot explore this matter in more detail at this stage, though I hope to do so in the future. Much of the data on the Estonian side, for example with regard to patterns of inheritance and collaboration among farmers in the present century, is only now becoming accessible to outside investigation. None the less, it is perhaps worth while to mention here one possibly related cultural phenomenon which I have already touched on in my discussion of the Finnish situation. In Finnish, the term *sisu* seems originally to have meant 'inside' or 'intestines', but nowadays it has a powerful symbolic reference approximating in some degree to the English concepts of 'guts', stamina and determination. The term has come to represent for many Finns a key feature of their national character, and it can at times take on almost religious overtones when glossed, as I once heard it, in terms of 'man's unremitting struggle with nature'. I understand, from an examination of dictionaries and discussion with Estonian scholars, that the same term exists in Estonian, but it does not carry this immense symbolic load. It simply refers in a relatively value-free way to the inner part or essence of an object or a concept.[27] Indeed one Estonian academic commented to me, when I raised this point with him, that perhaps Estonians had lost the Finnish sense of *sisu* in the course of their long and at times cruel subjection to foreign feudal domination.[28] It is perhaps more likely that the particular Finnish emphases in the term have been bolstered in the course of the ideological developments of the last century or so, and in any case there is reason to believe that comparable ideas are expressed in other ways, if not so strongly, in Estonian.[29] None the less, it is clear that the special nature of the *sisu* concept in Finland fits extremely closely with the commonly expressed ideals of independent individualism among family farmers there. It is also possibly significant of new developments and trends in Estonia that a recent American observer in the country reports that several people whom he met asserted that Estonians were more individualistic than the Russians.[30] In addition, it may be worth noting that I have encountered some small but not, perhaps, surprising evidence that independent Estonian farmers felt a strong sense of commitment to and respect for the land which they farmed. This seems closely comparable to the Finnish idea of *maahenki* (literally 'land-spirit'), which I discuss in a later section of this chapter. It is also interesting that the evidence in question – a detailed résumé of a novel about *kolkhoz* farmers – further suggests the absence of such deep-seated sensitivities among those recruited to the *kolkhoz* from an urban background.[31]

As my earlier discussion has implied, it is in general quite hard to predict the exact nature of the outcome of relations between family farmers and the wider world encapsulating them. This world may legally define the patterns of land holding and inheritance, and it may lay down important ground rules concerning the production and distribution of farm produce. In a highly oppressive feudal system, in which heavy demands are made on a serf population to work and produce for the manor, or in the case of private farmers taxed punitively by a Socialist regime, the meaning of a family farm will clearly differ radically from that of farming by free peasants, and by their successors as freehold farmers, working for themselves and even aided by state subsidy. Again the availability of alternative sources of income, in the urban world or in a range of rural off-farm settings such as forestry, also

[27] My thanks are due to the Estonian scholars Juhan Kahk, Eero Loone and Andrus Pork for their patient discussion of some aspects of this issue with me.

[28] It is probable that this comment also referred to the Soviet system. In similar vein, the use of terms such as 'red barons' to describe modern Soviet leaders seems to be a common form of conflation of the feudal and modern periods.

[29] The Estonian term *jonn* is perhaps the nearest equivalent Saagpaak (1982) glosses it as 'obstinacy, stubbornness, persistence, endurance, self-will', and notes the word *eestijonn*, which is translated as 'Estonian grit, Estonian enduring energy or persistence'.

[30] Shipler (1989, p. 73).

[31] See Lehiste (1973). The novel in question is *Tondiöömaja* by H. Kiik. Lehiste translates the title as *Where Hobgoblins Spend the Night*.

exercises a strong influence on the family-farming scene. Yet everywhere one finds examples of farming families negotiating their own terms of trade if only to a limited extent with the powers above. One finds a wide range of resources, such as the use of 'legal fictions' in a relatively free environment, and the development of an 'informal sector' and even smuggling in some more restrictive settings. In addition, it seems arguable that although the rationale of such external settings may vary considerably, the main premisses of a farming family tend to remain much the same. Of course, the interaction between family aims and values and those of the state and other structures may leave its mark upon behaviour in the family itself. Yet we have seen in Finland that even in situations where the family seems at first sight to have been thoroughly invaded by the spirit of capitalism and legality, reality turns out to be substantially more complicated.

Winners, losers and survivors
Beyond their implications for comparison across the centuries, continuity and change are also of importance at a different level of analysis of family farming. Here I have in mind the viability and persistence of individual farms and farming communities. There are several variables involved in this issue, and these can seriously affect the meaning of developments for the actors.

The complexity of the connection between farm and family, which I have already discussed at some length, is important in this as in other contexts. We know that a continuing link between a family and a farm is often likely to include an element of illusion, since such links commonly persist only because some members of the family withdraw from the farm. If, on the other hand, the land is divided among several heirs, the farm itself soon changes radically, and its ability to provide for those who live on it is likely to be seriously impaired.

As with other aspects of family farming, such internal problems of adjustment between a changing family and a farm cannot be understood simply in themselves. At the very least, technology and the environment are likely to be influential. Here one can usefully recall Voionmaa's broad historical contrast within Finland between eastern swidden and western field agriculture, even though the Vieki area itself does not seem to have fallen simply into the eastern patterns in question. As I noted briefly in the context of succession, he argues that the crucial element in the family–farm connection in the swidden area was the co-residence and labour input of the family members, with inheritance rights dependent upon these. Attachment to the family, in this special sense, was the predominant element in the situation. On the other hand, in the more fixed conditions of field agriculture, the farm itself became a lasting focus of individual family members' rights, and residence and participation in the labour process were not pre-conditions for inheritance. Coupled with this there seems to have been a special naming pattern in the west, whereby a family who moved to a different farm took the name of the farm as their family name. Thus a family might adopt the name Ollila as their surname, because they now owned a farm which had originally acquired this name through belonging to a man called Olli. In eastern Finland, however, the common pattern has been to call a farm by a name derived from the surname of its owners. Such names may stick, despite change of ownership, but they are not adopted as surnames by new owners, and they seem gradually to change over time. Thus the farm which had belonged to Helka Saarelainen's parents and grandparents in Vieki has been known for a long time as Saarela. As I have described in Chapter 5, it was taken over by her and her husband, and later by one of their sons, and it is now beginning to be known as Kiiskilä after the husband's surname, Kiiskinen.

Although the contrast drawn by Voionmaa is almost certainly too stark, the differences of emphasis and balance between farm and family which he posits as deriving from the different patterns of land use and settlement in question are extremely plausible, and they are well worth further exploration in other areas of swidden and field cultivation. More generally, his discussion usefully reminds us that land and family do not always carry the same meaning either within or between societies. Once again, it is easy to see that a wide range of political and economic factors can seriously affect such meanings. If farming families only have access to land in their capacity as a chief's subjects or as feudal tenants, they are likely to be differently disposed towards it than if they have clear rights to transmit it to their heirs or to benefit directly from investment in it. In Tanzania, Nyamwezi population movement has been connected with the different rights of chiefs and commoners in land, while political and legal rather than emotional bonds tied north European serf families, such as those on the south Baltic littoral, to their plots.[32] Also, the existence of alternatives to farming within the wider economy is a major variable affecting people's attitudes. A focus on the family farm itself readily leads one to assume that those who do not manage to acquire land are in some sense a deprived section of the population, but I have noted that in practice this may well not be the case. It is true that in North Karelia and other parts of Finland, there were by the beginning of this century substantial groups of crofters, cotters and landless labourers whose impoverishment constituted both a major source of hardship for themselves and a serious political problem for society at large. Yet even in the past, some of those who gave up farming in the rural areas

[32] See Abrahams (1967, p. 103, 1978b, p. 82), Palli (1983, p. 291), Plakans (1984, pp. 186–7) and Raun (1987, p. 291).

were able to develop prosperous careers for themselves either as émigrés or, sometimes, within Finland itself. In the present century, moreover, industrial, commercial and other developments have created major economic opportunities outside agriculture. Many farmers' children have been glad to take advantage of these, despite the fact that urban dwellers often miss the space and peace and quiet of the countryside, and many a son who has stayed at home to farm is, by most objective criteria, the loser as compared to siblings who have had the benefit of higher education and subsequent well-paid employment in the urban sector.[33] As I have noted in Chapter 5, the law has now begun to recognise this fact, and to provide some positive discrimination in favour of such farming sons.

Success and failure of farming families are, therefore, not immediately obvious phenomena these days, and they are certainly not exactly the same thing as the success and failure of family farms. Finnish farmers are not normally so devoted to their farms that they would sacrifice the interests of their children to those of the farm, and under pressure they are likely to be family members first and farmers second. One context where this emerges is the increased awareness of allergies which I mentioned in Chapter 4. During my research I was surprised at the number of families I encountered in which children suffered from allergies to farm animals and produce, and I was interested by the seriousness with which this problem was treated as a reason why a child should not go into farming. It is possible that there are more allergies today than in the past, for instance as a result of new forms of grain threshing and drying which may create finer dusts than older practices. But I suspect that there is more to it than this. One farmer humorously commented that he presumed that allergies had also existed in the old days, and that they were probably then diagnosed as 'laziness'.[34] Yet, he and his wife were proud of the fact that their own allergic children were university-educated and embarking on professional careers.

It is, though, sometimes possible, as I have shown, for farming couples to enjoy the best of several worlds in contexts of this sort. Providing that one son or daughter is happy to continue farming, the availability of good careers for other children outside agriculture is an unadulterated blessing, and the division of labour between such siblings may well provide a useful basis for good relations between them. Yet even if there is no available successor, one must be careful not to over-dramatise the situation. As I have already noted, the main issue for the senior generation may be to use succession to secure a materially and psychologically secure old age among

---

[33] See Tauriala (1979, p. 12).

[34] Paul Jorion (personal communication) has told me of a comparable situation with regard to sea sickness among Breton fishermen. In earlier days, those prone to this simply had to suffer, but nowadays it is considered an adequate reason to stay out of fishing.

family and friends. A corollary of this, however, is that if other means to this end are available, farmers may be reasonably satisfied to see their own lives out successfully, and to worry less about the future of the farm and farming generally, providing that their children are well catered for in other ways.

None the less, it is clear that many Finnish families have struggled to make a success of farming and to maintain connection with a farm over the generations, and it is also clear that large numbers of them have failed to do this. The reasons have varied somewhat at different times. Famine, often combined with other misfortunes, caused havoc to many Finnish families in the nineteenth century, and many farmers then and later have got badly into debt. A fondness for alcohol, and other character defects, have brought even prosperous past and present farms to rack and ruin in some cases, and ill health has also often been a problem, especially where there have been no alternative sources of labour for a farm. Beyond this, there have also been important structural factors, and it is certain that at different periods a large proportion of farms could not hope to survive in the prevailing social and economic conditions of the country. Like comparable programmes elsewhere, the attempts in the early years of independence to create large numbers of land-owning farming families out of the landless labourers and tenant crofters of the previous decades led to the creation of thousands of small farms which could scarcely hope to persist in the face of subsequent demographic and economic developments.[35] As I have described, it became steadily harder for many such farms to provide a decent living for those living and working on them. The depression years took their toll, and later the mechanisation of the timber industry deprived many farmers of vital extra income at the same time as jobs in industry and in the tertiary sector, both in Sweden and in Finland, beckoned them to seek a new life in the towns.

Despite these problems, and the large-scale movements out of agriculture, we have seen that there are still substantial numbers of families who have successfully remained in farming, even in the North Karelian 'outback'. The Loukku–Siltavaara 'agricultural village' experiment is a testimony to the resolve of such people to make a success of their farms, and one cannot help being struck by the positive outlook and determination of other Vieki farmers also. What sort of people are these survivors, and what sorts of factors have affected their capacity to survive?

One noticeable feature is that high levels of education and professional training are not very common in the area, and that many Vieki farmers have

---

[35] See Warriner (1964, pp. 154,. 166) for a useful general discussion of the longer-term problems which family-farming systems regularly face as population grows and the demand for new employment opportunities increases.

so far managed to survive successfully without them. It is well understood, however, that formal qualifications can be helpful to those who possess them, and it is also possible that they will loom larger in the future if competition both within and between farming areas increases sharply. Apart from the direct benefits of greater 'know-how' in the complex world of modern farming, such qualifications can also stand a farmer in good stead if he seeks to purchase extra land from the state or Commune, and when he applies for credit for such purchases and for support of other kinds. A number of the Loukku–Siltavaara farmers placed explicit emphasis on the fact that their participation in the *maatalouskylä* scheme would give them valuable access to up-to-date information and at least short-term instruction, but the amount available to them has of course been limited.

Credit availability has also been a vital factor for the success of many farmers. In addition to help which they received from the Vieki and other banks, several were wise enough to take advantage of government offers in the 1960s to buy timber land out of the state reserves. It seems that many of those who failed to do this were frightened by the spectre of debt that the accompanying credit arrangements raised for them, especially after the bitter losses of land and economic independence which so many families had experienced through indebtedness in the depression years and earlier decades. These were deep-seated fears, and the distress which such loss could bring to dependants as well as to oneself made debt both a moral and an economic danger. I was, however, often told that those who had the foresight, courage or foolhardiness to mortgage the future and seize whatever forest land the state could offer them had congratulated themselves many times in later years. As in many comparable contexts, inflation was the crucial factor, so that debts which looked like millstones when first entered into look nowadays almost like free gifts. Some war veterans, displaced Karelians and ex-crofters were also able to take advantage of debt cancellations in the post-war years. These were clearly helpful, and they created some resentment, as I noted earlier, among those who were not eligible for them. They are not, however, generally considered to have been decisive for the success or failure of those concerned.

One point which all farmers in the area tend to emphasise in discussions of survival and success is the importance of personal qualities. Three such qualities are particularly stressed. Firstly, there is here as in so many other contexts a strong emphasis on *sisu*, the capacity to work hard in the face of difficulties over a sustained period of time. This is a key quality, as I have described, but people are aware that it must be complemented by the further ability to work constructively, which turns upon the possession of organising skills. It seems likely that this quality can be acquired by training, but it tends locally to be seen as a talent. Thirdly, there is the question of wanting to farm, of having a feeling for the land and a commitment to it, which can help to take you through difficult patches and more generally to orientate yourself successfully to problems. My wife's aunt used to talk of this as *moahenki* (standard Finnish *maahenki,* literally 'earth-spirit'). The values and sentiments involved here have sometimes had complex political implications – an extreme form of them appears to have helped to fuel the right-wing activism of the Lapua League farmers whom I mentioned earlier – but they also seem to serve more directly as a genuinely important resource for many successful farmers. Such a feeling for and commitment to farming can show itself after some time, as the case of M. Myllynen, whom I discussed in Chapter 3, reveals. He had not planned to take over the family farm, and did so only when his younger brother died, but he has committed himself fully to the task, and he is much respected by his neighbours for his devotion to it.

It is also clear that, while it can be helpful, being born into a longstanding heritable farm (*perintötila*) is neither a guarantee of nor a prerequisite for success. There are many cases, including that of the T. farm in Loukku, where this has been of no help whatsoever. During the late nineteenth century, this was a large undivided farm belonging to K.T. and her in-marrying husband M., and it was divided formally in the 1920s and 1930s among three of their sons. Each son had many children, and a number of these left the farm but retained their ownership of plots which they inherited. Others stayed there on their own inherited sections, and one or two have tried to farm. No major reconsolidation of the now fragmented holdings has occurred, and much of the once prosperous farm remains divided into inviably small units. Apart from such instances of fragmentation, there are also many examples of successors who have failed to make a go of a good farm they have inherited, and others have tottered on the edge of disaster before mending their ways. Similarly, there are several cases known to me, such as that of the Huuro farm, where a former tenant crofter family has pulled itself up by a mixture of good character, good management and good fortune to become one of the more prosperous farming units in the area.

Other factors of importance for success include the ability to co-operate well with kin, friends and neighbours, as I have described in Chapter 6. It is also naturally valuable to have a substantial labour force available within the family, especially if this can be accommodated without future problems of succession and division. A small labour force, such as husband and wife alone, or even the odd case known to me of mother and daughter, can be very vulnerable, despite machinery, and may depend quite heavily on friendly help from others.

One notable element in many successful farms is the important role which women play in running them. There is much more involved here than women simply pulling their weight in the farm work-team in accordance with traditional patterns of labour division. In the first place, as I have described, the traditional division of labour is by no means always adhered to these days, especially when a small labour force is stretched to its capacity by the many demands made upon it. Men increasingly participate in the work of the cowshed, for example, and women are far more than dairy maids. This is obvious, of course, in the case of a farm like the Hn one in Loukku, where the only labour force is the women of the house. But it is also the case elsewhere to varying degrees. Women may look after a farm more or less completely if their husbands take winter timber work, as some still do, and there are some cases where functioning farms are largely run by women whose husbands have a full-time job throughout the year. Even on some farms with a large and active labour force of men, one can find the *emäntä* playing a strong part in running things, though she may sometimes disguise this and defer to her husband for the sake of appearances. Such farm-wives know a tremendous amount about agricultural techniques, developments and economics, and they display, at least as much as men, the organisational talents I referred to earlier.

A further point which may deserve some comment here concerns the relatively modest life style of several farm families known to me. For example, although things were changing fairly rapidly at the time of my research, there were still a number of farms which lacked modern indoor sanitation. This and other features of material comfort can, however, be deceptive guides to economic failure or success. A salient factor here is the somewhat puritanical pattern of investment priorities to which many families adhere. There is at least one case known to me where the *isäntä's* extreme miserliness led to bitter inter-generational conflict and eventually to homicide within the family, but such extreme cases are, not surprisingly, exceptional. The main point is that farming families often use their income when they can for capital investment in the farm itself, rather than on less productive creature comforts and consumer goods. It is only when they are satisfied that they have put enough into the farm that such families are willing to spend much on other things. Of course, other constraints may influence decisions of this kind. On one farm, for example, the family made several home improvements, including the installation of an inside toilet, and they were partly tempted to do this because the walk down to the old one by the cowshed was becoming rather dangerous for older members of the family on slippy winter days. And of course, as families expand, so too do their needs for living space, and this gives rise to renovations which accompany expansion.

It is hard to know whether the efforts of these Vieki farming families to maintain the viability of their farms and their communities will be sufficient in the longer term. Such villages and families live under constant threat. The age and sex structure of their populations do not bode at all well for the future. Schools have been closed in many areas already, and shops are few and far between. Often it is only summer trade brought in by visitors returning 'home' for holidays that keeps shops going as a profitable enterprise. As such services diminish, 'outback' villages appear increasingly remote, and they are less and less likely to attract new blood into their midst. Successors are often hard to find for ageing farmers, and many younger ones have difficulty in finding wives. Beyond this, it is also unclear whether farming in the backwoods can continue to compete with that in the more favourable zones of the country, which enjoy climatic advantages in addition to their greater proximity to main population centres. It is easy, however, as I have already noted, to misconstrue other people's priorities. We have seen that farming couples have often been glad to see their children educated out of farming, and that more generally they tend to choose the needs of family over those of farm. Yet this leads one to wonder even more at the energy and enthusiasm with which many farming families pursue their lives in such circumstances, and it seems clear that their relative independence is a partial base for this, despite the responsibilities and the risks and costs of failure it may entail. *Oma tupa, oma lupa* (literally 'own cottage, own consent') is a well-known proverb which encapsulates much of the spirit and significance of the freedom of action which Finnish family farmers enjoy. I hope that I have been able to capture at least some of the flavour of this spirit, and something also of the resilience and adaptability of farming villagers in this account of their life in a remote corner of north-eastern Europe.

Bibliography

Aarnio, A. 1975. *Jälkisäädökset*. Vammala.

Abrahams, R. G. 1967. *The Political Organization of Unyamwezi*. Cambridge.

1973. 'Some Aspects of Levirate', in J. Goody (ed.), *The Character of Kinship*, Cambridge.

1978a. 'Aspects of Labwor Age and Generation Grouping and Related Systems', in P. T. W. Baxter and U. Almagor (eds.), *Age, Generation and Time*. London.

1978b. 'Aspects of the Distinction between the Sexes in the Nyamwezi and some other African Systems of Kinship and Marriage', in J. S. LaFontaine (ed.), *Sex and Age as Principles of Social Differentiation*. London.

1981. *The Nyamwezi Today*. Cambridge.

(ed.) 1985. *Villagers, Villages and the State in Modern Tanzania*. Cambridge, African Studies Centre.

1988. 'Life Goes on Behind God's Back', in Ingold (1988b).

Agricultural Information Centre, 1981. *Agrifacts about Finland '81*. Helsinki.

Ahponen, P. 1979. *Kylä muutoksen objektina ja subjektina*. Joensuu.

Alapuro, R. 1980a. *Finland: An Interface Periphery*. Helsinki.

1980b. 'Mass Support for Fascism in Finland', in S. U. Larsen, B. Hagtvet and J. Myklebust (eds.), *Who were the Fascists?* Oslo.

Alapuro, R. and E. Allardt. 1978. 'The Lapua Movement: The Threat of Rightist Takeover in Finland 1930–32', in J. Linz and A. Stepan (eds.), *The Breakdown of Democratic Regimes II. Europe*. Baltimore.

Allardt, E. 1985. *Finnish Society: Relationship between Geopolitical Situation and the Development of Society*. Helsinki.

Allardt, E. and W. Wesolowski. 1978. *Social Structure and Change: Finland and Poland: Comparative Perspective*. Warsaw.

Andersson, E. et al. 1973. *Kodin Lakikirja*. Helsinki.

Arensberg, C. A. and S. Kimball. 1961. *Family and Community in Ireland*. Gloucester, Massachusetts.

Barnes, J. A. 1957. 'Land Rights and Kinship in Two Bremnes Hamlets', *Journal of the Royal Anthropological Institute*, 87, 31–6.

1962. 'African Models in the New Guinea Highlands', *Man*, 62, 5–9.

1979. *Who Should Know What?* Harmondsworth.

Baxter, P. T. W. and U. Almagor (eds.) 1978. *Age, Generation and Time*. London.

Beattie, J. 1964. 'Bunyoro: An African Feudality?', *Journal of African History*, 5, 25–35.

Berkner, L. 1972. 'Rural Family Organization in Europe: A Problem in Comparative History', *Peasant Studies Newsletter*, 1, 145–56.

Berkner, L. and F. Mendels. 1978. 'Inheritance Systems, Family Structure and Demographic Patterns in Western Europe (1700–1900)'', in C. Tilly (ed.), *Historical Studies of Changing Fertility*. Princeton.

Blomstedt, Y. 1973. 'Oikeutemme kehitys', in E. Anderson et al. (eds.), *Kodin lakikirja*, pp. 30–55. Helsinki.

Bohannan, P. J. 1957. *Justice and Judgment among the Tiv*. London.

Boholm, A. 1983. *Swedish Kinship*. Gothenburg Studies in Social Anthropology, No. 5. Gothenburg.

Carr, E. H. 1966. *The Bolshevik Revolution 1917–23*, Vol. I. Harmondsworth.

Central Statistical Office, Finland. 1940. *Suomen Tilastollinen Vuosikirja, 1939 (Annuaire Statistique de Finlande)*. Helsinki.

1965. *Suomen Tilastollinen Vuosikirja, 1964 (Statistical Yearbook of Finland)*. Helsinki.

1989. *Suomen Tilastollinen Vuosikirja, 1988 (Statistical Yearbook of Finland)*. Helsinki.

Chayanov, A. V. 1986. *The Theory of Peasant Economy*. Manchester.

Cole, J. W. 1977. 'Anthropology Comes Part-Way Home: Community Studies in Europe', in B. Siegel (ed.). *Annual Review of Anthropology*.

Cole, J. W. and E. R. Wolf. 1974. *The Hidden Frontier: Ecology and Ethnicity in an Alpine Valley*. New York.

Collomp, A. 1984. 'Tensions, Dissensions, and Ruptures inside the Family in Seventeenth- and Eighteenth-Century Haute Provence', in H. Medick and D. Sabean (eds.), *Interest and Emotion*. Cambridge.

Douglas, M. 1966. *Purity and Danger*. London.

Durkheim, E. 1893. *De la division du travail social*. Paris.

Epstein, A. L. 1967. 'The Case Method in the Field of Law', in A. L. Epstein (ed.), *The Craft of Social Anthropology*. London.

Fallers, L. A. 1961. 'Are African Cultivators to be Called "Peasants"?', *Current Anthropology*, 2, 2, 108–10.

Fortes, M. 1949. *The Web of Kinship among the Tallensi*. London.

1961. 'Pietas in Ancestor Worship', *Journal of the Royal Anthropological Institute*, 91, 166–91.

Fox, F. 1926. *Finland Today*. London.

Friedl, E. 1962. *Vasilika*. New York.

Galeski, B. 1971. 'Sociological Problems of the Occupation of Farmers', in T. Shanin (ed.), *Peasants and Peasant Societies*. Harmondsworth. Also in *Annals of Rural Sociology* (special issue, 1968).

Gaunt, D. 1983. 'The Property and Kin Relationships of Retired Farmers in Northern and Central Europe', in R. Wall, P. Laslett and J. Robin (eds.), *Family Forms in Historic Europe*. Cambridge.

Gluckman, M. 1950. 'Kinship and Marriage among the Lozi of Northern Rhodesia and the Zulu of Natal', in A. R. Radcliffe-Brown and D. Forde (eds.), *African Systems of Kinship and Marriage*. London.

1965. *Politics, Law and Ritual in Tribal Society*. Oxford.

Goldschmidt, W. and E. J. Kunkel. 1971. 'The Structure of the Peasant Family', *American Anthropologist*, 73, 5, 1058–76.

Goody, E. N. 1973. *Contexts of Kinship*. Cambridge.
Goody, J. 1958. 'The Fission of Domestic Groups among the LoDagaba', in J. Goody (ed.), *The Development Cycle in Domestic Groups*. Cambridge.
1962. *Death, Property and the Ancestors*. London and Stanford.
1971. *Technology, Tradition and the State*. Oxford.
1976a. *Production and Reproduction*. Cambridge.
1976b. Introduction to J. R. Goody, J. Thirsk and E. P. Thompson (eds.), *Family and Inheritance: Rural Society in Western Europe 1200–1800*. Cambridge.
'Inheritance, Property and Women: Some Comparative Considerations', in J. R. Goody, J. Thirsk and E. P. Thompson (eds.), *Family and Inheritance: Rural Society in Western Europe 1200–1800*. Cambridge.
1983. *The Development of the Family and Marriage in Europe*. Cambridge.
1984. 'Under the Lineage's Shadow', *Proceedings of the British Academy*, 70.
1986. *The Logic of Writing and the Organization of Society*. Cambridge.
Gould, R. A. 1988. 'Life Among the Ruins: The Ethnoarchaeology of Abandonment in a Finnish Farming Community', in Ingold (1988b).
Gripenberg, G. A. 1960. 'Finnish Neutrality', in U. Toivola (ed.), *Introduction to Finland 1960*. Helsinki.
Gulliver, P. H. 1955. *The Family Herds*. London.
1964. 'The Arusha Family', in R. F. Gray and P. H. Gulliver (eds.), *The Family Estate in Africa*. London.
Hakulinen, L. 1961. *Suomen kielen rakenne ja kehitys*. Helsinki.
Hall, Wendy. 1957. *Green Gold and Granite*. London.
Hann, C. M. 1985. *A Village without Solidarity*. Yale.
Harlock, W. E. and A. Gabrielson. 1951. *Svensk–Engelsk Ordbok*. Stockholm.
Hart, K. 1982. *The Political Economy of West African Agriculture*. Cambridge.
Hautamäki, L. 1979. *Elävä kylä*. Jyväskylä.
1980. 'Action-Oriented Village Research and Rural Development', in *Adult Education in Finland*, 17, 1, 18–23.
Hellman, B. 1989. 'The Reception of Russian Culture in Finland' (mimeo).
Honkanen, S. et al. 1975. 'Sukupolvenvaihdoksen ongelma maatilataloudessa', *Publications of the Pellervo Society Marketing Research Institute*, No. 16. Helsinki.
Honkaniemi, E. 1979. *Maidon tuotanto-olosuhteet ja tulevaisuuden näkymät vv. 1979–82 Joensuun ympäristön osuusmeijerin alueella*. Helsinki, Marketing Research Institute of the Pellervo Society.
Horsman, E. G. 1978. 'Inheritance in England and Wales: The Evidence provided by Wills', *Oxford Economic Papers*, 30, 3, 409–22.
Hurme, R., R.-L. Malin and O. Syväoja. 1984. *Finnish-English General Dictionary (Uusi suomi-englanti suursanakirja)*. Helsinki.
Hällström, E. af. 1934. 'Perimysmaasäännöstö', in *Juhlajulkaisu 1734 vuoden lain muistoksi*. Helsinki.
Ingold, T. 1984. 'The Estimation of Work in a Northern Finnish Farming Community', in N. Long, *Family and Work in Rural Societies*. London.
1988a. 'Land, Labour and Livelihood in Salla, Northeastern Finland', in Ingold (1988b).
(ed.) 1988b. *The Social Implications of Agrarian Change in Northern and Eastern Finland*. Helsinki.
Jackson, A. (ed.). 1987. *Anthropology at Home*. London.

Jarvenpa, R. 1988. 'Agrarian Ecology, Sexual Organization of Labour and Decision-Making in Northeastern Finland', in Ingold (1988b).

Jutikkala, E. 1958. *Suomen talonpojan historia*. Helsinki.

1960a. 'The road to Independence', in Toivola (1960).

1960b. 'Between the World Wars', in Toivola (1960).

Jäntti, A. 1960. 'Farming in a Cold Climate', in Toivola (1960).

Jägerskiöld, S. 1986. *Mannerheim Marshal of Finland*. London.

Kirby, D. G. 1979. *Finland in the Twentieth Century*. London.

Kula, W . 1976. *An Economic Theory of the Feudal System*. London.

Kuusi, M., K. Bosley and M. Branch (eds.). 1977. *Finnish Folk Poetry: Epic*. Helsinki.

Köppä, T. (1979). *Viljelijäperhe, yhteisö ja yhteistoiminta*. Pellervo Economic Research Institute. Helsinki.

Lander, P. S. 1976. *In the Shadow of the Factory*. New York.

Langbein, J. H. 1984. 'The Nonprobate Revolution and the Future of the Law of Succession', *Harvard Law Review*, 97, 5, 1108–41.

1988. 'The Twentieth Century Revolution in Family Wealth Transmission', *Michigan Law Review*, 86, 4, 722–51, 1988.

Le Roy Ladurie, E. 1976. 'Family Structures and Inheritance Customs in Sixteenth-Century France', in J. Goody, J. Thirsk and E. P. Thompson (eds.), *Family and Inheritance: Rural Society in Western Europe 1200–1800*. Cambridge.

Leach, E. R. 1960. 'The Sinhalese of the Dry Zone of Northern Ceylon', in G. P. Murdock (ed.), *Social Structure in Southeast Asia*. New York.

1961. *Pul Eliya*. Cambridge.

1972. 'The Influence of Cultural Context on Non-Verbal Communication in Man', in R. A. Hinde (ed.), *Non-Verbal Communication*. Cambridge.

1976. *Culture and Communication*. Cambridge.

Lehiste, I. 1973. 'Where Hobgoblins Spend the Night', *Journal of Baltic Studies*, 4, 4, winter 1973, 321–6.

Leskinen, J. 1979. *Finland. Facts and Figures*. Helsinki.

Lévi-Strauss, C. 1949. *Les Structures élementaires de la parenté*. Paris.

Lieksan Kaupunki. n.d. *Maatalouden perustutkimus*. Lieksa.

Lieksan Pääkirjasto. 1985. *Sodanjälkeinen asutustoiminta Suomesa v. 1945–58*. Lieksa.

Linna, V. 1959. *Täällä Pohjantähden alla*. Helsinki.

Löfgren, O. 1974. 'Family and Household among Scandinavian Peasants: An Exploratory Essay', *Ethnologia Scandinavica*, 17–52.

1980. 'Historical Perspectives on Scandinavian Peasantries', *Annual Review of Anthropology*, 9, 187–215.

McArdle, F. 1974. 'Another Look at "Peasant Families East and West"', in *Peasant Studies Newsletter*, 3, 3.

MacFarlane, A. 1978. *The Origins of English Individualism*. Oxford.

Maine, H. 1972. *Ancient Law*. Everyman edition. London.

Mattila, H. E. S. 1979. *Les Successions agricoles et la structure de la société*. Helsinki.

Mauss, M. 1954. *The Gift*. London.

Mead, W. R. 1958. 'Finns in Fact and Fiction', *The Norseman*, 14, 3–14.

1963. 'The Finn in English Fiction', *Neuphilologische Mitteilungen*, 44, 3, 243–64.

1982. 'Finland and the Finn as Stereotypes', *Neuphilologische Mitteilungen*, 83, 1, 42–52.

Mead, W. R. and H. Smeds, 1967. *Winter in Finland*. London.

Mendras, H. 1970. *The Vanishing Peasant*. Cambridge, Massachusetts.

Merton, R. K. 1968. *Social Theory and Social Structure*, enlarged edition. New York.

Mikkonen, E. 1975. 'Viekin osuuspankin historiikki 1905–75'. Unpublished MS.

Mitterauer, M. and R. Sieder. 1982. *The European Family*. Oxford.

Mäkelä, A. 1988. 'Elämän rikkaus – tutki sukuasi', in Tiitta (1988).

Naskila, M. 1982. *Emäntä Suomessa*. Helsinki.

Newby, H. 1977. *The Deferential Worker*. Harmondsworth.

    1980. 'Rural Sociology: Trend Report', *Current Sociology*, 28, 1, 1–141.

Nygård, M. 1983. 'Ammatillinen monitoimisuus maaseudulla', in Vuorela et al (1983).

Nykänen, J. 1977. *Pielisjärven työläisten Golgota*. Kuopio.

Oksa, J. 1985. 'The Social Function of a Provincial Centre – The Case of Joensuu', in J. Oksa (ed.), *Papers on Social Change in North Karelia*. Joensuu.

Palli, H. 1983. 'Parish Registers and Revisions', *Social Science History*, 7, 3, 289–310.

Parsons, T. 1951. *The Social System*. London.

Pellervo Seura. 1981. *Maatalouskalenteri 1981*. Helsinki.

Petrisalo, K. 1988. 'The Tourist Industry and Local Culture in the Countryside', in Ingold (1988b).

Pine, F. 1987. 'Kinship, Marriage and Social Change in a Polish Highland Village'. Unpublished Ph.D. dissertation, University of London.

Plakans, A. 1973. 'Peasant Families East and West: A Comment on Lutz K. Berkner's "Rural Family Organization in Europe: A Problem in Comparative History"', *Peasant Studies Newsletter*, 2, 3.

    1984. *Kinship in the Past*. Oxford.

Pokka, H. et al. 1979. *Sukupolvenvaihdos maatilalla*. Helsinki.

Rappaport, R. A. 1978. 'Maladaptation in Social Systems', in J. Friedman and M. J. Rowlands (eds.), *The Evolution of Social Systems*. Pittsburgh.

Raun, T. 1987. *Estonia and the Estonians*. Stanford.

Rautiala, M. 1975. *Perheoikeuden pääpiirteet*. Porvoo.

Richards, A. and J. Robin. 1975. *Some Elmdon Families*. Elmdon.

Riihimäki, A. 1970. *Perimys ja testamentin laadinta*. Porvoo.

Roberts, F. M. 1978. 'Kenttätutkimus hämäläisestä kylästä', *Suomen Antropologi*, 2, 65–79.

    1989. 'The Finnish Coffee Ceremony and Notions of Self', *Arctic Anthropology*, 26, 1.

Rouhinen, S. 1983. 'Uusimuotoinen kylätoiminta maaseudun kehittäjänä', in Vuorela et al. (1983).

Saagpaak, P. F. 1982. *Estonian–English Dictionary*. New Haven.

Sahlins, M. 1974. *Stone Age Economics*. London.

Saloheimo, V. A. 1953. *Nurmeksen Historia*. Kuopio.

    1954. *Pielisjärven Historia*, I. Lieksa.

Salpakari, K. 1963. 'Laatokan Karjalasta Egyptinkorpeen', in O. I. Laine (ed.), *Karjalan Vaaroilta*. Helsinki.

Santala, P. 1983. 'Uudet Maatilojen Perinnönjakosäännökset', *Defensor Legis*, 149–77.

Sarmela, M. (ed.). 1984. *Neljä pohjoista yhteistöä*. Helsinki.

Saul, J. and R. Woods. 1971. 'African Peasantries', in Shanin (1971).

Segalen, M. 1984. 'Avoir sa part': Sibling Relations in Partible Inheritance Brittany', in H. Medick and D. W. Sabean (eds.), *Interest and Emotion*. Cambridge and Paris.

Shammas, C., M. Salmon and M. Dahlin. 1987. *Inheritance in America from Colonial Times to the Present*. New Brunswick.

Shanin, T. (ed.). 1971. *Peasants and Peasant Societies*. Harmondsworth.

Shipler, D. K. 1989. 'A Reporter at Large', *New Yorker* (18 September), 52–99.

Siiskonen, P. 1988. 'The Role of Farmers and Farmwives in Agrarian Change', in Ingold (1988b).

Singleton, F. 1989. *A Short History of Finland*. Cambridge.

Sinkkonen, S., E. Ollikainen and E. Ryynänen. 1983. *Entäs nyt emäntä: naisen asema maataloudessa*. Kuopio.

Smith, M. S., B. J. Kish and C. R. Crawford. 1987. 'Inheritance of Wealth as Human Kin Investment', *Ethology and Sociobiology*, 8, 3, 171–82.

Soininen, A. M. 1974. 'Vanha maataloutemme', *Historiallisia tutkimuksia*, 96. Helsinki.

Spiegel, H. W. 1939. 'The Altenteil: German Farmers' Old Age Security', in *Rural Sociology*, 4.

Stenius, G. (ed.). 1963. *Introduction to Finland 1963*. Helsinki.

Strathern, M. 1981. *Kinship at the Core*. Cambridge.

1989. *The Gender of the Gift*. Berkeley.

Suolahti, E. 1973. *Helsinki: A City in a Classic Style*. Helsinki.

Suolinna, K. and K. Sinikara. 1986. *Juhonkylä*. Helsinki.

Sweetser, D. A. 1964. 'Urbanization and the Patrilineal Transmission of Farms in Finland', *Acta Sociologica*, 7, 215–24.

Talve, I. 1979. *Suomen kansankulttuuri*. Helsinki.

Tanttu, E. 1974, *455 Parasta*. Helsinki.

Tarvert, J. D. 1952. 'Intra-Family Farm Succession Practices', in *Rural Sociology*, 17, 266–71.

Tauriainen, J. 1982. 'Maaseudun väestökehityksen pääpiirteet 1950–1980', in Vuorela (1983).

Tauriala, J. 1979. *Väestön suhtautuminen Suomen maatalouteen ja maanviljelijöihin*. Helsinki, Pellervo Society.

Thiele, G. 1985. 'Villages as Economic Agents: The Accident of Social Reproduction', in Abrahams (1985).

Tiitta, A. (ed.). 1988. *Mitä Missä Milloin*. Helsinki.

Toivola, U. (ed.). 1960. *Introduction to Finland 1960*. Helsinki.

Toivonen, T. and S. Widerszpil. 1978. 'Changes in Socio-Economic Class Structure', in Allardt and Wesolowski (1978).

Toivonen, Y., E. Itkonen and A. Joki. 1958. *Suomen kielen etymologinen sanakirja*. Helsinki.

Tommila, P. and I. Heervä (eds.). 1980. *Muuttuva Kylä*. Helsinki.

Tompuri, E. 1947. *Voices from Finland*. Helsinki.

Uusitalo, E. 1979. *Part-Time Farming in the Light of Multi-jobholding*. Helsinki, Marketing Research Institute of the Pellervo Society.

Valkonen, T., R. Alapuro, M. Alestalo, R. Jallinoja and T. Sandlund. 1980. *Suomalaiset*. Helsinki.

Vilkuna, K. 1981. *Vuotuinen Ajantieto*. Helsinki.

Voionmaa, V. 1915. *Suomen karjalaisen heimon historia*. Helsinki.

Vuorela, P., M. Kosonen, and U. Virtanen. 1983. *Suomalainen maaseutu*. Helsinki.

Vuorela, U. 1987. *The Women's Question and the Modes of Human Reproduction: An Analysis of a Tanzanian Village*. Uppsala.

Warriner, D. 1964. *Economics of Peasant Farming*. London.

Wehrwein, C. F. 1932. 'Bonds of Maintenance as Aids in Acquiring Farm Ownership', *Journal of Land and Public Utility Economics*, 8.

Wijeyewardene, G. 1969. 'Taxation, Inheritance, and the Structure of Peasant Communities: Some Thoughts on the Manorial Model', *The Australian and New Zealand Journal of Sociology*, 5, 1, 2–13.

Williams, R. 1973. *The Country and the City*. London.

Wily, E. 1988. 'The Political Economy of African Land Tenure: A Case Study from Tanzania'. Unpublished Ph.D. dissertation, University of East Anglia, Norwich.

Wolf, E. R. 1966. *Peasants*. Englewood Cliffs.

General index

Affleck, S. 30, 175
ageing (*see also* inheritance and succession, retirement) 112, 128, 136, 193
agriculture 11, 27, 168
  field 131, 186–7
  swidden 25, 31, 131, 135, 186–7
alchohol 6, 18, 189
Alen (Ahola), O. 35, 147, 148
allergies 84, 188

bachelors (*see also* marriage) 73, 99–103, 119
banks 16, 35–6, 147, 148, 153ff.
Bobrikov, N. I. 24
bread 171, 173ff.
  symbolic importance of 173–4
Britain 169–70

churches (*see also* religion)
  Lutheran 16, 17–18, 30, 34–5, 144
  Orthodox 17–18, 30, 39
civil war 26–7, 37
co-operation 19, 34–6, 39, 56, 78, 79, 90, 143–66, 168
cousins 95ff.
credit 1, 39, 46, 138, 139, 154, 155, 190

education 14, 23, 34–6, 189
Egyptinkorpi 38
Engel, C. L. 15, 22
Estonia 10, 184ff.

family 70ff.
  as farming unit 2–3, 83ff., 87, 113, 123, 128, 131, 167, 170ff., 183, 188
  different conceptions of 71

flexibility of 74, 168, 183
perhe and *suku* 75–7, 79, 81, 83, 103
stem-family 114, 142
famine 25, 32, 33, 48, 189
farms 29–33, 42, 46, 61, 72, 83–4
  as family property 1, 22, 71ff., 123, 167
  dairy farming 42, 46, 55, 56, 57, 61, 72
  size 40, 52, 54–5, 56, 57, 67, 69, 88, 90, 92, 151
feudalism 51, 174, 180, 181, 184, 187
fictions 124–5
fieldwork 3–10, 52
Finland 10ff., 169ff.
  history 21ff.
  language 10, 21–4, 49, 75
  literature 7, 143
forest 25, 31, 40, 45–6, 54, 56, 57, 60, 88, 90, 168, 169, 190
France 141
friendship 81, 152, 155
funerals 6, 42, 124

Greece 131, 133

health 84–5, 88, 189
Helsinki 15, 22, 166
holidays 13–14, 153
horses 87–8, 156
households 70,. 83ff., 101–3
housing 60, 138ff.

Iisalmi 55
illegitimacy 93–4
Ilomantsi 29, 150
independence 13, 21, 25ff.
  war of 26–7, 37

individualism 143ff., 185
inheritance and succession 19, 48, 57, 58,
    59, 60, 67ff., 72, 73, 77, 78, 80ff., 97–8,
    101–2, 104ff., 112ff., 124ff., 131ff., 150,
    154, 181, 188–9, 190, 191
  dowry as inheritance 97, 104–5
  impartible 73, 101, 114ff., 175, 181
  partible 73, 114ff., 181
  patrilineal 77
  pre-mortem 56, 57, 61, 110–11, 114–15,
    122–8
  retrait lignager 22, 80, 81, 117
  son-in-law 48, 53, 66, 67, 127, 128–37
  unigeniture 115
Ireland 131, 141

Joensuu 15–16, 92

Kekkonen, U. 29
Kinnunen, A. 35
kinship 51, 70, 74, 75ff., 81, 112, 152ff.
  descent groups 51, 77ff., 130
Kolkki, E. 35–6
kotivävy (see also inheritance: son-in-law)
    58, 133, 135

labour 83ff.
  division of 32, 56, 83ff., 126, 192
  for others 32–3, 41, 45, 86, 132, 155, 156,
    157
  off farm 41, 46, 55, 58, 60, 74, 84–5, 189
land 71, 72ff., 79
  as a factor of production 72ff.
  reforms 22, 27, 31, 37–8, 52, 55, 56, 58,
    66, 67, 144
  rental 55, 56
Lapuan movement 27–8, 170, 191
law (*see also* inheritance, land, marriage)
    15, 22, 103–11, 114ff., 119, 134ff., 141,
    177
liberalism 24, 80
Lieksa 11, 15–16, 34, 44, 48, 92, 147, 150
livestock 3, 55, 61, 72, 83, 88, 157, 173
Loukku 38, 149ff., 189, 190

machinery 2, 54, 57, 83–4, 85, 87–92, 145,
    150, 151, 152, 154ff., 172ff., 189
Mannerheim, C. G. 26, 27, 28
marriage 74, 83–4, 92–9, 100, 103ff., 121,
    126, 143
  daughters-in-law 127, 139, 141
  divorce 94–5
  living together (*avoliitto*) 94
migration 8, 14–15, 25, 38, 41–2, 47, 113,
    129ff., 135, 169–70

nationalism 23–4
Nurmes 18, 30, 47, 56, 76, 105, 107, 147
Nyamwezi 72, 74, 178–9, 187

Paasikivi, J. K. 29
peasants 180
  in Finland 24, 175ff.
  in southern Baltic lands 51, 175, 187
  in Sweden 175
pensions 41, 43, 57, 122ff.
politics 10, 25ff., 41, 43–5
  Centre Party 4, 43–5
  communists 26, 27
  elections 24, 25, 43–5
  political parties 25, 43–5
  Social Democrats 27, 41, 43–5
population 11, 14–15, 29–33, 38–41, 42, 48
  Karelians 38–40

railways (*see also* transport) 13, 16
records (civil and parish) 49–52
religion 17–18, 144, 165, 177
  fundamentalism 140
  pietism 17–18, 140
retirement 43, 122–8, 137ff.
Runeberg, J. L. 24
Russia 21–6, 29–30
  war with 23, 26, 144

Savolanvaara 44
schools 14, 23, 34–5, 149, 161, 193
seasons 11–14
Siltavaara 44–5, 96, 149ff., 189
sisu (inner strength) 143, 172, 184ff., 190
Snellman, J. V. 23
social categories and strata 31, 32–4, 36–7,
    82ff., 86, 93, 165
  herrasväki (gentry) 165
  lampuodit (tenant farmers) 31ff., 59
  loiset (dependent lodgers) 31ff., 54, 82
  mäkitupalaisat (cotters) 31ff., 82
  talolliset (farm owners) 31ff., 82
  torpparit (crofters) 31ff., 37–8, 55–6, 82
Soviet Union 10, 167, 170, 181
  war with 28–9
Speransky, M. M. 22
spinsters (*see also* marriage) 99–103
Stalin, J. 26
state (*see also* law and politics) 113, 126,
    137, 177, 190
succession (*see* inheritance and succession)
Svinhufvud, P. E. 26
Sweden 8, 10, 21, 30, 31, 41, 80, 103, 104,
    130, 167
syytinki (see also pensions) 122ff.

Tanttu, E. 161
Tanzania 1, 3, 5, 71, 72, 78, 167, 173, 178,
181, 187
tractors (*see also* machinery) 2, 54, 57, 87ff.,
159, 171
transport 2, 13, 16
Tsars
Alexander II 23
Alexander III 23
Nicholas II 23

Uusikylä 33, 40

Vieki 11, 16, 29ff., 47ff., 73, 76, 78, 84, 88,
92, 99, 100–1, 108, 118, 131, 135,
145ff., 149ff., 151, 162, 166, 171, 186ff.,
189ff.

Viekijärvi 57
Viensuu 57
village
'agricultural' (*maatalouskylä*) 150ff.
committees 148ff.
facilities 16, 34, 42, 172, 193

war, *see* civil war, independence, Russia,
Soviet Union
wills (*see also* inheritance and succession)
105, 106, 109, 110, 111, 114, 116–22,
127, 133, 134, 174
women 22, 83–6, 103–11, 192
work 5, 18, 83ff., 144, 168, 172, 190

Zambia 177, 178

Index of family and farm names

Eskelinen 76, 78

Harjula 60
Heikura 63
Honkanen 95
Huuro 56, 190
Hämäläinen 34

Kainula 57
Kainulainen 56, 96–7
Karjalainen 96
Kiiskilä 90–2, 187
Kiiskinen 36, 57–8, 67–9, 90, 102, 133, 135, 153ff., 187
Kärki 34, 36, 55–6, 96, 150, 151, 152
Kärkkäinen 36, 47, 55, 56, 62, 76, 78, 96, 108

Lehtola 59–60, 83

Meriläinen 57, 76
Mikkonen 108
Mustola 37
Mustonen 56, 120ff.

Myllynen 52–5, 63
Männikkölä 57, 88–90

Nevalainen 76, 107, 118

Pyykkö 37

Repola 152
Ryynänen 57, 120ff.
Räisänen 63

Saarela 187
Saarelainen 36, 58, 102, 107–9, 153ff., 187
Savelius 57, 96–7
Savolainen 47
Stahlman 108

Toivanen 53
Turula 83
Turunen 35, 53, 56, 57, 59–66, 78, 88, 96–7, 102, 118ff., 146, 156

Wallius 57

Index of authors cited in main text

af Hällström, E. 80
Alapuro, R. 21
Allardt, E. 11, 21
Arensberg, C. 71

Barnes, J. 77
Berkner, L. 115, 181–2
Bohannan, P. 177

Chayanov, A. 71
Cole, J. 115
Collomp, A. 141

Durkheim, E. 153, 176

Fortes, M. 112
Friedl, E. 133

Gluckman, M. 162, 177
Goody, E. 178
Goody, J. 70, 77, 112, 114, 122, 123, 125, 174
Gulliver, P. 71

Hautamäki, L. 148

Jutikkala, E. 50, 122, 125, 132

Kimball, S. 71
Kula, W. 175, 181
Köppä, T. 163

Leach, E. 77

Maine, H. 110, 112, 114, 116, 122, 176
Malinowski, B. 115
Mauss, M. 145
Mendels, F. 115, 181–2
Mendras, H. 173
Merton, R. 181
Morgan, L. 176

Newby, H. 169

Plakans, A. 51–2, 77, 175

Richards, A. 71
Roberts, F. 160

Sahlins, M. 71
Saloheimo, V. 50, 105, 135
Sweetser, D. 128ff., 136

Tönnies, F. 176

Voionmaa, V. 50, 72, 97, 117ff., 119, 120, 131ff., 135, 137, 186

Warriner, D. 75
Weber, M. 181
Williams, R. 169
Wolf, E. 115

Cambridge Studies in Social and Cultural Anthropology

Editors: Ernest Gellner, Jack Goody, Stephen Gudeman, Michael Herzfeld, Jonathan Parry

1 The Political Organisation of Unyamwezi
  R. G. ABRAHAMS
2 Buddhism and the Spirit Cults in North-East Thailand*
  S. J. TAMBIAH
3 Kalahari Village Politics: An African Democracy
  ADAM EUPER
4 The Rope of Moka: Big-Men and Ceremonial Exchange in Mount Hagen, New Guinea*
  ANDREW STRATHERN
5 The Majangir: Ecology and Society of a Southwest Ethiopian People
  JACK STAUDER
6 Buddhist Monk, Buddhist Layman: A Study of Urban Monastic Organisation in Central Thailand
  JANE BUNNAG
7 Contexts of Kinship: An Essay in the Family Sociology of the Gonja of Northern Ghana
  ESTHER N. GOODY
8 Marriage among a Matrilineal Elite: A Family Study of Ghanaian Civil Servants
  CHRISTINE OPPONG
9 Elite Politics in Rural India: Political Stratification and Political Alliances in Western Maharashira
  ANTHONY T. CARTER
10 Women and Property in Morocco: Their Changing Relation to the Process of Social Stratification in the Middle Atlas
  VANESSA MAHER
11 Rethinking Symbolism*
  DAN SPERBER. Translated by Alice L. Morton
12 Resources and Population: A Study of the Gurungs of Nepal
  ALAN MACFARLANE

13 Mediterranean Family Structures
   EDITED BY J. G. PERISTIANY
14 Spirits of Protest: Spirit-Mediums and the Articulation of Consensus among the Zezuru of Southern Rhodesia (Zimbabwe)
   PETER FRY
15 World Conqueror and World Renouncer: A Study of Buddhism and Polity in Thailand against a Historical Background*
   S. J. TAMBIAH
16 Outline of a Theory of Practice*
   PIERRE BOURDIEU. Translated by Richard Nice
17 Production and Reproduction: A Comparative Study of the Domestic Domain*
   JACK GOODY
18 Perspectives in Marxist Anthropology*
   MAURICE GODELIER. Translated by Robert Brain
19 The Fate of Shechem, or the Politics of Sex: Essays in the Anthropology of the Mediterranean
   JULIAN PITT-RIVERS
20 People of the Zongo: The Transformation of Ethnic Identities in Ghana
   ENID SCHILDEROUT
21 Casting out Anger: Religion among the Taita of Kenya
   GRACE HARRIS
22 Rituals of the Kandyan State
   H. L. SENEVIRATNE
23 Australian Kin Classification
   HAROLD W. SCHEFFLER
24 The Palm and the Pleiades: Initiation and Cosmology in Northwest Amazonia*
   STEPHEN HUGH-JONES
25 Nomads of Southern Siberia: The Pastoral Economies of Tuva
   S. J. VAINSHTEIN. Translated by Michael Colenso
26 From the Milk River: Spatial and Temporal Processes in Northwest Amazonia*
   CHRISTINE HUGH-JONES
27 Day of Shining Red: An Essay on Understanding Ritual*
   GILBERT LEWES
28 Hunters, Pastoralists and Ranchers: Reindeer Economies and their Transformations*
   TIM INGOLD
29 The Wood-Carvers of Hong Kong: Craft Production in the World Capitalist Periphery
   EUGENE COOPER
30 Minangkabau Social Formations: Indonesian Peasants and the World Economy
   JOEL S. KAHN
31 Patrons and Partisans: A Study of Two Southern Italian Communes
   CAROLINE WHITE
32 Muslim Society*
   ERNEST GELLNER

33 Why Marry Her? Society and Symbolic Structures
   LUC DE HEUSCH. Translated by Janet Lloyd
34 Chinese Ritual and Politics
   EMILY MARTIN AHERN
35 Parenthood and Social Reproduction. Fostering and Occupational Roles in
   West Africa
   ESTHER N. GOODY
36 Dravidian Kinship
   THOMAS R. TRAUTMANN
37 The Anthropological Circle: Symbol Function, History*
   MARC AUGE. Translated by Martin Thom
38 Rural Society in Southeast Asia
   KATHLEEN GOUGH
39 The Fish-People: Linguistic Exogamy and Tukanoan Identity in Northwest
   Amazonia
   JEANNIE JACKSON
40 Karl Marx Collective: Economy, Society and Religion in a Siberian
   Collective Farm*
   CAROLINE HUMPHREY
41 Ecology and Exchange in the Andes
   Edited by DAVID LEHMANN
42 Traders without Trade: Responses to Trade in two Dyula Communities
   ROBERT LAUNAY
43 The Political Economy of West African Agriculture*
   KEITH HART
44 Nomads and the Outside World
   A. M. KHAZANOV. Translated by Julia Crookenden
45 Actions, Norms and Representations: Foundations of Anthropological
   Inquiry*
   LADISLAV HOLY AND MILAN STUCKLIK
46 Structural Models in Anthropology*
   PER HAGE AND FRANK HARARY
47 Servants of the Goddess: The Priests of a South Indian Temple
   C. J. FULLER
48 Oedipus and Job in West African Religion*
   MEYER PORTES
49 The Buddhist Saints of the Forest and the Cult of Amulets: A Study in
   Charisma, Hagiography, Sectarianism, and Millennial Buddhism*
   S. J. TAMBIAH
50 Kinship and Marriage: An Anthropological Perspective (available in
   paperback/in the USA only)
   ROBIN FOX
51 Individual and Society in Guiana: A Comparative Study of Amerindian
   Social Organization*
   PETER RIVIERE
52 People and the State: An Anthropology of Planned Development*
   A. F. ROBERTSON
53 Inequality among Brothers: Class and Kinship in South China
   RUBIE S. WATSON

54 On Anthropological Knowledge*
   DAN SPERBER
55 Tales of the Yanomami: Daily Life in the Venezuelan Forest*
   JACQUES LIZOT. Translated by Ernest Simon
56 The Making of Great Men: Male Domination and Power among the New
   Guinea Baruya*
   MAURICE GODELIER. Translated by Rupert Swyer
57 Age Class Systems: Social Institutions and Politics Based on Age*
   BERNARDO BERNARDI. Translated by David I. Kertzer
58 Strategies and Norms in a Changing Matrilineal Society: Descent,
   Succession and Inheritance among the Toka of Zambia
   LADISLAV HOLY
59 Native Lords of Quito in the Age of the Incas: The Political Economy of
   North-Andean Chiefdoms
   FRANK SALOMON
60 Culture and Class in Anthropology and History: A Newfoundland
   Illustration
   GERALD SIDER
61 From Blessings to Violence: History and Ideology in the Circumcision
   Ritual of the Merina of Madagascar*
   MAURICE BLOCH
62 The Huli Response to Illness
   STEPHEN FRANKEL
63 Social Inequality in a Northern Portuguese Hamlet: Land, Late Marriage,
   and Bastardy. 1870–1978
   BRIAN JUAN O'NEILL
64 Cosmologies in the Making; A Generative Approach to Cultural Variation
   in Inner New Guinea*
   FREDRIK BARTH
65 Kinship and Class in the West Indies: A Genealogical Study of Jamaica and
   Guyana*
   RAYMOND I. SMITH
66 The Making of the Basque Nation
   MARIANNE HEIBERG
67 Out of Time: History and Evolution in Anthropological Discourse
   NICHOLAS THOMAS
68 Tradition as Truth and Communication
   PASCAL BOYER
69 The Abandoned Narcotic: Kava and Cultural Instability in Melanesia
   RON BRUNTON
70 The Anthropology of Numbers
   THOMAS CRUMP
71 Stealing People's Names: History and Politics in a Sepik River Cosmology
   SIMON J. HARRISON
72 The Bedouin of Cyrenaica: Studies in Personal and Corporate Power
   EMRYS L. PETERS. Edited by Jack Goody and Emanuel Marx
73 Property, Production and Family in Neckerhausen
   DAVID WARREN SABEAN
74 Bartered Brides: Politics, Gender and Marriage in an Afghan Tribal Society
   NANCY TAPPER

210

75 Fifteen Generations of Bretons: Kinship and Society in Lower Brittany,
    1720–1980
    MARTINE SEGALEN. Translated by J. A. Underwood
76 Honor and Grace in Anthropology
    Edited by J. G. PERSTIANY and JULIAN PITT-RIVERS
77 The Making of the Modern Greek Family: Marriage and Exchange in
    Nineteenth-Century Athens
    PAUL SANT CASSIA AND CONSTANTINA BADA
78 Religion and Custom in a Muslim Society: The Berti of Sudan
    LADISLAV HOLY
79 Quiet Days in Burgundy: A Study of Local Politics
    MARC ABELES. Translated by Annella McDermott
80 Sacred Void: Spatial Images of Work and Ritual among the Giriama of
    Kenya
    DAVID PARKIN

* available in paperback